Understanding the European Communities

William Nicoll has been a Director-General in the Council of the European Communities in Brussels since 1982. Earlier, he had two spells in the United Kingdom Permanent Representation to the European Communities: 1972–5, dealing with external relations, and 1977–82, as Deputy Permanent Representative (including Chairmanship of the Committee of Permanent Representatives in 1981). He has published a score of articles on EC subjects, mainly the budget and inter-institutional relations.

Trevor C. Salmon, Jean Monnet Professor of European Integration Studies at the University of St Andrews, has taught undergraduate courses on the European Communities for fifteen years. Having initially worked in the Irish Republic for five years, he moved to the University of St Andrews in 1978. He has published a number of articles on European issues, especially security, and is the author of a detailed analysis of the compatibility of Community membership with neutrality, *Unneutral Ireland*.

Understanding the European Communities

WILLIAM NICOLL

Council of the European Communities

TREVOR C. SALMON

*Jean Monnet Professor of European Integration Studies,
University of St Andrews*

PHILIP ALLAN

NEW YORK   LONDON   TORONTO   SYDNEY   TOKYO   SINGAPORE

First published 1990 by
Philip Allan
66 Wood Lane End, Hemel Hempstead
Hertfordshire HP2 4RG
A division of
Simon & Schuster International Group

Typeset in 10/12pt Ehrhardt
by Inforum Typesetting, Portsmouth

Printed and bound in Great Britain by
Billing and Sons, Worcester

British Library Cataloguing in Publication Data

Nicoll, William
  Understanding the European Communities.
  1. European Community
  I. Title   II. Salmon, Trevor C.
  341.24'22

ISBN 0-86003-409-7
ISBN 0-86003-709-6 pbk

3 4 5 94 93 92 91

Contents

Preface

Another introduction to Europe! Does the world need it?

Yes, we think, for four reasons.

The creation of the single market by 1992 brings the Europe of directives and of ministerial gatherings closer to everyone.

Yet there is still widespread unawareness of how the European Communities (EC) are involved in the business of government. We think that the quality of judgement and opinion about the EC will be enhanced if more is known about how they came about, how they work and what they do.

Our own contribution is to combine the resources of an academic political scientist and a serving employee of one of the community institutions.

Finally, we can offer to a British readership French bibliographies not always translated into English.

Tables

Abbreviations

ACP	African Caribbean and Pacific countries
CAP	Common Agricultural Policy
CCP	Common Commercial Policy
CE	Compulsory expenditure
CFP	Common Fisheries Policy
CMEA (COMECON)	Council for Mutual Economic Assistance
COREPER	Permanent Representatives Committee
COST	Co-operation on Science and Technology
CSA	Special Committee for Agriculture
DNO	Non-compulsory expenditure
DO	Compulsory expenditure
EAGGF	European Agricultural Guarantee and Guidance Fund
EC	European Communities
ECJ	European Court of Justice
ECOFIN	Council (Economics and Finance)
ECSC	European Coal and Steel Community
ECU	European Currency Unit
EDC	European Defence Community
EDF	European Development Fund
EEC	European Economic Community
EFTA	European Free Trade Association
EIB	European Investment Bank
EMS	European Monetary System
EMU	Economic and monetary union
EP	European Parliament

EPC	1 European Political Co-operation
	2 European Political Community
ERDF	European Regional Development Fund
ERM	Exchange rate mechanism (in EMS)
ESC	Economic and Social Committee
ESCB	European System of Central Banks (proposed)
ESF	European Social Fund
GATT	General Agreement on Tariffs and Trade
MCA	Monetary Compensation Amount
MFA	Multi-Fibre Agreement
NATO	North Atlantic Treaty Organization
NCE	Non-compulsory expenditure
OEEC	Organisation for European Economic Co-operation (later OECD: Organisation for Economic Co-operation and Development)
OOP	Office for Official Publications of the European Communities

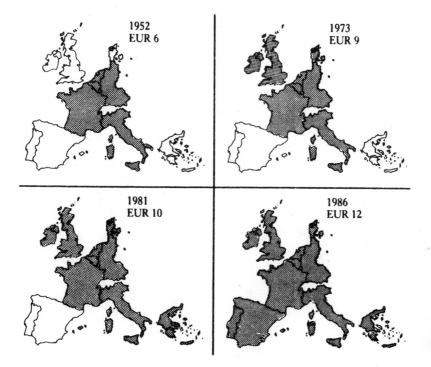

The Europe of the European Communities.

1

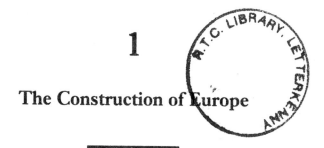

The Construction of Europe

The Construction of Europe to the Treaties of Rome

Throughout its history, the European continent has been restless, fragile and contradictory,[1] competitive and pluralist.[2] Responding, unlike the subjects of the Chinese, Japanese and Ottoman Empires, to no central rule-making authority, and divided from each other by language and religion, and by princely, and later national, aspirations, the Europeans vied with and stimulated each other to create a civilisation, proprietorially described simply as 'civilisation', which it became their manifest destiny to spread across the planet.

But if there were common strands in their expansionism – Christianity, the Greco-Roman heritage of philosophy and law, the humanism of the Renaissance, and (much later) the principles of representative democracy – the Western Europeans were in more or less constant strife with each other in the four centuries up to the middle of the twentieth.[3] With exponential growth of efficiency in the technology of killing and maiming, there was a massive rise in the numbers of combatants involved in any fighting and the effective disappearance of the distinction between combatant and non-combatant.[4] War-making also served to promote industrial development. War was even ideologically glorified as the means of cultivating the noblest instincts of man[5] and the chivalry which had formed part of a martial code was diluted in the assertion of a principle of hegemony, whether because the belligerent maintained that he had the monopoly of respectable peace aims, or because his was rightfully a master race. A European born in 1900 and still alive in 1955 would have spent one-fifth of his or her life in war years, would have known of the killing fields of Flanders, witnessed the blighting of the Brave New World of the League of Nations, seen in the news reels the horror of Belsen, the fire storm of Dresden and the vaporisation of Hiroshima, lived through the breakdown of the Great Alliance which was supposed to underpin and enforce the peace-keeping objectives of the United Nations, and listened to the debate about whether the third atom bomb might be used to stem the advance of Chinese–North Korean forces.[6] He or she would also have known that since the end of the Second World War the seat of power had moved east and west, from the chanceries of the European capitals to Moscow and to Washington. The Europeans' home continent was no longer a world power.

Over the years, many prepared for or waged war, irrespective of whether they wished peace, but others devoted themselves to the cause of ending war and making peace last. It seemed to most of them that the guarantee of peace would be the acceptance of laws and the setting up of international institutions. Just as law prescribes the relations between citizens, so law could do the same between states and, if directly applied, between citizens of these separate states. Various thinkers applied themselves to suggesting how this could be put into practice.

The 'Grand Design' attributed to Henry IV of France (1553–1610) and notably to his minister Sully is almost certainly apocryphal. It was, in its legendary form, for a 'Great Republic' of Europe, bringing together the divided kingdoms and principalities (and religions within Christendom) to co-exist in peace.[7]

William Penn (1644–1718), the great English and later American Quaker, having been obliged by his unpopularity within his family and with the law in England to travel extensively in Europe, had been an eyewitness of the devastation of the long-lasting seventeenth-century wars. In 1693 he published an essay on the present and future peace of Europe. He advocated the institution of a European estates general or parliament which would mediate on disputes among the sovereigns and, in an anticipation of what the UN would call 'uniting for peace', would enforce the result of its deliberations against any dissidents.[8]

The German philosopher Immanuel Kant (1724–1804) published in 1795 his treatise *Zum Ewigen Frieden* ('Towards Perpetual Peace'). For Kant the existence of the state implied aggression: the state of nature was the state of war. Man's power over nature, the power to make law, could change this state. Disputes could be resolved, not by victory in war but by judicial means.[9] These means were not, however, what would today be called international law, because the latter existed then only because of war, actual or imminent. Kant's version of pacific law was for a federation of free states, freely consented to. Kant, as he himself acknowledged, had no greater success than any other thinker in resolving the paradox of structural imbalance: how can the federation be strong enough to co-exist with its members without being dominated by them, but not so strong as to destroy them and subject them to an imperial sway?

Saint-Simon (1760–1825) had lived through the War of American Independence and its constitution-building aftermath. He published in 1814 with Augustin Thierry 'On the Reorganisation of European Society'. Unlike Penn and Kant he moved from the notion of the participating state to the participating people, to be represented by a European parliament, independent of the national states and empowered to settle disagreements among them. Saint-Simon did not take up the Kantian paradox.

The Italian Carlo Cattaneo (1801–69) did so, and based his solution on what in the 1980s came to be known as 'subsidiarity'. This principle teaches that government can be organised in layers – from the local community up to world level – each layer possessing the competence which it can discharge better than those above or below it. Seen from the viewpoint of a unitary state this is decentralisation. Seen from the smallest unit it is federation, and one in which there need be no contradiction between the loyalties paid to each layer – a Yorkshireman can comfortably be a Northerner, an Englishman, a Briton, a European and a citizen of the world.[10]

These and other appeals and treatises were not greatly heeded. Nation states consolidated themselves by conquest, satellisation of their neighbours, and rebellion against a foreign ruler, in the name of freedom and national unity. This was an alternative path to European unity – the one followed by Napoleon. But it was predestined to evoke the opposition and armed response of the nations which did not want to be subservient or which feared to share the continent with too powerful a partner.

The outbreak of European war in 1914 affirmed the reality of the existence and consolidation over four centuries of the nation state, unified within its frontiers, governed by a single decision centre which engaged all its subjects, and devoted to increasing the relative power of the state by all available means: war if not diplomacy or commerce. The brotherhood of man, an airy vision,[11] was dissipated when, notably, the socialists in the Reichstag voted through the war credits in 1914. The Treaty of Versailles, signed on 28 June 1919, five years to the day from the assassination of the Archduke Ferdinand, demonstrated again that war and victory do not make lasting law. A fundamentally insecure and self-igniting system had been put together and the League of Nations, the peace-seeking and peace-making organ, stood no chance of success.

To some it was clear from the beginning that another structure was needed to provide stability in Europe, correctly seen as the key to stability in the world. This was the advocacy of Richard Coudenhove-Kalergi, a Hungarian nobleman who founded in 1923 the Pan-European movement (his 'Pan-European manifesto' was published in 1924) and won the support of several leading and active politicians, especially in France.[12] Aristide Briand, Prime Minister of France, having obtained in advance the support of his German colleague Gustav Stresemann, delivered on 7 September 1929, at the 10th General Assembly of the League of Nations, a speech in which he outlined a plan for European union. At the request of the League's members, the French Government elaborated the plan into a memorandum, 'The Organisation of a Régime of European Federal Union', presented in May 1930 to a world racked by economic depression.

The British reaction was crucial and negative. While warmly disposed towards intergovernmental European economic co-operation, and perhaps later extending it to political co-operation, His Majesty's Government gave weight to 'the peculiar and indissoluble connexion of the British Isles with the world-wide territories of the British Empire and ... the prestige and efficiency of the League of Nations which is the sheet anchor of British policy'.[13] The French memorandum, remitted to the attentions of the Committee for the Study of European Unity, was rejected by the General Assembly of the League.

British names are conspicuously missing from the roll call of Europeanists. This is not to say that there was no awareness of the problem of European fractiousness and of the insecurity of the classic British pursuit of European balance. In 1897, diamond jubilee year, in the heyday of British imperialism, the Prime Minister, Lord Salisbury wrote:

The federated action of Europe, if we can maintain it, is our sole hope of escaping from the constant terror and calamity of war, the constant pressure of the burdens of an armed peace, which weigh down the spirits and darken the prospect of every Nation in this part of the world. The Federation of Europe is the only hope we have.[14]

As war clouds gathered in Europe, Lord Beveridge (later known as the architect of the post-war welfare state) founded the Federal Union, drawing together the efforts of such as P.H. Kerr (Lord Lothian), author in 1935 of 'Pacifism is not enough, nor patriotism either'.[15] To this movement, which enjoyed little support, a federal community of nations, which need not initially be world-wide, was the only way of abolishing the institution of war: patriotism was not enough and non-violent resistance, which also had powerful and sincere advocates,[16] would not succeed either. Neither would international socialism, unless it also created the federal community. Kerr observed that the search for national advantage through trade protectionism and the drive for markets was being supported by capitalists and socialists alike. Miss Barbara Wootton, socialist and co-founder of the Federal Union, reached a similar conclusion in her pamphlet 'Socialism and federation' in 1940. As long as there was 'international anarchy', international no-law, a socialist had to choose between taking up arms against his comrades or giving in to aggression. He had usually chosen the former. Hence international socialism lay in ruins.

The 1930s saw the world economic and trade war, the closing in of markets, the search for self-sufficiency, the command economy of the Third Reich[17] and the collapse of world trade.[18]

This was the economic expression of the nation state, pursuing national advantage in a zero-sum game. The nation states went to the political and shooting war of the 1940s, appeasement having failed to curtail the territorial demands of Hitler's Germany. Britain and France drew the line after the occupation, in the spring of 1939, of the parts of Czechoslovakia which had not already been ceded by the Munich Pact of 1938. The German offensive against Poland in September 1939, followed by the occupation of Luxembourg, Belgium, the Netherlands, Denmark and Norway, the Italian invasion of Greece and the attack on France in June 1940, ushered in five years which were to prove the final demonstration of international anarchy. The execution in December 1941 of the long-prepared plan for the Strike South by Japanese imperialism made warring anarchy global, from Murmansk to Midway.

On either side, the first war aim was the defeat and probably the territorial occupation of at least part of the opposition. The Reich envisaged a New Order under German hegemony in Europe and in Russia, as well as in the African colonies of the defeated nations. Japan wanted to create the Greater Asia Co-Prosperity Sphere in the service of its empire. But neither was able, under the stresses of waging war, or willing to give much attention to the economic restructuring of the lands they had conquered. Occupied Europe did not become a single market.

British war aims were simple: to win. Harold Nicolson has described[19] how, as a junior minister at the Ministry of Information in 1940, he was charged with preparing a statement of war aims (in essence 'socialism' at home – that is, the welfare state – and pooled resources in Europe), which the War Cabinet decided against adopting. But the problem of a future Europe at peace did not go away. On 21 October 1942, when there was still a long dark way to go towards victory, Winston Churchill, the Prime Minister, sent Anthony Eden, the Foreign Secretary, the following minute:

I must admit that my thoughts rest primarily in Europe – the revival of the glory of Europe, the parent continent of the modern nations and of civilisation. It would be a measureless disaster if Russian barbarianism overlaid the culture and independence of the ancient States of Europe. Hard as it is to say now, I trust that the European family may act unitedly as one under a Council of Europe. I look forward to a United States of Europe in which the barriers between the nations will be greatly minimised and unrestricted travel will be possible. I hope to see the economy of Europe studied as a whole . . . Of course, we shall have to work with the Americans in many ways and in the greatest ways, but Europe is our prime care . . . It would be easy to debate upon these themes. Unhappily the War has prior claims on our attention.[20]

The winning of the war and Anglo-American planning for post-war world organisation[21] were the leading preoccupations of allied statesmen but some Europeans, including those who were suffering grievously, were searching for answers to the questions of economic and political organisation in Western Europe. In London, the governments in exile of the Netherlands, Luxembourg and Belgium were discussing co-operative and integrational plans which laid the basis for the Benelux organisation (Belgium and Luxembourg had been in economic union since 1921). In imprisonment in Italy in 1941 the renowned anti-fascist and pro-European Altiero Spinelli was writing the manifesto for a free and united Europe (the 'Ventotene manifesto'). The central theme was the awful and inevitable consequences of the existence of separate sovereign states: the global war.

Meanwhile in Washington Jean Monnet (1888–1977), a French businessman, was organising (as he had also organised in the 1914–18 war) allied war supply. It was Monnet who had inspired Churchill's proposal in 1940 that France, on the brink of military defeat, and the United Kingdom, resolved to fight on, should merge into a single state. Monnet had travelled widely in the family business and in banking and had become convinced of the essential need for European integration.

After the Second World War he joined the French Planning Commission where he further enriched his experience of organising and negotiating, in preparation for the unparalleled service he was to render to the unification of Europe.

With democratic governments reinstalled in liberated Europe, a series of initiatives were taken to pursue federalist objectives. The structure of post-war Europe had also been extensively discussed in resistance movements in the latter stages of the war. This searching phase culminated in a Congress of Europe, held in The Hague in May 1948. It brought together leading figures from France (including twelve former prime ministers and the future president, François Mitterrand), Britain (Churchill, Eden and Macmillan, belonging to the Conservative opposition, all future prime ministers), the Netherlands, Belgium, Germany, Italy and elsewhere. The outcome may have been something of a disappointment or perhaps at most a very small beginning for the federalists. While the Congress had called for the constitution of a European parliament, the ensuing negotiations followed the path of the intergovernmental relationships which the British Government had favoured: the setting up of a Committee of Ministers and a non-elected Consultative Assembly, these forming the Council of Europe, founded in May 1949. The Council of Europe aimed only at 'closer unity' as against The Hague demand for 'economic and political union'.

Churchill's speeches in Zurich in September 1946 and at The Hague conference, and his references to 'a kind of United States of Europe', made a powerful impact: although out of office, he was still a great statesman. But he was not offering Britain as a founder member of the union – a friend and collaborator certainly, but a country which also had competing ties to the USA and to the British Empire. (In his Fulton Missouri speech in March 1946 about the special relationship between Britain and the USA he looked forward to a permanent defence agreement between the USA and the Commonwealth and to possible common citizenship.)

A separate initiative led to the creation of another European body, the Organisation for Europe Economic Co-operation, in response to the offer by US Secretary of State George Marshall at Harvard in June 1947 of massive US aid for the rebuilding of Europe (without distinction of East from West) on condition that the beneficiary countries would co-operate with each other in the use of the resources which the USA would make available. General Marshall was convinced from a visit to Moscow in April 1947 that the Soviet Union would do nothing to help to build the war-shattered economies of Europe and that it was intent on increasing Soviet influence in Western Europe. The OEEC represented only governments and had no elected or nominated consultative organ. It was a classic intergovernmental operation, acting by consensus or not at all.[22] These movements, although bold, generous and full of hope, fell far short of the integrationist objectives of those who sought to escape from national rivalries. They also did not touch a number of unresolved problems. There was the question of Franco-German relations, within which the Saar was a specific problem. The Saar was a German province, once again (as in 1918) split from Germany, being administered by France and potentially incendiary. Heavy industry in Germany and elsewhere needed to be restored, but with the guarantee that it would not, as in the past, encourage military production and adventure.

This was the basis of Monnet's plan, which he presented to the French Foreign Minister, Robert Schuman, early in May 1950 and which the latter announced on 9 May in the Salle de l'Horloge in Paris after an anxious wait for clearance from the German Government. From this moment the flagship of European integration is the European Communities,[23] of which the Coal and Steel Community was the first. Schuman's stated objective was 'to make war not merely unthinkable but materially impossible'.

The European Coal and Steel Community (Treaty of Paris, signed on 18 April 1951) removed the coal and steel industries of its participants, whether publicly or privately owned, from full national control, placing them under supranational stewardship. The supranational authority was to be the decision centre for production, prices (under certain conditions), investment and social conditions. It was not in the buying and selling business and it was not the negotiator of commercial treaties with non-member countries. France, Germany, Belgium, the Netherlands, Luxembourg and Italy announced their willing participation. The United Kingdom had an option to join but declined to submit itself to supranational authority for reasons which will be examined in Chapter 5.[24] This decision was taken under the Labour Government; the Conservatives, who came into power in 1951, considered changing it but decided against.

The European Coal and Steel Community Treaty is of federal inspiration. The High Authority which it created and whose members were designated by the governments of the member states was a decision-taking body, independent of the member states save where it needed their assent, which was obtained in some cases by a qualified majority of nationally weighted votes. It consulted an Assembly, but was not bound by its opinions. The Assembly was not in the first instance directly elected but direct election could come.

Outside events combined to hasten progress. The outbreak of the Korean War in June 1950 sharply increased world demand for steel, showing the economic value of co-ordination in production and offering a reminder of the linkage between steel production and war making. Already in the summer of 1948 the post-war hopes of world co-operation had been broken and the vulnerability of Western Europe had been re-exposed when Russia sealed off the surface routes into Berlin. The North Korean crossing on the 38th parallel in June 1950 was a further reminder, if any were needed, of the artificial post-war carto-graphy where East joins on West.

The first community was regarded only as a starting point. The success foreseen in this sector was equally confidently expected to spread to others according to the functionalist theory of integration. In particular, the Coal and Steel Community was a selected trial run for dealing with something far more significant: Western security. The treaty preamble has little to say about coal and steel. It speaks of safeguarding world peace, of establishing an economic community, and of substituting for age-old rivalries and bloody conflicts the merging of the essential interests.

The loss in the first phase of the Korean War of most of the peninsula showed the United States in particular how ill-prepared it was for any kind of war. In 1950 only one complete army division existed in the United States. Setting out to rearm, and assessing its European com-mitments, the USA called on its allies to follow suit. It also called for German rearmament within NATO command.[25] This was touching the most sensitive of nerves.

Western Europe, although protected by the American nuclear bomber shield, was aware of its own military weakness and of the undesirability of a specifically German contribution to rearmament. The safest way to assert some military independence and insure against an American withdrawal, or American tactical choices which would leave part of Western Europe less than fully protected, seemed to be the creation of integrated European armed forces obeying no neo-nationalist command. Allowance would be made for out-of-theatre operations which remained in national hands, such as the colonial involvements of France and Belgium. But just as the Coal and Steel

Community took the infrastructure of war away from national machination, so the European Army would serve the interests of all of Western Europe.

Here again, as often before, Churchill provided inspiration. On 11 August 1950, at the Fifth Session of the Consultative Assembly of the Council of Europe, he successfully proposed a motion calling for the immediate creation of a unified European Army subject to proper democratic European control and acting in full co-operation with the United States and Canada. He asked the Assembly to assure the German representative present that if the Germans threw in their lot, 'we shall hold their safety and freedom as sacred as our own'.[26]

It fell, however, to René Pleven, the French Prime Minister, to formulate the corresponding plan for the European Defence Community, presented to the French National Assembly on 24 October 1950 and later to NATO. The plan was in ECSC vein, providing for an Assembly, a common budget and a Council of Ministers as well as for a European Ministry of Defence. The plan received a favourable vote in the National Assembly. A conference was called in Paris, representing the six ECSC countries. The UK did not attend; its aloofness was later to be criticised by the USA which for its part, under President Eisenhower, strongly supported the plan. (The Richards Amendment to the Mutual Security Act of July 1953 allocated half of US military aid to Europe to the future EDC.) The EDC Treaty and accompanying protocols with NATO were signed on 27 May 1952, another high point of European integration.[27] A security structure without foreign policy cohesion would have been incomplete. Accordingly, Article 38 of the EDC Treaty called on the Assembly which it would set up to evolve a European Political Community (EPC). Taking time by the forelock, this task was pragmatically assumed by the ECSC Assembly, enlarged for the purpose and presided over by Paul Henri Spaak, the Belgian socialist. A draft treaty was prepared providing for a directly elected 'Lower House', a Senate elected nationally, an Executive, a Court and a Council of Ministers, all common to the ECSC, the EDC and the EPC. The treaty also provided for the establishment of a common market with free circulation of goods, capital and persons.[28] The draft was remitted to ministerial consideration, but they embarked on a virtually new version, less supranational. For example, the Upper House looked as if it would be nominated by governments.

Four member states had ratified the EDC Treaty by April 1954, and in the summer the Italians were close to ratification. In Germany the

Socialist Party opposed ratification, as it had also opposed the ECSC Treaty, but was outvoted. In France successive governments, besieged by innumerable problems and of changing political persuasion, either hesitated to press for ratification or lost procedural votes. The US Government remained strongly in favour of the EDC. On 14 December 1953 Secretary of State Dulles threatened an 'agonising reappraisal' of US European policy if the treaty were not ratified. In August 1954 the Government of Mendes-France, a Radical who had Gaullist support, demanded a major revision of the treaty but the other participants refused. At the end of the month his Government – with no expectation of success – proposed that the ratification debate be placed on the Assembly's agenda, but the Assembly voted to pass on to the next item. It was the end of the European Defence Community and the stillbirth of the European Political Community.

The fast track to European union was blocked. A fresh start, on a longer path, was needed. European security would pursue its course within the North Atlantic Treaty Organisation and in Western European Union (WEU), a new creation built on the Brussels Treaty Organisation. WEU became a forum in which the UK met and collaborated with the Six.

Opinion was divided on whether and, if so, how the construction of Europe should proceed. Supranational was for the time being a dirty word, and it was clear that the ECSC and the drafts of EDC and EPC could no longer serve as a model. In Italian government circles there was a preference for the 'OEEC method', intergovernmental and reaching out beyond the Six. In the Netherlands there was a call to proceed with the economic content of integration, a tailpiece of EPC included at Dutch insistence and lost with it. In Germany there was a desire to press forward with policies which gave West Germany a European vocation – although the Economics Minister, Dr Erhardt, did not believe in a Europe of the Six, preferring a wider trading structure.

Monnet, President of the High Authority of the Coal and Steel Community, used his contacts and influence in government and private circles to promote a resumption of the dialogue. He persuaded the foreign ministers of the Six to meet at Messina on 1 June 1955. The conference owed much to the sensitive preparatory work of the Benelux countries and in its conclusions took over much of their argument and language. The governments of the Six resolved that 'the moment has come to go a step further towards the construction of Europe. In their opinion this step must, first of all, be taken in the economic field.'

Specifically, they agreed on objectives for co-ordinating the development of transport and of energy generally and nuclear power particularly and for establishing a European common market free of customs duties and quantitative restrictions.[29]

The study of the removal of trade restrictions was also part of the mandate of the OEEC, but in the OEEC it had been more or less confined to the liberalisation of quota restrictions. Britain and others considered that tariff-cutting and free trade arrangements belonged properly to the General Agreement on Tariffs and Trade (GATT), where they could be placed in a world trade context. Atomic energy was an inviting and exciting prospect. Europe suffered from a technology gap, possessed (that is, Belgium possessed, in the Congo) uranium resources, and foresaw both shortages of fossil fuels and, unless something was done, undue dependence on the Middle East for essential oil supplies.

The Messina Conference set up a committee of government representatives, under the chairmanship of Spaak and assisted by experts. They invited Britain 'as a power which is a member of WEU and is also associated with the ECSC' to take part. Britain responded by appointing as its representative (not 'observer') on the expert committee R.F. Bretherton, Under-Secretary at the Board of Trade (the precursor of the Department of Trade and Industry).

The work settled down to study a possible Atomic Energy Community and a common market, the second being given lower priority and regarded (even by Monnet himself) as nebulous and too long-term to offer much political dividend.

In the atomic energy discussions, which took centre stage, the position of a non-participant, the USA, was a major factor. The USA led in nuclear know-how. Much of the information needed to build and operate nuclear reactors was classified, because they had been built not to generate power but to produce fissile material for bombs. But there were openings. In a speech at Penn State University on 11 June 1955, President Eisenhower announced the US 'Atoms for Peace' programme. The USA was ready, on appropriate terms, to conclude bilateral agreements which opened up prospects for US exports or, as in the US–Belgian bilateral agreement, ensured a supply of raw uranium. Other European countries were also interested in acquiring US know-how and assistance, and negotiations were prepared. US policy makers were faced with the problem of balancing their national security interests and their foreign policy objectives. The latter prevailed. Within the

State Department the view was taken that:

the most hopeful avenue for relaunching the movement towards European integration now appears to be the creation of a European common authority, along the lines of the Schuman Plan, to be responsible for the development of atomic energy for peaceful purposes.[30]

In pursuance of this conclusion and in response to rumours that the individual European countries could get a better deal bilaterally than via an Atomic Energy Community, on 30 March 1956 US Secretary of State Dulles authorised his ambassadors in Bonn, Brussels, The Hague, Paris, Rome and Luxembourg to inform foreign ministers that:

US Government could make available substantially greater resources and adopt attitude of substantially greater liberality towards real integrated community possessing effective common responsibility and authority than would be possible for countries separately.[31]

A difficult issue confronting the negotiators was the insistence by five of them that the member states of a European Atomic Energy Community should forswear the manufacture of atomic bombs. This was unacceptable to France, both on military grounds and because there was thought to be no possibility that the National Assembly would ratify such a self-denying ordinance. The compromise was a provision that no member state would explode a device before 1 January 1961, which was simply a recognition of the lead-time which France would need in its military programme.

The common market discussions in the Spaak Committee took less of the limelight (and gave rise to less debate within the US Government). The Six wanted to proceed, as the German states had proceeded eighty years before, to a customs union with no internal tariff barriers but a common external tariff.[32] They also wanted to find a way of including agriculture within the system. The difficulty was that in most of the Six – where mass famine was a vivid recent memory – agricultural production was heavily protected, with the aim of raising self-sufficiency levels (and, historically, of maintaining a rural population which could provide manpower for the conscript land army). Various plans for agricultural cross-frontier trade such as 'green pools' had been discussed earlier but had foundered.[33] For Britain, membership of a customs union was out of the question. Under imperial (later Commonwealth) preference it gave (largely) free entry to the raw materials and manufactures of Commonwealth countries and it received a certain amount of tariff preferences for its exports to them.[34] It was not prepared to overthrow this system and subject its imports from Commonwealth countries to 'reverse preferences' – that is, to see them move from free entry towards taxation whilst imports from the partners in the customs union went the other way.

The alternative to a customs union was a free trade area (without agriculture). There would be no tariffs between the members, but each would maintain its own external tariffs and the origin of goods from outside the area would be controlled. (Origin controls would in any case be necessary in the initial phases of a customs union as members transited to the common external tariff.) Agriculture raised a threat to British cheap food policies. Food imports were largely free of duty and the domestic price was subsidised down to world levels. An increase in food costs would push up the cost of living and unit wage costs in industry.[35] Britain sought to interest the USA in the negative consequences for the USA of a European customs union, but it was not until far on into the negotiations, which the USA had consistently supported, that the latter turned its mind to the possible damage to its agricultural exports. It then looked to the GATT to find a solution.

As the work of the Spaak Committee proceeded, the question of linkage between the two chapters, atoms and common market, became acute. France, for example, wanted progress on atomic energy but lacked interest in the common market. Germany and especially German industry thought that a purely national programme of atomic energy (with US help) was likely to be more effective and profitable. On the common market, Germany was decidedly reserved on bringing the African colonies into the arrangements, the proposal being pressed by France.

In November 1955 Spaak asked the non-Messina participants in his committees – Britain, the Council of Europe, the OEEC, the ECSC and the Committee of European Ministers of Transport (a free-standing organisation) – to take a position on the arrangements which were emerging. Since Britain was unable to commit itself to any part of the emerging proposals, it effectively ceased from then on to play a part in the preparatory work. Spaak pressed on in 1956, reporting at intervals to meetings of the Six foreign ministers and producing in April the second Spaak Report, which was considered briefly by foreign ministers meeting at Venice in May 1956. Treaty drafting began in earnest after the summer break, and new compromises on disputed points (several remained outstanding from Spaak's reports) were negotiated at foreign minister level and at the meeting of Heads of State or Government[36] in February 1957. The two treaties, establishing a European Economic Community and a European Atomic Energy Community (Euratom), were signed in Rome on 25 March 1957, although only the EEC Treaty is colloquially known as the Treaty of Rome.

The Construction of Europe 1957–72

The EEC Treaty takes as its premise that there will be an ever closer union of the peoples of Europe. (In the German text the usual words for 'union' are not used. The word selected is *Zusammenschluss*, which has none of the historical connotations of other synonyms like *Einheit* or *Einigkeit*.) The treaty stipulates that customs duties and other trade barriers among the member states will be abolished. A customs union will be formed. Cartels, trusts and the abuse of dominant market positions are outlawed. State aids which distort competition are incompatible with the common market. The free circulation within the Community of goods, services, capital and persons is to be secured partly by means of legislation which by harmonising divergent rules, standards and practices, will eliminate non-tariff barriers. The agricultural market of the Community is to be organised in accordance with stated principles.[37] The member states transfer to the Community the power to conclude treaties with international organisations and with third countries in matters for which the Community has competence. Provision is made for a special relationship between the Community and the former or existing colonies or overseas dependencies of its member states.

The Community is composed of four institutions. Their functioning is discussed in Chapter 2. The Commission is responsible for making legislative proposals, for executing policies which have been decided and which are entrusted to it, and for monitoring member states' compliance with the obligations which they have entered into. This gives rise to the much-used characterisation of the Commission as the driving force of European integration (because of its right of initiative) and as the guardian of the treaties (because it can intervene with the member states to demand compliance with their obligations).

The Council (often colloquially called the Council of Ministers although this expression is not used in the treaties) is composed of representatives of the governments of the member states, each government deciding on its own representation. The Council decides on Commission proposals.

In the more mature Community some decisions were to be taken by a majority vote, weighted according to the size of the member: Germany, France and Italy in one band, Belgium and the Netherlands in another, Luxembourg in a third.[38] Broadly speaking, all decisions involving new policies would continue to require unanimity. Although the Commission has some decision-making powers, the Council is the Community's legislator, which is a marked shift towards the recognition of the role of national governments in contradistinction to the Coal and Steel Community where the High Authority was the decision maker.

The Assembly is consultative. It can, if it musters a sufficient majority, express its non-confidence in the Commission and dismiss it. Its members were initially nominated by national parliaments from within their ranks. It was charged to propose to the Council arrangements for universal direct elections and the Council was to commend them to the member states for adoption under the latter's constitutional procedures.

The Court of Justice is the supreme constitutional authority for giving judgment on the obligations of the institutions, the member states, and legal and physical persons.

The Economic and Social Committee, officially an 'organ' rather than an institution, is consultative. Its members are appointed by the Council on the basis of nominations made by the governments of the member states and are representative of employers, workpeople and independent persons.

Thus a programme was written and institutions established for the creation of a customs union including agriculture and for the means of reducing or eliminating non-tariff barriers. These went far beyond the intra-European trade liberalisation measures adopted and discussed in the OEEC.

The Community was to pass laws binding on its members, who placed themselves unreservedly under the jurisdiction of a constitutional court. This legal order is often called the 'originality' of the European Community. There was a distinct transfer of sovereignty from the member states to the Community. But the member states, meeting in the Council, had the final say on most issues and often could decide only by unanimity. The electorates were not directly represented in the parliamentary body and it was only consultative, its opinion having no binding force. And apart from the high-minded phraseology[39] in the preambles to the treaties, talk of political co-operation, co-ordination or integration was taboo.

The parliaments in the member states ratified the treaties and they entered into force on 1 January 1958.

One reaction deserves notice: the total opposition of the Soviet Union, which regarded the European Communities as part of the war-making plot against it. It had sponsored its own world (and European) peace initiatives and in March 1957 tried a spoiling manoeuvre. The new Soviet leadership proposed an All-European Economic Agreement.[40] This was swiftly brushed aside.

The prospective coming into being of the European Common Market within the customs union created precisely the situation which the UK had sought to avoid: a trade split in Europe. Picking up discussions which had begun in the OEEC the UK embarked on a new objective. It could no longer be a question of a free trade area as the chosen form of economic organisation for Europe, but of a free trade area in which the EEC would be a unit, along with the UK and the other members of the OEEC who wished to belong to it. Accordingly it was no longer for the UK to negotiate alongside the Six; the discussions (which the members of the Six desired and for which the National Assembly in Paris had asked in its ratification vote on the EEC Treaty) were within the OEEC – although the UK was a leading participant. Prior to the completion of the EEC negotiations and the ratification of the treaty, the free trade area talks could not make much headway. Work began with the publication in January 1957 of the report of the OEEC working party followed by the appearance of a British memorandum setting out proposals for a European industrial free trade area. The UK's preconditions were formidable. There was to be no agricultural content. The Commonwealth preference system was to be maintained. No significant institutional structure was required. The various compensating insurances built into the EEC Treaty would not be taken up and could be replaced by a complaints procedure. The British cause was not helped by its separate presentation in May 1957 of its 'Grand Design' for rationalising the mushrooming parliamentary-type bodies in Europe. The British proposal, though sound technically, caused suspicion that an attempt was being made to sap the solidarity of the Six and to impose NATO on the neutrals.[41] Another development was to be of more significance: on 1 June 1958, after major political upheaval in France, General de Gaulle returned to power.

At the request of the Six, OEEC ministerial discussions were deferred from July to October 1957. The OEEC Council then agreed to form a ministerial committee to pursue the Council's stated resolve to establish a free trade area. The chairman of the committee was Reginald Maudling, who in August 1957 had been appointed to the non-portfolio post of Paymaster-General in the British Government to head up the European negotiations. The Community began to negotiate as one, and the Commission which had taken office on 1 January 1958 began to participate (strictly under Article 113 of the treaty it should have been the sole Community negotiator). The Maudling Committee worked through the catalogue of differences with little success until in November 1958 the French delegation announced to the press that it would not be possible to establish a European industrial free trade area between the Six and the other eleven members of the OEEC. The French had, in fact, concluded that free trade as proposed was a soft option, lacking the rigour which the EEC Treaty imposed on its members. This announcement was seemingly not cleared with the other members of the Community but they did not repudiate it. In a first and very early test the cohesion of the Community took precedence over other considerations.

In the sequel, a series of proposals were made inside the Community and in the OEEC for averting the discrimination (although the use of this word was contested) which the Six would practise when they began on 1 January 1959 to implement cuts in the intra-Community tariffs and increases in quotas, and which would worsen so far as the low-tariff EEC countries were concerned when they began on 1 January 1962 to move to the Common Customs Tariff. None of the proposals stood up to the scrutiny to which it was subjected. Seven OEEC countries – Britain, which took the lead, Denmark, Norway, Sweden, Switzerland, Austria and Portugal – then decided to form a free trade area. The Stockholm Convention founding the European Free Trade Association (EFTA) was worked out at Saltsjöbaden near Stockholm in July 1959. The parties planned and expected to:

- obtain trade benefits for themselves;
- keep in step with the 'intra' tariff reductions among the Six;
- continue to work for an agreement with the Community (an activity known as 'bridge building').

The UK strictly and formally opposed the journalistic phraseology which spoke of the 'Inner Six' and the 'Outer Seven'. But after almost a decade of negotiations, the three European Communities were in business and Western Europe was divided into two trading groups.

Within the Communities a vast work programme had been laid out. One primary task was to put flesh and bones on the general provisions of the EEC Treaty relating to agriculture. This work was inaugurated by the holding of a conference of all interested parties at Stresa on 3 July 1958. The ensuing Commission proposals provoked the first of the 'marathon meetings' which, for the next thirty years, were to be a feature of Community life. (Initially, the meetings were of foreign ministers; later agricultural ministers took over.) The guiding principles which emerged and which determined subsequent agricultural legislation were:

- common prices;[42]
- common financing (that is, an agricultural budget);
- Community preference (over imports).

As a major world trader, and with commercial policy as a Community competence rather than one within the sovereign control of the member states, the Community was sought after by other trading states which wished to establish or improve their commercial relations. The Commission became the Community's spokesman in GATT discussions and was immediately involved in defending the Community against claims that the tariff changes arising from the customs union should give rise to compensation for third countries. The Community had its own commercial relations agenda, notably the question of the African territories linked to member states. Following decolonisation, eighteen African countries took the 'European option' and entered into negotiations which resulted (in July 1963) in the Yaoundé Convention.[43] This gave them tariff freedom in the EEC. In return they were required to give duty-free and quota-free access to EEC exports, subject to maintaining duties and quantitative restrictions to meet their development needs, including revenue. The African countries used this right, but the principle of reciprocity for imports from the EEC was established. The Convention was also a vehicle for aid in the form of the European Development Fund (EDF).

In the Coal and Steel Community, however, the situation was unpromising. By the end of the fifties demand for coal was being squeezed by the rapid increase in oil consumption. The international oil companies, responding to the nuclear challenge, marketed vigorously and successfully. Moreover, coal was being imported into the Community (especially into Belgium) at a price which Community producers could not match. The High Authority judged that this was a 'manifest crisis' in the terms of the treaty and it proposed a limitation on Community output as well as restructuring measures. For diverse reasons, France, Germany and Italy demurred. France considered that the crisis was not of its making: measures had already been taken to modernise coal production and the closure of French coal mines was economically and politically unacceptable, especially if done at the insistence of an external authority. In the free market of the German economic miracle nurtured by the Economic Minister Dr Erhardt, there was resistance to interventionist measures and a conviction that Germany could find its own best way forward. At a specially convened meeting on 15 May 1959 the High Authority's proposals for introducing production quotas were rejected by France, Germany and Italy. Although Belgium accepted mine closures under the High Authority Plan, other coal producers successfully pressed the High Authority to approve national measures, including subsidies. This was a serious reverse for European integration and for the standing of the High Authority.

Euratom, once also seen as the great hope of European construction, did not take long to run into difficulties at the hands of the member states. Although, with some German hesitations, they had felt the need to come together to establish a civil nuclear industry, they found that the prospects for nuclear power were less promising than they had appeared. Considerable difficulties arose over the allocation by the Brussels authorities of research contracts among the member states, each of which had its own idea of what constituted a fair share (*juste retour*). Euratom was financed by national contributions and these gave the measure of what contributors expected to get back. The sign of crisis and of the diminishing authority of Euratom was the French refusal to renew the term of office of Etienne Hirsch of France, President of the Euratom Commission and a convinced European, when his appointment expired at the beginning of 1962. It was perhaps from this moment, only shortly after the entry into force of the EEC and Euratom Treaties, that the creation of the common market of the EEC assumed primary importance and that the other Communities were relegated to a secondary status.

It remained the strategy of Monnet, President of the Action Committee for the United States of Europe, which he had founded when he resigned from the presidency of the Coal and Steel Community, that economic Europe should be the path to political Europe: to European union. This view was not shared by President de Gaulle. He had already made a major contribution to economic Europe by the economic and monetary reforms that he had carried through in France and by insisting on the creation of the Common Agricultural Policy. But he did not wish to see a structure which was divorced from governments become the gathering point for political union. His own European plan was for a 'Europe of the states'.[44] He regarded all else as an illusion or delusion. He envisaged a Europe which proceeded by co-operation, which took its decisions by unanimity, which would become less dependent on the USA and which would dialogue with the USSR on equal terms, and under French leadership.

At his first meeting in 1958 with Chancellor Adenauer, whom he otherwise assured of his attachment to the Alliance and to the Communities, de Gaulle proposed regular meetings of foreign ministers, assisted by a small secretariat. When this proposal was put out more widely among the Six it provoked opposition, notably from the Netherlands, which saw it as further excluding Britain from European political affairs and weakening the Atlantic community. Other EEC members also feared a weakening of the role of Community authorities. After some exchanges with his EEC partners, on 5 September 1960 de Gaulle held one of his dramatic press conferences at which he launched his plan for Europe. Although his downgrading of the European institutions caused alarm, the principle of a new drive for union was welcomed by Monnet as opening up a prospect for progress. The Heads of State and Government of the Six met in Paris on 10–11 February 1961. In their communiqué[45] they declared their intention to lay the foundation of a union which would develop progressively and they spoke of a new type of relationship based on the development of the common market and on political co-operation. At a follow-up meeting in Bonn on 18 July 1961 they agreed that they would meet regularly 'to compare their views, to concert their policies and to reach common positions in order to further the political union of Europe, thereby strengthening the Atlantic Alliance'. They also called on the committee which they had established at their earlier meeting to 'submit proposals on the means which will, as soon as possible, enable a statutory character to be given to the union of their peoples'.[46]

The French representative and chairman of the committee was Christian Fouchet, a career diplomat. On 2 November, Fouchet presented to the committee a French draft treaty ('Fouchet I'). This provided for a 'union of the states' working through the adoption of a common foreign policy and a common defence policy. The Council of the Union was to take decisions by unanimity. Meetings of the Council would be prepared by a European Political Commission consisting of senior officials from foreign offices. After three years there would be a review, having as its main object the introduction of a unified foreign policy and

the gradual establishment of an organisation centralising, within the Union, the European Communities referred to in the Preamble to the present Treaty. (Article 16)

The draft provoked adverse comment among the other committee members and elsewhere. In particular the Assembly, in an opinion prepared by René Pleven, while approving the idea of regular Summit meetings insisted that nothing in the new treaty should call in question the existing institutions. It criticised the reference to 'union of the states' and asked for a return to the 'union of the peoples' used in the Bonn communiqué. It disapproved of the Political Commission, advocating instead an independent secretary general (who could be dismissed by the Assembly). It also opposed the unanimity rule.

On 18 January 1962 Fouchet presented a new draft to his committee (Fouchet II), following critical discussion of Fouchet I. This maintained all the disputed provisions of the first draft and added that the union was to act also in the economic field. Intergovernmental co-operation was to become the apex of the work of the three European institutions. The aim of the modified revision clause was to strengthen the union in general:

or, in particular, for simplifying, rationalising and coordinating the ways in which the Member States cooperate. (Article 16)

The reception given to this proposal was even colder.

Negotiations continued, especially between France, Germany and Italy. Foreign ministers met in Paris on 17 April 1962 to make a final attempt at agreement, and failed. Spaak, the main opponent of Fouchet II, along with Luns of the Netherlands proposed that discussion should be adjourned until Britain had joined the EEC, and they were able to cite a speech by Edward Heath on 10 April 1962 in which, changing front from an earlier position, Britain had asked to take part in the discussion of political union. (Leo Tindemans, the long-serving Belgian statesman, has referred to discussion of a Fouchet III, which Monnet urged Spaak and Luns to consider. They would have none of it. The text has never been published.) The subject was dead and de Gaulle, in a further press conference on 15 May 1962, poured scorn on his opponents and their 'Europe of the stateless' (*apatrides*) and said disobliging things about the Atlantic Alliance, thereby provoking the resignation from his government of Maurice Schumann, Pierre Pflimlin and other members of the pro-European Mouvement Populaire Républicain which was in coalition with the President's own party. (Twenty-two years later Pflimlin became president of the second directly elected European Parliament.)

The sequel was the consolidation of the Franco-German *entente*. A Treaty of Franco-German Co-operation was signed on 22 January 1963 and instituted regular joint meetings of the ministerial teams.[47] The regular meetings of the foreign ministers of the Six which had begun, on French initiative, in 1959 were now abandoned.

Thus the first attempt at a European Political Community (via the Pleven plan) failed because France could not fall in with it. The second attempt failed because the Five could not follow the Fouchet plans. Given British attitudes to European integration, as discussed in Chapter 5, Britain had no difficulty with Fouchet II. But the staunchest supporters of British entry into the Community were also the strongest opponents of both Fouchet plans. Meanwhile, the British themselves had lost the initiative. Installed in the EFTA camp they now had no leverage to obtain the wider European free trade area which they had been promised after the formation of the EEC and which – they claimed – was the basis of their support for it. Worse, the context of the negotiations had changed. First the Commission and later the Six reasoned that alleged tariff discrimination was not a European but a world-wide problem. Solutions should be pursued in the world forum – the GATT. 'Globalism' was supported by the USA, which also continued to back the European integration process. In doing so it parted company with Britain which opposed the EEC plans to accelerate the tariff adjustments towards the customs union, which the USA supported. Time was also running out. Throughout 1960 the Six, at French insistence, were hammering out their common agricultural policy, an incubus for the UK in its economic relations with the Six.

The fresh start came in the decision to apply for EEC membership announced by the British Prime Minister, Harold Macmillan, on 31 July 1961. The leader of the UK negotiating team was Edward Heath, appointed Lord Privy Seal but also acting as Foreign Office minister (when Reginald Maudling embarked on the free trade negotiations his base was not in the Foreign Office). British Government spokesmen made it clear that the decision was primarily political. Denmark applied for EEC membership on 10 August 1961 and Norway on 30 April 1962. Ireland, not an EFTA member but in free trade with the UK,[48] applied on 30 July 1961. Austria, Sweden, Switzerland and Portugal applied to become associates. The focus of the discussion was on the UK negotiations, which are considered in Chapter 5.

On 15 December 1962 Macmillan visited de Gaulle at Rambouillet. They discussed the accession negotiations and defence. Macmillan explained that he was shortly to meet President J.F. Kennedy to discuss the implications of the expected US discontinuation of the Skybolt nuclear missile development. Britain depended on this weapon following the cancellation of its national project, Blue Streak. In the event Britain and the USA agreed on the Polaris programme. The USA would provide the missiles for the British-built launchers (submarines) and warheads. Kennedy offered Polaris missiles on the same terms to France as he had already negotiated with Britain. The offer was declined (France had no launchers or warheads)[49] and was seen in Paris as part of a US strategem to dominate the European nuclear weapon capability. A second controversy arose over whether Macmillan had rebuffed de Gaulle by not evoking the possibility of Anglo-French collaboration on nuclear weapons.

On 14 January 1963, the day before Heath was due to begin one of two scheduled marathon sessions with the Six in Brussels, de Gaulle announced at a press conference that in the French view the UK was not ready to accept the conditions of EEC membership. He answered in the negative the (planted) question of whether:

Great Britain can at present place itself, with the Continent and like it, within a tariff which is truly common, give up its preference with regard to the Commonwealth, cease to claim that its agriculture be privileged and, even more, consider as null and void the commitments it has made with the countries which are part of its free trade area.

Despite the French veto administered in Paris, the accession negotiations continued in Brussels until 29 January 1963. Spaak, whose European credentials were beyond dispute, pronounced judgement:

On 14 January we were faced with a spectacular reversal of French policy . . . without being forewarned . . . and without even being permitted to discuss the reasons . . . It will be extremely difficult, I am convinced, to continue to develop the economic Europe. As for the political Europe about which we had dreamed as a necessary consequence of economic organisation, I do not know when it will be possible to speak of this again.

Thereafter the EEC and EFTA remained apart as the other EFTA countries and Ireland also abandoned their negotiations. The EEC proceeded to implement the treaty.

One organisational matter required attention. For the three Communities there was a single Assembly, a single Court of Justice and in practice a single Council, but three different executives each with a president. The Assembly and several member states were in favour of the fusion of the executives, in order to enhance the authority of a single new Commission. France agreed, subject to the later fusion of the treaties (which never occurred). The Fusion Treaty – which also legally created a single Council – was signed in Brussels on 8 April 1965. It innovated by referring specifically in Article 4 – the only treaty reference – to the Committee of Permanent Representatives (COREPER), responsible for preparing Council meetings. The new Commission was transitionally composed of fourteen members, then reducing to nine which gave France, Germany and Italy two members each. Fusion brought with it the problem of the seat. The ECSC High Authority had its seat in Luxembourg. The new Commission was in Brussels, which exerted a centripetal force. The Assembly had its headquarters in Luxembourg but also met in Strasbourg, sharing premises with the Consultative Assembly of the Council of Europe. The transfer of the Assembly (now the European Parliament) to Brussels, where it holds most of its committee meetings, remains undecided (1989) despite much urging by a majority of its members.

The actual installation of the new Commission was hit by a rift within the Council, nominally over budgetary matters, but reaching out to the whole span of Community activity. The budgetary question concerned the financing of agricultural expenditure, which was likely to rise from 1964 when according to a Commission proposal there would be a single cereal price across the Community. According to the EEC Treaty (Article 200) the Economic and Euratom Communities are financed by national contributions which the member states vote in their own national budgets. (The ECSC was financed by a levy on production.) Article 201 of the EEC Treaty enjoined the Community to replace the national contributions of Article 200 by the creation of 'own resources'. The Commission accordingly proposed on 31 March 1965 that the Community should possess, as its own resources, the agricultural levies (on imports) and customs duties collected by the member states and hitherto retained by them as national revenue. In parallel the Commission proposed a treaty amendment which would make the Assembly a joint budgetary authority with the Council – a logical development since national parliamentary control over the sums in question would come to an end. The proposal was, however, ahead of its time. In addition, the German President of the Commission, Dr Hallstein, unveiled the proposal before the the Assembly, to the irritation of member states. In discussion France proposed the continuation of the existing national contributions system for a period of years; others proposed shorter periods and there was a blockage. France, in the chair, then closed the meeting down on 15 June 1964. It then boycotted Community meetings[50] and listed its grievances. Under the EEC Treaty, from 1 January 1966 a large number of Council decisions were to come under the rule of majority voting. This was not acceptable to the Government of President de Gaulle. It was only in January 1966 – after de Gaulle had failed to obtain a sufficient majority in the first round of the presidential elections in December 1965 – that France agreed to attend a meeting with the five foreign ministers. This was held in Luxembourg rather than Brussels to show that it was not a normal meeting. The French Foreign Minister presented his country's demands: unanimity was to be required when a country had major interests at stake, there should be a code of good conduct for the Commission ('the Decalogue') and a work programme was to be agreed.

The first point gave the greatest difficulty to the Five united against France – although France had not been alone in opposing the original 'own resources' proposal. The outcome of a second meeting held on 28–30 January and largely shaped by Spaak was the Luxembourg Compromise:

I   Where in the case of decisions which may be taken by a majority vote on a proposal of the Commission very important interests of one or more partners are at stake, the Members of the Council will endeavour, within a reasonable time, to reach solutions which can be adopted by all the Members of the Council, while respecting their mutual interests and those of the Communities, in accordance with Article 2 of the Treaty.

II With regard to the preceding paragraph, the French delegation considers that where very important interests are at stake the discussion must be continued until unanimous agreement is reached.

III The six delegations note that there is a divergence of views on what should be done in the event of a failure to reach complete agreement.

IV The six delegations nevertheless consider that this divergence does not prevent the Community's work being resumed in accordance with the normal procedure.[51]

Often described as an agreement to disagree, the Luxembourg Compromise was, on the contrary, determining. The Council did not proceed to majority voting on those issues to which it applied according to the treaty and the normal procedure became a search for unanimity achieved through the Council and its preparatory bodies negotiating within themselves to amend Commission proposals.

With the 'empty chair' again occupied, the Council had to catch up with its arrears including the adoption (on 11 May) of a financial regulation and the nomination of the new (single) Commission. Hallstein, who had been President of the EEC Commission since its inception, was not reappointed. Jean Rey of Belgium was the new President.

In October 1964 the Labour Party, led by Harold Wilson, came to power in Britain. The new Government felt it necessary to impose a 15 per cent import surcharge, a move which was contrary to EFTA rules and which upset Europe in general. It took some time to repair relations with both. However, an apparently profound change in British attitudes, examined in Chapter 5, resulted on 11 May 1967 in the UK applying for membership of the European Communities. Ireland and Denmark applied on the same day; Norway on 24 July.

As required under Article 237 of the EEC Treaty, the Commission gave an opinion – generally favourable – on the UK application and the Five prepared to proceed towards negotiations. De Gaulle, however, demurred. At a press conference on 10 May 1967 he administered the 'velvet veto' and on 27 November 1967 he commented on the weakness of the UK economy (the pound had been devalued on 19 November), and predicted that the entry of the UK would damage Community structures and would transform the Community into a simple free trade area. In internal discussion in Brussels, France maintained its position: there could be no entry negotiations until the UK took the necessary measures to repair its economic weaknesses, as France had done before the entry into force of the EEC Treaty. Franco-British relations were set back by the 'Soames Affair' in February 1968.[52] In discussion with the British Ambassador, Sir Christopher Soames, de Gaulle spoke of his own concept of Europe. Specifically, he reportedly envisaged replacing the Community system by a more flexible arrangement, embracing all the EFTA states, and with long-term bilateral agreements for agricultural trade. Politically Europe would assert its independence under a Directorate consisting of France, Germany, Italy and the UK. The British, embarrassed by these proposals, with which they in any case could not agree, decided to inform the Five – although France disputed the Foreign Office version of the conversation (Soames had taken the precaution of showing his reporting telegram to the French Foreign Minister) and although Wilson himself was against disclosure. The upshot was that the Six were unable to agree on the opening of negotiations with the applicant countries. The UK announced that it 'did not take no for an answer' and that its application, to which it had received no response, remained on the table of the Community.

President de Gaulle resigned on 28 April 1969, after losing the referendum he had called on the reform of the regions and the Senate. The successful Gaullist candidate in the ensuing election was Georges Pompidou, a former prime minister under the General, who defeated the ardent European, Alain Poher. Pompidou moved in short order to obtain a meeting of Community heads of state and government. The agenda could not possibly have left unmentioned the dormant applications for membership. Another item, of special interest to France, was a new financial regulation, the means of financing the Common Agricultural Policy. Many straws were in the wind, including Pompídou's remark at his first press conference on 10 July 1969, 'We have no objection of principle against a possible UK accession.' The summit meeting took place at The Hague on 1–2 December 1969. Apart from launching the initiatives for European Political Co-operation, which are examined in Chapter 4, it came out with the triptych: completion (which meant essentially secure financing of agricultural expenditure); deepening; and widening – the admission of more members. It was understood that the negotiations should open in the first half of 1970, and 30 June became the date. In February 1970 the Labour Government published as a White Paper an economic assessment of membership (Cmnd 4289) which was generally objective but reaffirmed the Government's commitment to reaching a successful conclusion. Eight days before 30 June 1970 the Conservative Party won a general election in Britain and Edward Heath formed the Government. It inherited (and accepted) the preparations which its predecessor had made for the entry negotiations. Ireland, Denmark and Norway also prepared to negotiate.

In the Maudling days, the negotiations had the appearance of being among seven states. In the first Heath negotiations it was the Six (aided by the Commission), plus one. Third time round it was to be the Six as one, plus one. The Six arranged that, with the help of the Commission, they would speak only through the President of the Council – although the Six would all be present at negotiating sessions, silently observing and on hand to caucus if the session needed a new contribution from them. For the Six the ground rules were that the applicants accepted the treaties and the *acquis* (translated as 'what the communities have achieved'), and that there would be transitional arrangements, but that their purpose was solely to allow for the adhering states to adjust to the conditions of membership. It was also perhaps in the mind of all that this time around there were not to be discussions at the level of what to do about kangaroo meat – but in the event, matters such as tariff arrangements for mimosa wattle had to be di cussed and agreed. By early 1971 the negotiations were running into log-jams which made recourse to bilateral diplomacy at all levels necessary. (The leader on the UK side was Geoffrey Rippon, in another non-portfolio post as Chancellor of the Duchy of Lancaster, and having his base in the Foreign and Commonwealth Office, as it had come to be called following the post-1965 reorganisation of the Diplomatic Services.) From 19 to 21 May Heath met Pompidou in Paris. At the close, Pompidou was able to conclude that: 'it would be unreasonable to believe that agreement is impossible at the Conference in June'.

So it was in Luxembourg in June that the last four big issues were settled. The first was the UK budgetary contribution, where the UK opened with a (knowingly) low bid. The solution was a relatively low starting position, a growth formula and an anti-surge rule for the last year of the transition. The second was the transitional period. The British opener had been a longer period for moving to agricultural prices than for abolishing internal tariffs, regarded by the Six as having the cake and eating it. The solution was to make the periods approximately the same. The third divide was over Commonwealth sugar, which had contractual access to the British market and a favourable price there for 1.4 million tons. The UK wanted the equivalent to become a Community obligation and demanded 'bankable assurances' but finally accepted that the enlarged Community *'aura au coeur'* the interests of Commonwealth producers, including sugar producers, especially in the forthcoming association negotiations with Caribbean, African and Pacific countries.[53] A fourth problem was New Zealand dairy produce, resolved in a protocol fixing access and price for an import quota which gave satisfaction to the New Zealand representative John Marshall, who was on hand in the building, and his Government. The complete results of the negotiations were set out in a White Paper in July 1971 (Cmnd 4715).

Denmark, Norway and Ireland concluded their negotiations and the

Accession Treaties were signed in Brussels on 22 January 1972. They provided for the four new members to join on 1 January 1973.

One immediate task for the Ten was to establish a relationship with what would be left of the European Free Trade Association when three of its members left it. All had accepted the proposal of the Six that bilateral free trade agreements should be negotiated with each of the EFTA members, not with EFTA as a bloc. Such agreements were signed in July 1972 with Sweden, Switzerland, Austria, Portugal and Iceland. Signature of an agreement with Finland was deferred to October 1973, pending Finland's discussion of its European relations with the Soviet Union. In Ireland and in Denmark referendums were held on the terms of membership (Ireland 83 per cent yes; Denmark 63.3 per cent yes) and parliamentary ratification followed. In the UK the European Communities Bill was enacted. At third reading in the Commons on 13 July 1972 the vote was 301 for, 284 against. In Norway the consultative referendum went against membership (53.49 per cent no)[54] and Norway concluded a Free Trade Agreement with the enlarged Community in May 1973.[55]

This then redrew the economic map of Western Europe so far as those states were concerned that had, since the Second World War, wanted to create a new structure, or had been obliged by those who wanted it to find their place in it.

The construction of Europe post-1972

Early in its existence the new structure came under a strain which was to prove too much. In October 1973 the Arab oil producers embargoed exports to the Netherlands, which they regarded as pro-Israeli, and began to force up oil prices. Community solidarity was not enough to defend a member state (although the oil majors did so). The UK and France were quick to make oil deals with Arab states and the Community was seen to show little backbone when Arab ministers showed up in Copenhagen at a summit meeting in December 1973.

With the change of government in the UK on 28 February 1974, the Community was propelled into further difficulty with the renegotiation of the terms of British membership (see Chapter 5). This culminated in the positive vote in the British referendum of 5 June 1975. With membership questions thus settled the Communities could turn to an institutional problem, although some of the old problems soon came back.

Each of the three treaties creates an Assembly; the Convention on Certain Institutions Common to the European Communities provides that the same Assembly serve each of the three. Each treaty stipulates that the Assembly:

- consists of delegates who shall be designated by the respective Parliaments from among their members – between 1973 and 1975 the Labour Party did not designate members, showing its opposition to Britain's membership;
- shall draw up proposals for elections by direct universal suffrage in accordance with a uniform procedure in all member states – the Council shall, acting unanimously, lay down the appropriate provisions which it shall recommend to member states for adoption in accordance with their respective constitutional requirements.

In 1960 the (single) Assembly drew up and adopted a draft convention for direct elections. The Council did not act on it. There was disagreement over details and reservation on the principle of creating a body which would have supranational status and which would rival the democratic legitimacy of the parliaments and governments of member states. Italy, which did not share these hesitations, at one point initiated measures to secure the direct election of Italian members.

The Heads of State and Government meeting in Paris on 9–10 December 1974 took two institutional decisions. One was to create and arrange for meetings of the European Council in which they would come together regularly in future. The other was in favour of universal direct elections to the European Parliament. Some commentators saw a trade-off between the two. The UK and Denmark reserved their position on direct elections.

The Assembly itself had campaigned for direct elections at every opportunity and on 14 January 1975 it adopted a new draft convention (the Patijn Resolution, from the name of its draftsman). The draftsman had concluded that a uniform procedure, exactly the same in every member state, created too many problems. The European Council majority in 1974 had spoken of direct elections in 1978 but the UK needed more time for 'internal consultations', including difficulties with the Conservative opposition. In the event, the first European direct elections were held in June 1979. The turnout was generally low, except where voting is compulsory and the campaigns were largely fought on national issues. The House elected as its first president Mme Simone Veil, a French member of the Liberal group, and for the second half of its mandate Piet Dankert, a Dutch socialist. When Greece acceded to the Community, its members were initially designated by the Greek Parliament, pending direct elections. The second direct elections (still conducted on national lines) were held in June 1984. The first Spanish and Portuguese members in 1986 were designated but direct elections were held shortly afterwards in both countries.

The holding of direct elections made no formal differences to the Assembly's advisory and supervisory functions. But it could speak with greater authority – for example, in rejecting the budget – and could reinforce its demand to be given legislative or co-legislative functions. On 30 March 1962 the Assembly had decided to change its name to European Parliament, although this was not used in legislation. The Single European Act of 1986 formally changed the name.

It was said above that some old problems soon came back. The problem of budgetary imbalance – the net amount transferred by the UK to the Community budget – did not go away after renegotiation and the British referendum of 1975. It had been to some extent tempered by transitional arrangements, but with continuing growth in agricultural expenditure it became a major issue for Britain – and for the Community – when the Conservative Government under Margaret Thatcher came to power in 1979. Britain pressed with some vigour its argument that seven of the nine member states, including five more prosperous than the Community average, were net beneficiaries of the budget. In fact, the budget transferred resources from member states with relatively small agricultural sectors to those which are net exporters of agricultural products regardless of their relative prosperity. Two member states, Britain and Germany, were left to make transfers to the others. After a stormy session of the European Council in Dublin on 29–30 November 1979, it was agreed that there should be 'complementary measures' in favour of Britain, in the form of additional projects financed by the Regional and Social Funds. In May 1980, after difficult discussion of a series of issues in the Council, the Commission was given a mandate to produce the proposals which would enable the Community to fulfil its pledge to resolve the problem by means of structural change. The new Commission (under the presidency of Gaston Thorn) responded to this mandate in June 1981. Meanwhile the complementary measures continued and became a dispute between the Council and the European Parliament, which as a budgetary authority had the right to scrutinise them, to vote on them and to subject them to budgetary control. As the debate on lasting solutions to the Community's financial problems was pursued from Council to Council and European Council to European Council – including the failure of the European Council in Athens in December 1983 to adopt any conclusions at all – *ad hoc* refunds in Britain's favour were agreed for 1983. For 1984 a new correcting mechanism was established as a fixed amount for that year and, for future years, as relief in the amount of VAT which Britain was due to pay into the budget. This changed from one which compensated Britain by channelling additional Community expenditure there to one which reduced the amount transferred by Britain to the Community budget. It was accompanied by a decision to increase the total size of the budget (in revenue and expenditure) and was to be examined *ex novo* before the new revenue ceiling was reached (European Council, Fontainebleau, 25–6 June 1984). This examination was integrated into the task of 'making the Single Act succeed', which was brought to a conclusion at the European Council meeting in Brussels, under German Presidency, in February 1988.

The two major rounds of financial negotiation, pre-Fontainebleau 1984 and pre-Brussels 1988, covering the future financing of the Community, the development of new policies, problems of enlargement, budgetary discipline, 'budgetary imbalances' (the UK problem) and the cost of the CAP took heavy toll for eight years of the Council's time and negotiating capacity, as well as touching off acrimony among members of the Council and between it and the Parliament. In particular, the protracted and sometimes sterile negotiations could not but delay progress in the Community's further enlargement. The applicants wished to see what kind of community they were applying to join, and the member states had to find time to address the enlargement negotiations.

Relations with countries eligible for membership

For six countries which are European in the sense of Article 237, and are therefore eligible for membership of the Communities, relations limited to trade or to association have been found insufficient. Greece had been quick to establish a relationship with the Communities. An Association Agreement under Article 238 of the EEC Treaty was concluded in July 1961 and came into force on 1 November 1962. It looked to later membership.[56] On 21 April 1967 units of the Greek armed forces rebelled and assumed power in what was known as the 'Rule of the Colonels'. The Community thereupon 'froze' the Association Agreement, confining its operation to day-to-day matters. On 24 July 1974, following the ill-fated intervention by the Colonels in Cyprus, democracy (but not monarchy) returned to Greece. The Association Agreement was brought out of the cold. On 12 June 1975 the new Greek Government applied for EEC membership, the first time that an associate had done so. For the Council, there was no question of turning down the application, which was regarded as an expression of Greek desire to consolidate democratic government. On 28 January 1976, however, the Commission noted that in its opinion Greece and Turkey had hitherto been on an equal footing, as associates. It proposed that the rights guaranteed to Turkey by its associate status should not be affected by the examination of the Greek application. The Greek Accession Treaty was signed in Athens on 28 May 1979. Greece became the tenth member state on 1 January 1981.

Spain, under General Franco, stood aside from the democratic movements of post-war Europe. In 1962 Spain proposed to the EEC that it should become an associate, but the proposal languished in Brussels. At the end of the sixties, the Community became concerned to develop what it called an 'overall Mediterranean approach'. Some member states had important interests in the Mediterranean area and there were loose ends in the EEC Treaty, which had special and now outdated provisions for Algeria. Within the overall approach a Trade Agreement (Article 113 of the EEC Treaty, not Article 238) was concluded between the EEC and Spain in 1970. It did not envisage membership. From 1975, when King Juan Carlos ascended to the vacant throne, Spain set out to improve and strengthen its relations with its European neighbours. It submitted an application for membership on 28 July 1977. The negotiations were long drawn-out, less because of the problems intrinsic to them than because of the Community's preoccupations with its own internal problems, especially of finance. It fell to the Italian Presidency, in the first half of 1985, to give a new impetus. The Accession Treaty was signed in Madrid on 12 June 1985 and Spain entered the Community on 1 January 1986.

Portugal, a member of EFTA, concluded a Free Trade Agreement with the EEC in 1972. Democracy was restored to Portugal in 1974. On 28 March 1977 Portugal applied for membership of the Communities.

In its opinion on the application the Commission said that there was no choice, 'The Community cannot leave Portugal out of the process of European integration.' The Portuguese and Spanish negotiations proceeded in parallel. The Accession Treaty was signed in Lisbon on 12 June 1985 and Portugal entered the Community on 1 January 1986.

Turkey is classified a European country as a member of the Council of Europe and as a member of the North Atlantic Treaty Organisation. Like Greece, Turkey acted quickly to establish a relationship with the European Communities, becoming an associate in 1964. The Association Agreement gave rise to problems over the years, notably over the question of free movement for Turkish workers to and within the Community. This was foreseen in the agreement, but by the time it should have become operative employment conditions had drastically changed. After considerable preparations, Turkey lodged an application for membership on 14 April 1987. In accordance with precedent and treaty procedure, the Commission was asked for its opinion on the application. The Turkish Prime Minister said in a press conference in September 1988 that he had in the past talked of membership by the year 2000, but that it could be later. The Turkish application will be the first use of the new procedure under which the majority of the membership of the European Parliament must give its consent.

Malta concluded an Association Agreement with the Communities in 1971. This agreement did not refer to the possibility of ultimate membership. In mid-1988 the new Maltese leaders announced that there would be an application for membership by 1992, and perhaps by 1990. At the same time the Maltese Prime Minister said that Malta would remain not only neutral but non-aligned.[57] Cyprus concluded an Association Agreement in 1973; the text does not refer to possible membership of the Communities. An agreement on moving to a customs union was concluded on 19 October 1987. In late 1988 there was talk of a possible application for EC membership.

The EFTA countries (Iceland, Norway, Sweden, Finland, Austria and Switzerland) were led to re-examine their relations with the Communities in 1986–8 in the light of the single market to which they would not belong. It is clear from the public statements of several of them that the membership option has been considered. For example, the Austrian Chancellor said in 1987 that the State Treaty of 1955 (which ended the occupation) and the Austrian Constitution of the same year which established the country's perpetual neutrality, would not in his Government's view – contrary to what had often been thought – be a bar to membership. An Austrian application for membership was lodged in July 1989. The Swiss authorities announced in 1988 that their federal structure and the devolution of power to the cantons would, apart from any other consideration, make it impracticable for Switzerland to assume the obligations of membership. The Norwegian debate appears to continue. In Sweden neutrality remains an issue but the debate on relations with the European Communities has been reopened.

Yugoslavia, which concluded a Co-operation Agreement in 1973, is usually regarded as an impossible applicant. Albania remains in self-imposed isolation. There is a pledge in the Spanish Accession Agreement to examine the Communities' relations with Andorra, and negotiations to create a customs union began in the first half of 1989. Morocco, which concluded an Association Agreement in 1969, applied for membership on 8 July 1987. This application could not be entertained, Morocco not being a European country.

Major constitutional reform

A new round of constitutional and institutional reform opened at the meeting of the European Council in London in November 1981, when the German and Italian delegations, acting jointly, gave notice of a new plan to promote European union. The German side elaborated its ideas at an internal meeting on Epiphany (*Dreikönigstag*). The plan was for the adoption of an Act of European Union and was known as the Genscher–Colombo initiative. The plan took as its principles the need to provide a firmer orientation to political objectives, a more effective decision-making structure and a comprehensive political and legal framework capable of development. The detailed provisions included an organisation which placed the European Council at the apex both of the work of the Communities and of political co-operation and which recognised the central importance attached to the work of the European Parliament in the development of European union.

An attempt was made to define the use of the notion of 'vital interest'. A country claiming that its vital interests were at stake would be required to give its reasons in writing. The Council would defer its decision until its next meeting. If, at the meeting, the member state concerned again invoked its vital interests (in writing) a decision would again not be taken. There was to be a review of the European Act after five years with a view to preparing a treaty on European union. An accompanying statement on economic integration called for a functional internal market, an adjustment of the Common Agricultural Policy, an improvement in budgetary structure and closer co-ordination of economic policy.

The Council found it hard going to discuss a paper which had not come to it from the Commission or from its own Presidency and progress was slow and difficult. Having taken a forward public position, the authors found it difficult to compromise. Even when the incoming German Presidency in January 1983 began to compile a final version, the text which emerged from the European Council meeting in Stuttgart on 19 June 1983 – no longer an Act but a Solemn Declaration of European Union, not involving constitutional procedures in member states – was subject to reservations set out in footnotes. Five out of the Ten (Denmark, Greece, France, Ireland and Britain) upheld the Luxembourg Compromise; Denmark opposed any extension of the Council/Parliament conciliation procedure; Greece did not accept the desirability of reaching more rapidly common positions in political co-operation. The Solemn Declaration did not achieve what the Genscher–Colombo plan wanted and the outstanding problems had to be faced again two years later.

From 1980 to mid-1984, spanning the Genscher–Colombo initiative, the major preoccupation within the Community was 'budgetary imbalance', the catchword for the British demand for relief from what it regarded as its excessive gross and net payment to the Community budget. This was linked with the (generally) rising cost of agricultural guarantee expenditure. By a quirk of nature, agricultural spending in 1980 was relatively low. In 1982, when the Council came to fix agricultural prices for the coming season, Britain was at war in the Falklands and was seeking and obtaining support from Community institutions and from the governments of member states for economic measures against Argentina.[58] It opposed the proposed price increases and invoked the Luxembourg Compromise. This was not accepted by a majority of member states, on the grounds that the British objective was not intrinsic to the matter for decision but belonged to its attempt to obtain budgetary reform. By majority vote substantial price increases were agreed. Agricultural spending continued to rise. As described above, at the European Council meeting in Fontainebleau in June 1984 the French Presidency successfully put through a series of measures which took the sting out of the budgetary problem and laid a basis for the further development of the Communities.

Apart from budgetary issues, the European Council at Fontainebleau decided to set up two new committees to prepare reports on the future of the Communities. Each took the name of its chairman: Dooge, an Irish Senator who had been Minister of Foreign Affairs, presided over the *ad hoc* Committee on Institutional Questions, and Adonnino, a former Italian member of the European Parliament, took the Committee on 'Citizen's Europe'. Although the passage in the European Council conclusions appointing the Dooge Committee likened it to the Spaak Committee of foundation days, there was a major difference. Dooge had a completely open mandate because nothing had been decided. Spaak had worked on the commitments entered into at Messina. The Dooge Committee did not set out to be consensual, and its report is qualified by dissent. In all there are thirty-seven reservations and two closing unilateral declarations. The mainstream report (March 1985) looks towards a single market by the end of the decade; the improvement of competitiveness; the promotion of common values (including cultural); the search for external identity (including security and defence); more regular recourse to voting in decision making (with a saving for very important national interests); the strengthening of the role of the Commission; the participation of Parliament in legislating (including co-decision in defined matters); and operationally the convocation of a conference to draft a treaty of European union (Danish, Greek and British disagreement).

The European Council meeting in Milan in June 1985 did not follow mainstream Dooge. A series of further proposals were on its table (including British and Franco-German ideas about political co-operation) but the Council confined itself to an agreement in principle, taken for the first time in a European Council by vote – Denmark, Greece and Britain being outvoted – to convene a conference under Article 236 of the EEC Treaty to discuss treaty amendment.[59]

The Single European Act

It fell to the ensuing Presidency, Luxembourg, to organise the conference and to discharge the preparatory procedures under Article 236. All this could be done by qualified majority but the final outcome needed common agreement and ratification by the parliaments in each member state. This was the genesis of the Single European Act, which emerged after less than six months, to be signed on 17 February 1986 by nine member states, followed on 28 February by Denmark, Italy and Greece. The Danish Government had been required by the Folketing to ascertain that no revision of the Act was possible and had done so. It then held a referendum in which the electorate voted in favour of acceptance of the Single European Act.

'Single' recalls that the Act both concerns the revision of the three treaties under Article 236 of the EEC Treaty and corresponding clauses of the other treaties, *and* contains separate (and for the first time) treaty provisions on political co-operation, including the establishment of a small secretariat consisting of officials temporarily seconded from foreign ministries.

In the Community section, Title II, the Single European Act makes four main innovations:

- It provides that certain decisions hitherto subject to unanimity (for example, Article 100 of the EEC Treaty, harmonisation of standards) are brought under the qualified majority rule (for example, new Article 100A).

- It formalises Community concern with research and development and with the environment, hitherto actively pursued in the Community but under general enabling provisions (for example, Article 235).

- It devises a 'co-operation procedure' between the Council and the Parliament which gives Parliament more say but without co-decision. The procedure applies to measures aimed at creating the single market. The Commission r ;ains the monopoly of legislative initiative. The Parliament gives an opinion on the Commission proposal. The latter may, but is not obliged to, modify its proposal accordingly. The Council takes, by qualified majority, or by unanimity if it amends the (possibly revised) Commission proposal, a 'common position'. The Parliament then examines and votes on the common position, needing a qualified majority (of at least half its members) to propose amendments. The Council considers Parliament's second reading and decides. Parliament and Council have three months each for their second readings (extendable by common agreement to four months) and the Commission has one month in which to express an opinion on the Council's 'common position'. If at the end of the period the Council has not decided, the proposal is dead.

- It gives the Parliament the right to grant or withhold assent when consulted by the Council on the entry of new member states into the Community (Article 237) or new agreements with third countries for association with the Community (Article 238).

The majority in the European Parliament regarded the Single European Act as disappointingly meagre compared with its own aspirations but resolved to 'exploit it to the limit'. Full ratification was delayed when, in Ireland, a private citizen, Raymond Crotty, obtained a judgment on 9 April 1987 that the political co-operation part of the Single European Act could not be ratified without a constitutional amendment. A referendum was held to change the Constitution. Turnout was 44 per cent, and 69.9 per cent of votes cast were in favour. The Act entered into force on 1 July 1987.

A negotiation which had opened in disagreement ended in consensus. The final package had the required 'something for everyone' character. For example, new Article 100A, paragraph 4, provides that if following Council decision a member state needs (stronger) national measures, for the reasons adduced in Article 36 (the escape clause of the EEC Treaty) or for the protection of the environment or the working environment, it can be authorised by the Commission to keep them in being. This is helpful to Denmark, which had difficulties over the years with what it regarded as the low standard of Community environment legislation. The Single Act explicitly provides for economic cohesion, on which Greece, as a country below average GNP, had insisted in its note of dissent in Dooge. For the UK a major preoccupation, new in the negotiations, was the programme for the completion of the single market. This gave treaty effect to the White Paper which the Commission had produced in June 1985 under the leadership of Vice-President Lord Cockfield,[60] setting out an annotated, precise and timed programme for the completion of the single market in 1992.

The single market was predicated on the elimination of all controls at frontiers, such that the circulation of goods, services, capital and people across frontiers would be as free as circulation within national frontiers. The White Paper set out proposals for Community decisions which would replace nationally divergent rules such as those concerning product standards, pharmaceutical and phytopathological controls, professional qualifications, indirect tax rates (VAT and excise) and passport control. Although the member states strongly backed the programme (without committing themselves to accept every measure exactly as the Commission proposed it), several of them had major reservations about the fiscal proposals and about abolishing all frontier controls on travellers, mingled among whom are terrorists, drug traffickers and international criminals.

The Single European Act needed accompanying financial measures, to cost the programmes and to arrange for their financing by curtailing the growth of agricultural expenditure and increasing the resources available to the Community budget. The Commission filled in this part of the mosaic in the documents (COM)100 and (COM)101 which it published in February 1987 under the headline 'Making the Single Act succeed'. This set the member states off on a new round of negotiations, first with each other and the Commission and then with the European Parliament, the joint budgetary authority.

To bring agricultural spending under control the Commission proposed a maximum annual growth rate (modelled on one already in use), a reserve fund for fluctuations in the exchange-related price of agricultural produce, and the introduction or extension to other products of stabilisers, which limit the quantities to which Community price guarantees apply. For additional revenue the Commission proposed a new resource, proportionate to member states' gross national products. Under the principle of cohesion, it proposed the doubling of the structural funds (Regional, Social and Agricultural Guidance), along with new objectives for backward and declining areas. Finally, it proposed that budgetary expenditure should be programmed five years ahead. At European Council meetings in Brussels (June 1987, Belgian Presidency) and Copenhagen (December 1987, Danish Presidency) the member states inched towards agreement. At Brussels in February 1988 the German Presidency carried through a package, subject to reaching an inter-institutional agreement with the European Parliament, on what could be variously regarded as containing expenditure ('budgetary discipline') or planning its growth. Such an agreement, almost the last piece in the jigsaw, was signed at the European Council meeting in Hanover in June 1988. It remained for the governments to obtain national parliamentary ratification of the decision to increase the Communities' 'own resources'.

European union?

The long march of European Councils from Stuttgart to Hanover via every other country in the Community of Ten had provided the Community's new statutory and budgetary base – and had taken it to within a few months of the appointment of a new Commission (of which Jacques Delors had been redesignated President) which would be responsible for transforming the common market into the single market of twelve members (for goods, capital, services and people) by the end of its mandate in December 1992.[61]

In one year only in the cycle of twenty a new Commission and a new Parliament take office; 1989 is such a year. This renewal, coming on the heels of the Single European Act and the operation called 'Making the Single Act succeed', may stimulate at least new reflection about where the Communities are going next. A leading player in the next act will be the European Parliament, the advocate of European union.

European union is a concept with many connotations. Whatever else it means in the minds and sayings of those who use it, it usually implies that some of the powers and functions of the governments of the member states will pass to the organs of the Union. It usually also means that the Union will undertake a wider range of responsibilities than those exercised by the Communities.

When the short cut to 'political union' was blocked, the approach to closer integration became circuitous. Some of the milestones were the first modest revisions of the EEC and Euratom Treaties in 1970 and 1975 to give the (nominated, not elected) Parliament budgetary power, a characteristic of most parliaments. On 19–20 October 1972 the Heads of State and Government at their meeting in Paris (including the new member states) set themselves the major objective of transforming, before the end of the 1970s, the whole complex of the relations of member states into a 'European union'. The strain placed on the Community in the oil crisis of 1973 put paid to such intentions. The European Council meeting in Paris in December 1974 asked its Belgian member, Leo Tindemans, to write a report on European union and his report (*Bulletin of the EC*, Supplement 1/76) was considered at the meeting in The Hague in 1976. In a 'high road to European Union'[62] Tindemans proposed a common foreign policy, on a legal basis; a monetary policy within an economic policy; a 'citizen's Europe'; and a reform of the institutions (including direct elections, majority voting in the Council, an annual Council Presidency, delegation of powers to the Commission and the right of the president of the Commission to choose his or her team). Tindemans' report was not followed up at the time, but many of the ideas came back strongly later.

Another report on Community institutions by 'three wise men', Biesheuvel of the Netherlands, Dell of the UK and Marjolin of France (OOP 1980), was examined at the European Council meeting in Brussels in December 1978, without significant effect. The holding in June 1979 of the first direct European elections was a landmark, and strengthened the already dominant European spirit of the body. While the Council proceeded via the Solemn Declaration of European Union of Stuttgart in June 1983 towards the Single European Act, the new Parliament tried a more direct route. It appointed on 9 July 1981 a Committee on Institutional Questions, charged with producing proposals for establishing a European union. The Committee, led by Altiero Spinelli, set to work to prepare a draft treaty. (Spinelli had been expelled from the Italian Communist Party in 1937 but was an affiliate of it in the European Parliament. He was a Commissioner from 1970 to 1976.)

On 14 February 1984 the European Parliament (membership of 434) adopted by 237 votes for, 31 against and 43 abstentions the Draft Treaty Establishing the European Union. Parliament sent the draft treaty to the parliaments and governments of member states, and charged the new Parliament (from the elections of 17 June 1984) to pursue contacts with national parliaments. These contacts subsequently gave rise to a proposal that national referendums should be held on European union.

The Draft Treaty of European Union (OOP February 1984) is so far the most fully articulated plan for a united Europe. As such – although it remains only a parliamentary proposal and one on which little has happened between 1984 and 1989 – it is worth some study. The draft treaty identifies the European Communities, the European Monetary System and European Political Co-operation as 'first achievements'. It entrenches in the Union the fundamental rights and freedoms derived from the constitutions of the member states and from the European Convention for the Protection of Human Rights and Fundamental Freedoms. Within five years the Union is to formulate its own declaration on fundamental rights.

The institutions of the Union would be:

● A directly elected Parliament, co-legislator.

- The 'Council of the Union' consisting of representatives appointed by governments and headed by a minister. The Council participates in legislation. For a transitional period of ten years a representation can invoke a vital national interest to postpone a decision which could be voted. When legislating or budgeting, the Council meets in public.

- A Commission, the President of which is appointed by the European Council and able to select the Commission. The Commission can be dismissed by Parliament with a majority of two-thirds of votes cast.

- A Court of Justice, half the bench being appointed by the Parliament and half by the Council.

- The European Council, composed of the heads of state or government and the president of the Commission.

There would be four organs: Court of Auditors, Economic and Social Committee, European Investment Bank, and European Monetary Fund.

In the legislative process, draft laws are to be proposed by the Commission, or by the Council or Parliament if their request for a draft law is declined. Parliament votes and sends the draft (possibly amended) to the Council. Council votes and if the draft does not pass or is amended a conciliation committee, drawn from Parliament and Council, meets. If disagreement persists the draft falls, unless either institution fails to submit it to a further vote within a given time limit. In this case, a draft which has been expressly approved by either legislative authority passes into law. The law of the Union is directly applicable and takes precedence over national law. A member state which violates democratic principles or fundamental rights and has judgment given against it by the Court can have its treaty rights suspended.

The Union is to comprise a single market with free circulation of persons, services, goods and capital. All member states must participate in the European Monetary System wherein part of the reserves of the member states are taken into the European Monetary Fund and the ECU becomes a reserve currency and a means of payment. Full monetary union is to be achieved progressively. The revenue of the Union budget is the own resources of the Communities, including a VAT share which the Union can determine. Expenditure is based on a multiannual financial programme, which is adopted via the Union's legislative procedure. Parliament and the Council of the Union are the budgetary authority.

The draft treaty is open to ratification by all the member states of the European Communities. It can come into force when ratified by member states making up two-thirds of the population of the Communities (200 million). The draft treaty is silent on how the residual Communities conduct themselves if a number of their members have declared for the Union and brought it into being.

Little of the draft treaty found its way into the Single European Act. The two share treaty status for political co-operation, and explicit mention of a series of objectives – for example, social, environmental, and research and development. The multiannual expenditure plan came through in the 1988 Inter-Institutional Agreement. The 'two readings' type of legislative procedure has a distinct analogy in the co-operation procedure instituted by the Single European Act, but it eschews the conciliation committee (a feature of bicameral Germany and USA). The thrust of the draft treaty is towards majority voting in the Council of the Union and the Single European Act went some way in the same direction. It is implicit in the draft treaty that Union budgetary expenditure will increase, and that increases in the availability of revenue will be decided by the Union, not by the governments and parliaments of the member states. Although this has also been proposed in the Community, it did not happen in the Single European Act or in its inter-institutional sequels.

The call for national referendums did not evoke much echo – except in Italy – during the mandate of the second directly elected Parliament (1984–9). It was addressed directly to parliaments, bypassing governments, whereas the latter are normally the instigators or at least the organisers of referendums. The Draft Treaty of European Union was undercut by the Single European Act, the general inference being that it would take some considerable time for the member states to return to constitutional redrafting, especially in view of the effort they need to devote to realising the objectives of the Single Act and the single market.

A study of some of the wider implications of European union appears in the final chapter.

Appendix 1.1 European (and wider) organisations

	EC	Council of Europe	NATO	OECD	EFTA	WEU	Benelux	Schengen (travel area)	G7 world economic summits[3]	Nordic council[4]	COCOM strategic embargo
Belgium	X	X	X	X		X	X	X			X
Denmark	X	X	X	X						X	X
Germany (FR)	X	X	X	X		X		X	X		X
Greece	X	X	X	X							X
Spain	X	X	X	X		X					X
France	X	X	X	X		X		X	X		X
Ireland	X	X		X							
Italy	X	X	X	X		X			X		X
Luxembourg	X	X	X	X		X	X	X			X
Netherlands	X	X	X	X		X	X	X			X
Portugal	X	X	X	X		X					X
UK	X	X	X	X		X			X		X
Austria		X		X	X						
Cyprus		X									
Iceland		X	X	X	X					X	
Liechtenstein		X			X[2]						
Malta		X									
Norway		X	X	X	X					X	X

San Marino	X					
Sweden	X		X	X		X
Switzerland	X	X	X			
Turkey	X		X²			X
Yugoslavia				X		
Finland	X		X		X	
USA		X	X		X	X
Canada		X	X			X
Japan			X			X
Australia			X			
New Zealand			X			

¹ See also *Yearbook of International Organisations*, (London, K.G. Saur).
² Special status.
³ Plus Commission of E.C. and Presidency of Council of E.C, if not already represented.
⁴ Greenland and Faeroes separately represented within Danish delegation; Åland within Finnish delegation.

Notes

1. Richard Hoggart and Douglas Johnson, *An Idea of Europe* (London, Chatto and Windus, 1987).
2. Paul Kennedy, *The Rise and Fall of the Great Powers* (London, Unwin Hyman, 1988).
3. H.A.L. Fisher, *A History of Europe* (London, Edward Arnold, 1938).
4. Training manuals for British conscripts in 1939 talked of the nation going from peace to total war overnight. It was expected that from the first hours of hostilities there would be air attacks on civilian populations (as at Guernica during the Spanish Civil War), using poison gas (as in the Italian conquest of Abyssinia).
5. Brian Bond, *War and Society in Europe 1870–1970* (London, Fontana, 1984).
6. Claude Delmas, 'Corée 1950', *Editions Complexe*, Paris, pp. 111–31.
7. The Edict of Nantes, by which Henry gave the Huguenots religious freedom was 'the first public recognition of the fact that more than one religious communion can be maintained in the same polity', Fisher, op. cit., p. 579.
8. W. Nicoll, 'Pour la constitution en 1963 d'un Parlement européen composé de délégations nationales siégeant en hémicycle avec pondération de vote', *Révue du Marché Commun*, Paris, No. 302, December 1986, p. 592.
9. 'Law is to do what blood and iron have for centuries failed to do. For only unity based on a freely-taken decision can be expected to last; unity founded on the fundamental values such as freedom and equality, and protected and translated into reality by law', Commission of the European Communities, *The ABC of Community Law* (OOP, 1986), p. 28. This is the milk of Kant's doctrine.
10. Barthalay.
11. The vision was common to Burns in 'A man's a man for a' that' and Schiller in 'An die Freude', which to Beethoven's setting became the 'European Hymn'.
12. Coudenhove-Kalergi appears at vital points over the years. In 1943, in exile in New York, he proposed a 'European Federation' which the Roosevelt administration disfavoured, anxious to avoid trouble with the USSR. See Boyd France, *US–European Community Relations*, (Washington, European Community Information Service, 1973), p. 6. In 1965 Coudenhove-Kalergi supported General de Gaulle's perception of European unity. His movement had already been written off in 1952 by out-and-out federalists like Spinelli.
13. James Joll (ed.), *Britain and Europe: Pitt to Churchill 1793–1940* (London, Adam and Charles Black, 1961), p. 15, footnote. In his semi-fictional biography of Briand, 'Moi, Artistide Briand' (Paris, Plon, 1981), Vercors has him 'proposing as a first step the creation of a Common Market, which by facilitating the movement of goods, capital and people would show that something coherent and complete was happening . . . The governing idea would be union, not unity, with no danger of the stronger nations dominating the weaker . . . The replies showed the fierce tenacity of national egoisms' (pp. 307–8).
14. Quoted by Harold Macmillan. *Tides of Fortune 1945–1955* (London, Macmillan, 1969), p. 151.
15. 'Patriotism is not enough, I must have no hatred or bitterness towards anyone' were the last words of Edith Cavell, killed by firing squad in Brussels on 12 October 1915 for aiding escaped British prisoners of war.
16. Passive resistance, *ahimsa*, was the Gandhian response to British police power.

17. W. Shirer, *The Rise and Fall of the Third Reich* (London, Secker and Warburg, 1974), pp. 259–62.

18. Christopher Saunders, *From Free Trade to Integration in Western Europe?* (London, Chatham House/PEP, 1975), p. 10; Sidney Pollard, *European Economic Integration 1815–1970* (London, Thames and Hudson, 1974), Chapter 6.

19. Nigel Nicolson (ed.), *Harold Nicolson: The War Years 1939–45: Diaries and Letters Vol. II* (London, William Collins, 1967), pp. 101–2, 139.

20. Macmillan, op. cit., Appendix 1.

21. Boyd France, op. cit., p. 6.

22. For the scale of the US contribution to the European Economic Recovery Programme, 1947–53, see Paul A. Samuelson, *Economics* (New York, McGraw-Hill, 1955), p. 672. Although it was not US policy to push the OEEC countries towards economic or political organisation which they might not want, the first administrator of the Economic Co-operation Administration, Paul G. Hoffman, did not take long to become forthright. In late 1949 he looked forward to 'a single large market within which quantitative restrictions on the movement of goods, monetary barriers to the flow of payments and eventually all tariffs are permanently swept away'.

23. The Schuman plan launched the first of the European Communities, for Coal and Steel. The others are the Economic Community and Euratom. Together they are described as the European Communities, despite the expressed wish of the European Parliament that the official name should be 'The European Community'. The 'Common Market' is a colloquial name for the European Economic Community. European Political Co-operation is not a Community, or regarded as belonging to the European Communities as defined above.

24. British ministers were not told of the announcement of 9 May 1950 in advance and were irritated when they learned that others, including the US Secretary of State, Dean Acheson, had had advance notice. On 19 May President Truman said 'Mr Schuman's proposal is an act of constructive statesmanship. We welcome it'. Britain declined to attend the conference which Schuman called on 20 June 1950 to discuss details of the plan.

25. The North Atlantic Treaty was signed on 4 April 1949 by the USA and Canada; by the five countries which had signed the Brussels Treaty on 17 March 1948 (France, the UK, Belgium, the Netherlands and Luxembourg); and by Italy, Portugal, Denmark, Norway and Iceland.

26. Consultative Assembly, Council of Europe, 11 August 1950: *Proceedings*, pp. 222–8.

27. Fondation Paul-Henri Spaak, *Pour une Communauté Politique Européenne* (Brussels, Bruylat, 1984), Ch. 3.

28. European Parliament (Text of the Statute of the European Community), p. 57 *et seqq.*

29. European Parliament, pp. 95–9.

30. William Slany (ed.), *Foreign Relations of the United States 1955–57: Vol. IV Western European Security and Integration* (Washington DC, US Government Printing Office, 1986), p. 323.

31. Ibid., p. 421.

32. Pollard, op. cit., pp. 112–16.

33. François Clerc, *Le Marché Commun Agricole*, (Paris, Presse Universitaire de France (Que sais-je?), 1970), p. 20.

34. Britain abandoned free trade when it passed the Import Duties Act in 1932. The Act imposed a 10 per cent tariff. Imports from the colonies were exempt. Imports from

India and the Dominions were also provisionally exempt, as an autonomous measure. This exemption became contractual in the Ottawa Agreements concluded in 1932. Under these agreements Britain secured 'preferences' in India and the Dominions. The creation of these preferences had been pioneered from 1904 to 1906 by Joseph Chamberlain. See R. Grinter, *Joseph Chamberlain*, (London, Edward Arnold, 1971), pp. 33–8, 46–61. The 1932 Act was promoted by his son, Neville Chamberlain, better known as British Prime Minister at the time of the 1938 negotiations with Hitler.

35. D. Jay, *After the Common Market* (London, Penguin, 1968).
36. This nomenclature recurs throughout. France is the one EC country whose head of state (president) has executive responsibilities and attends summit meetings.
37. Articles 39 and 40 of the EEC Treaty, which provides that the common organisation of agricultural markets *may* include all measures required to attain the objectives set out in Article 39, in particular regulation of prices.
38. W. Nicoll, 'Historique de la composition de la majorité qualifiée en vertu des traités', *Révue du Marché Commun*, Paris, No. 295, March 1980, p. 135.
39. 'Determined to lay the foundations of an ever closer union among the peoples of Europe . . . Resolved thus by pooling their resources to strengthen peace and liberty. . . .'
40. In the Note which it handed to the Six the USSR said that, since they all belonged to NATO, 'it is obvious that the entire activity of the Common Market and of Euratom will be subordinate to the objectives of NATO, whose aggressive character is well-known'. France, Belgium, Germany and Italy replied in identical terms that their aims were peaceful and that the Soviet proposals could be discussed at the May meeting of the Economic Commission for Europe, a UN body in which East and West participate.
41. Pierre Gerbet, *La Construction de l'Europe* (Paris, Imprimerie Nationale, 1983), p. 237.
42. Cf. n. 36.
43. The Yaoundé countries were: Burundi, Cameroon, Central African Republic, Chad, Congo, Dahomey, Gabon, Ivory Coast, Madagascar, Mali, Mauretania, Niger, Rwanda, Senegal, Somalia, Togo, Upper Volta and Zaïre. Mauritius (a Commonwealth country) became a member of the Yaoundé Convention in 1973.
44. General de Gaulle stated that he never used the phrase 'L'Europe des patries' which was attributed to him.
45. European Parliament, op. cit., p. 106.
46. Ibid., pp. 107–8.
47. On the silver jubilee of the Franco-German Treaty the two countries concluded a new agreement, which provides for the setting up of a Finance Council and a Defence Council. It also provides for a Franco-German infantry brigade, which has been formed.
48. Harold Wilson, *The Labour Government 1964–1970* (London, Weidenfeld and Nicolson, and Michael Joseph, 1971), pp. 184–5.
49. France exploded its first atomic bomb (under the Euratom dispensation) in the Sahara on 13 February 1960. The first French nuclear submarine was launched on 29 March 1967.
50. The boycott was not total. French delegates came to meetings in Brussels of CAP Management Committees.

51. W. Nicoll, 'The Luxembourg Compromise', *Journal of Common Market Studies*, Vol. 23, No. 1, September 1984, pp. 35–43.

52. Uwe Kitzinger, *Diplomacy and Persuasion* (London, Thames and Hudson, 1973), pp. 45 *et seqq*.

53. This statement by the Six was reinterpreted in London as 'a firm assurance of a secure and continuing market in the enlarged Community on fair terms for the quantities of sugar covered by the Commonwealth Sugar Agreement'. In the event the assurance was respected in the Lome Convention (*Hansard*, 9 June 1971, Col. 1062).

54. Norwegian representatives immediately stopped attending the EC meetings to which they had been invited and returned all the documents they had received since January 1972.

55. In February 1982, following home rule for Greenland and a referendum there, it withdrew from membership of the European Communities, although there is no provision or procedure for withdrawal in the treaties.

56. Only two association agreements – those of Greece and Turkey – provide for membership of the Communities to be examined when association has sufficiently prepared for it.

57. *Le Figaro*, Paris, 17 November 1988.

58. *The Falklands War* (Sunday Times Insight); (London, Sphere Books, 1982), pp. 116–18. Max Hastings and Simon Jenkins, *The Battle for the Falklands* (London, Pan, 1983), p. 124.

59. For a commentary on the European objectives of the Italian Presidency, see 'European union: one character in search of an author' by Signor Andreotti, Italian Foreign Minister, Eighth Jean Monnet Lecture, OOP, 23 November 1985, especially pp. 17–24.

60. 'Completing the internal market', OOP.

61. Commission of the EC, 'Le Défi' (Introduction to the Cechinni Report), Flammarion, 1988.

62. P. Ludlow, *The Making of the European Monetary System* (London, Butterworth, 1982), p. 22.

2

The Institutions at Work

The Commission

The Commission, sometimes called the European Commission, more formally the Commission of the European Communities, consists – in the Community of twelve member states – of seventeen Commissioners. Two come from each of Germany, Spain, France, Italy and Britain, and one from each of the other member states. Those with two can share the appointments among political parties (as Britain has always done). Commissioners must be nationals of member states. They have mostly been active politicians.

Commissioners are appointed by common accord of governments, but in practice this agreement is taken for granted and each government announces its choice unilaterally and in its own time.[1] The original appointment is for four years and is renewable. Several Commissioners have had several terms but many have had only one. In performing their duties Commissioners are required to be independent and neither to seek nor to take instructions from any quarter.[2] Once appointed, a Commissioner can be dismissed only if the Court of Justice, on application by the Council or the Commission, retires him or her. If a vacancy occurs, a successor can be appointed on the same conditions, or the Council may decide that the vacancy need not be filled, as happened in 1976 when Altiero Spinelli resigned in order to campaign for election to the European Parliament.

Commissioners must resign as a body if in the European Parliament a motion of censure is carried by a two-thirds majority of the votes cast and a majority of members. Censure motions have been proposed but no such vote has ever carried. It used to be considered that a refusal by Parliament to grant discharge of the budgetary accounts presented by the Commission would also be regarded as a vote of no confidence, but when discharge of the 1982 accounts was refused, the Commission did not resign. (It was in any case close to the end of its term.)

The president and vice-presidents of the Commission are appointed by common accord of the governments for a period of two years, renewable. The European Parliament is consulted before the name of the president is announced. The president can belong to any member state.[3] One of the Commissioners from the five dual-member countries normally becomes a vice-president (unless the president comes from that country). Other vice-president posts rotate among the other member states. Until 1989, when Greece appointed Madame Papandreou and France Madame Scrivener, all Commissioners had been men.

The Commissioners meet weekly (about forty-five times a year), and take their decisions by the procedure on which they agree: vote, consensus, unanimity, nem. con., etc.[4] In 1987 the Commission adopted 8,212 instruments and sent the Council 699 proposals and 192 other communications. The Commission's proposals may be the brain-child of a Commissioner. They may flow from the treaties, or from legislation already adopted under them. They may be consequent upon a judgment of the Court. They may respond to a demand of the Parliament, or of the Council, or of a member state, or of an interest group. They may have their origins in the Commission staff, following a study or a piece of research or participation in a programme run by an outside body. Wherever they come from, they must be accompanied by a budgetary statement (of their cost to the Community) and a statement, in the name of deregulation, on their effect on small and medium-sized firms. They must also come in all nine official languages.

Each Commissioner has a portfolio of subjects for which he or she is responsible, but decisions are collegiate and all Commissioners keep themselves informed of the whole of the work of the Commission. They travel extensively, meeting their ministerial counterparts in the member states, political personalities in their home countries, and individuals and groups who have points to make or to whom points are to be made. Commissioners also attend plenary sessions of the European Parliament and committee meetings to answer questions, present Commission proposals and take part in debates. There is a monthly working luncheon in Strasbourg of the presidents of the three institutions.

Each Commissioner has a private office, or *cabinet* (the French word). The *cabinet*, which has a *chef*, consists of four or five people selected by the Commissioner as his personal staff. Some come from the institutions, especially the Commission itself. Others come from outside, often from national government service, and hold temporary appointments. Between them, the cabinet members help their Commissioner to cover the whole of the work of the Commission and to run his or her particular responsibilities. The chefs de cabinet meet weekly under the president's chef to prepare the weekly Commission meeting. The chef de cabinet has heavier responsibilities and a higher public profile than a typical private secretary in a British minister's private office.

Before or on taking up office, the incoming Commission meets to allocate the portfolios. This used to be a 'night of the long knives' and a time for vigorous lobbying, but more recently has been arranged in a more gentlemanly manner. Each Commissioner (sometimes including the president) thus acquires responsibility for a range of subjects, which are handled by the Directorates General of the Commission. The number of Directorates General varies, but is usually a little over twenty. In addition, there is a Secretariat General, under the Secretary General of the Commission, which holds the operation together, ensures coordination and under that heading is specifically responsible for data processing; a Legal Service; a Spokesman's Service, centralised under the president and replacing the arrangements for media liaison which each Commissioner used to make; a Joint Interpreting and Conference Service, which also provides interpreters for the Council and the Economic and Social Committee; and a Statistical Office. The Directorates General and the services plus the College of Commissioners is often collectively described as 'The Commission'. Most of the Commission staff are in Brussels but there are some in Luxembourg and in the Joint Research Centre at ISPRA in Italy. The Commission maintains information offices in each member state and delegations in some eighty-five countries and to four international organisations.

The terms of employment of the staff of the Commission (and of all the institutions) are governed by the Staff Regulations, which have legal force and are much invoked in proceedings before the Court of Justice.[5] Staff are subjects of member states (although there are and have been exceptions). The institutions are required to recruit on the widest possible geographical basis and they seek to maintain a geographical balance among the nationalities. The Commission is responsible for all appointments to its staff. Recruitment at the entry grade is by open competition, usually involving both written work and interview. Candidates must have a working knowledge of a Community language other than their own. Although there is a good deal of mobility within the Commission, and rather less between different institutions, there is a tendency towards specialisation and some staff, such as scientists, are recruited for their skills. Redundancy is rare: the staff of the Commission (and of other institutions) grows steadily. At the higher ranks, and usually after informal consultations with member states, staff are appointed from outside ('parachuting') often from national government service. As in the other institutions, a very large part of the staff is concerned with the translation (into eight languages from an original) and physical production and distribution of papers. The remuneration of staff of the institutions is exempt from national income taxes but subject to a Community income tax, which accrues to the Community budget.[6] There is a contributory pension scheme and sickness insurance.

The Council

The Council of the European Communities is theoretically a single body but in practice it meets in different compositions. Its members are representatives of governments, normally ministers (including junior ministers). The Presidency rotates among the member states for six-month spells in the alphabetical order of the countries' names in their own language, thus: Belgium, Denmark, Germany, Greece, Spain, France, Ireland, Italy, Luxembourg, the Netherlands, Portugal, and the United Kingdom. With an even number of member states, this means that each would have the same semester every six years, although the burden of work is not evenly distributed throughout the year. (August is not a working month. The budget falls in the second half. Farm prices are a heavy responsibility in the first half.) For the cycle which begins in 1993, the normal annual order is reversed: Denmark, Belgium, Greece, Germany, France, Spain, Italy, Ireland, the Netherlands, Luxembourg, the UK, and Portugal.

The Foreign (or General) Affairs Council, the Agriculture Council, and the Economic and Finance Council (ECOFIN) meet monthly. The Internal Market Council meets four or five times a year. The Fisheries and Budget Councils meet three or four times, Councils such as Industry, Research, Steel, Transport, Energy, Education, Development, Environment, Culture, and Social Affairs meet two or three times, and those such as Consumer Affairs, Tourism, Health, Tele-communications once or twice. Council meetings are held in Brussels, and in Luxembourg in April, June and October. The Budget Council sometimes meets in Strasbourg in December, during a parliamentary session. The work of the Council(s) is prepared by meetings of officials of the member states. According to Article 4 of the treaty creating a single Council and single Commission (1965, as amended) the work of the Council is prepared by a committee consisting of Permanent Representatives. By use and wont, this rule does not apply to the Agriculture Council, where the same task is performed by the Special Agricultural Committee (CSA).

The Committee of Permanent Representatives (COREPER) is split in two. Part II, consisting of Ambassadors, works (broadly speaking) for the Foreign (or General) Affairs Council, for ECOFIN, for the Energy Council, for the Research Council and via the Foreign Affairs Council for the European Council. The work of COREPER II is itself facilitated by the 'ANTICI Group' of Ambassadors' assistants, with whom the presidency discusses agenda planning, work programming and pro-cedural matters. Part I of COREPER consists of deputy permanent representatives and works for the other ('specialised') councils.[7] The 'preparation of a Council meeting' is the process of agreeing on the matter to be submitted to the Council and in what terms.

In the 'Community method' the starting point is a Commission proposal, sent to the Council. The Commission has a virtual monopoly, under the treaties, of the power to make proposals. As a general rule, the Council can take decisions only on Commission proposals. Every proposal (and decision) rests on a legal base – one or more articles of the treaty concerned. The choice of legal base determines:

- the majority required for the proposal to pass;
- the procedure to be followed with and in the European Parliament.

The voting rules provide for simple majorities (mainly for procedural questions), qualified majorities (for the infilling of existing policies) or unanimity (for new policies, or if the Council wishes to change a Commission proposal without the latter's agreement). A qualified majority is made up of 70 per cent of the votes of the member states, weighted by size. In the Community of twelve the weighting is 10 votes each: Germany, France, Italy, the UK; 8 votes: Spain; 5 votes each: Belgium, Greece, the Netherlands, Portugal; 3 votes each: Denmark, Ireland; 2 votes: Luxembourg. The qualified majority is fifty-four.

Conversely the blocking minority, which will prevent a positive vote, is twenty-three. Unanimity can be obtained with abstentions. In qualified majority voting, however, abstentions have the same effect as votes against because votes do not build up to the qualified level. The Council needs a quorum of six members. A member may give its proxy to another.

Although the Luxembourg Compromise was a note of disagreement, and although the European Council decided in Paris in 1979 that there should be more regular recourse to voting, up to the mid-1980s Councils generally preferred to reach consensus. This took time, usually involved amending the Commission's proposal, and could result in no decision being taken. The successive enlargements, adding to the spectrum of interests, further complicated the attempts to find solutions acceptable to all. This, however, is the principal task of the 'Council bodies'. Their work consists of examining a Commission proposal, first of all to ensure that there is a common understanding of it and then to establish whether it can be accepted – and if not, what changes or glosses might make it acceptable.[8]

This kind of preparatory work is organised hierarchically. It begins in the 'working groups'. These meet under the serving presidency and with the Commission present. They consist of member states' officials. Some are manned by Brussels residents, members of the 'permanent representations'. A permanent representation typically has thirty to forty staff with diplomatic status, plus support services. The staff are either members of the national diplomatic service or are seconded to it from national ministries. They receive their instructions from capitals, where the different agencies are organised to co-ordinate national positions. In some working groups the Brussels residents are supplemented or replaced by visitors from capitals (often referred to as 'experts') who come with instructions.[9]

The working group sets out to prepare a report which will show what can be agreed and what remains disputed at its level. The chairman, Commission representative and individual delegates may also seek to devise compromises or otherwise to act as brokers between different viewpoints. This includes bilateral negotiations outside the conference room, and negotiations between delegations and the Commission. On major points such negotiations may be taken over by senior officials and ministers in capitals, telephoning their opposite numbers or travelling to meet them.[10]

In the search for compromise, the Council has the help of its

Table 2.1 Number of days spent on Council meetings and meetings of preparatory bodies

Year	Ministers	Ambassadors and ministerial delegations	Committees and working parties
1958	21	39	302
1959	21	71	325
1960	44	97	505
1961	46	108	655
1962	80	128	783
1963	63.5	146.5	744.5
1964	102.5	229.5	1,002.5
1965	35	105.5	760.5
1966	70.5	112.5	952.5
1967	75.5	134	1,233
1968	61	132	1,253
1969	69	129	1,412.5
1970	81	154	1,403
1971	75.5	127.5	1,439
1972	73	159	2,135
1973	79.5	148	1,820
1974	66	114.5	1,999.5
1975	67.5	118	2,079.5
1976	65.5	108.5	2,130
1977	71	122	2,108.5
1978	76.5	104.5	2,090
1979	59	107.5	2,000
1980	83	106.5	2,078.5
1981	83	110	1,976
1982	86	107	1,885
1983	121.5	105.5	1,912.5
1984	133	86	1,868.5
1985	118	117	1,892

Secretariat General. This body has no treaty basis, its only official manifestation being its administrative budget, incorporated in the general budget. It numbers some 2,000 staff, the larger part being translators and services for providing conference facilities, printing and distribution. Some 150 staff are recognisably committee secretaries, whose responsibilities are to record the result of discussions, to brief presidents and to help them in any initiatives they want to undertake, including the search for compromise. This search goes on at all levels: Council, COREPER, committee. Only the Council has the power of decision. What is done at the lower level is informal and rests on the understanding that the Council will, in due course, endorse it. The

Council infrastructure is substantial. Each presidency has to find chairmen or women for some 150 working groups. The number of 'meeting days' is shown in Table 2.1.

As long as the Council wanted consensus (and in its absence, refrained from deciding) the work of 'Council bodies' was devoted to this aim. This in turn led to the charge that the bureaucrats had captured the Council and prevented or discouraged ministers from taking decisions which required political will.

In the Single European Act the member states agreed that a number of key treaty articles, and especially those concerned with the completion of the single market, should be modified to provide that decisions on proposals made under them should be taken by qualified majority voting in place of unanimity. This does not, of course, mean that the Council has no choice but to vote for or vote down a Commission proposal. It can still, if it wishes, and acting by unanimity, modify the Commission proposal, and it can still find itself without a qualified majority for a proposal. But it can also find that a qualified majority can be obtained if, after hearing the arguments, the Commission is ready to change its proposal. Such a qualified majority is what would often have been unanimity in a smaller Community. Consequently, the readiness of the Council to vote does not at a stroke eliminate the preparatory work. It is still necessary for the member states to make sure that they have a common understanding of the Commission proposal, to explore at working level whether it is generally acceptable, or what changes would make it so, to test whether the Commission may be prepared to make changes and, where there is disagreement, to report to ministers the reasons for it. In the light of their discussion, and under the political responsibility of their president, ministers decide whether they wish to vote, to negotiate for compromise at their level, to allow time for reflection, to remit the matter for more work at official level or, where major questions are open, to involve the European Council.

To create the material conditions for greater use of voting, the Council modified its internal rules of procedure in 1987. The Commission or a member state can now ask in Council for a straw poll to be taken on the procedural question of whether the Council should now vote on a proposal. This procedural question is settled by a simple majority (seven member states for) and, if it passes, the Council then votes on a qualified majority basis. If no qualified majority exists, the Council does not regard the proposal as lost and it may return to its search for a compromise. The Council also cleared the way for voting by marking on its agenda notices, sent out in advance of meetings, the points on which a vote could be taken.

No exact statistics exist to mark the evolution, since about 1983, towards the use of voting. This is because the Council does not, and did not in the past, always need to record votes cast. A chair can infer from discussion that agreement exists without polling delegates. If he or she concludes that it does, and this conclusion is not challenged, the decision-making process has worked.

Council agendas are divided into two parts. 'A' points are those on which delegations, acting under instructions, have found that there is agreement and Council discussion is not required. 'A' points are formally approved in Council meetings and can relate to matters which are not within the ambit of the Council approving them. 'B' points are those which require ministerial discussion.

The Budget Council was always an exception to the consensus rule. In Article 203 of the EEC Treaty an annual timetable is laid down. The draft budget has to reach Parliament from the Council by 5 October. When it returns from Parliament in early November, the Council has fifteen days to make any changes. Because of this time constraint and perhaps because the Council can, in this sole case, change the Commission's preliminary draft by qualified majority, not by unanimity, the draft budget has always been voted in the Council. This does not always guarantee a result: in 1987 the Council was unable to find a qualified majority for any budgetary proposal.

There were eighty Council meetings in 1986. The Council adopted 74 directives, 473 regulations and 184 decisions. In addition to these meetings there are two variants on 'normal' Council meetings. Councils sometimes meet 'informally', and then usually in the Presidency country at the invitation of the Presidency. At informal Councils there is no set business, rather general discussion and no intention of reaching decisions. The Presidency may take the opportunity to prefigure ideas which it may have for the agenda and handling of the next formal meeting. Some Presidencies (and individual presidents) set more store by informal Councils than others.

There are also meetings of 'The Council and Ministers of [. . .] meeting within the Council'. This indicates that there was discussion of matters which are not within the competence of the Community, or on which Community competence is accepted by some but opposed by others. These meetings are distinct from those which are outside the Community altogether but which bring together ministers of member states, such as the regular (since 1986) meetings of ministers responsible for immigration.

European Council

Meetings of the European Council have become formidable affairs, far removed from the fireside chat which may have been their original conception. Usually held in the custom-built Conference Centre with which every Presidency equips itself, sometimes held away from the capital city, they bring together the large entourages which accompany each Head of State or Government, although the latter are accompanied in the meeting room itself only by their foreign ministers, without attendant national officials.[11] The media and police are present in strength. There is (in principle) no set agenda, but each presiding prime minister has sent to colleagues, well before the meeting, a letter telling them what should be discussed, perhaps along with papers. The Commission also puts in papers. The Political Committee (of European Political Co-operation discussed in Chapter 4) usually meets *in situ* to run a last eye over any statement to be adopted. Heads of the official teams meet as the session proceeds to agree on the terms of the Conclusions which will be published after the meeting. The Conclusions are, however, usually described as those which the Presidency has drawn, on its own responsibility. At breaks in the session, prime ministers meet bilaterally, whether to pursue matters covered by discussion, or to discuss matters outside the sphere of the European Council, such as Anglo-Irish matters. Their delegations brief the media and there is a final round of press conferences, including the central one at which the president of the European Council is accompanied by the president of the Commission.

There used to be debate about whether the European Council could take decisions in the name of the Community. There is, in fact, nothing to prevent the European Council, if it wishes, from taking decisions in the same way as Councils take decisions and subject to the same procedural processes: a Commission proposal exists, the Commission is present for the discussion, opinions have been received, if required, from the European Parliament and from the Economic and Social Committee, due notice has been given of the proposed discussion, or participants have agreed to waive such notice, a quorum exists, and unanimity or qualified majority, whichever is required, is available.

In practice, however, the European Council, having a lot of ground to cover in a meeting which cannot go much beyond a day without provoking media reports of crisis, prefers to reach 'political agreement' on a subject, then charging the appropriate Council to proceed to the formal adoption of the Community instrument which the European Council agreement has unblocked. The Council thus charged may, for its part, need further help from the Commission or from the Council's subordinate bodies.[12]

At the first parliamentary part-session in Strasbourg after a meeting of the European Council (December and June or July), its president reports on what happened and the president of the Commission also makes a statement. This opens a debate which is concluded by a parliamentary vote on a resolution giving Parliament's views on the proceedings.

Up to 1985 the European Council met three times a year. It later settled down to one meeting per Presidency. The Single European Act provides in Article 2, second paragraph, that it will meet at least twice a year.

The Council Presidency

The rotating Presidency, serving for six months, has acquired increasing responsibilities. Its elementary function is to arrange dates of meetings, provide chairmen or women for them and propose agendas. But a Presidency would not be human if it discharged these functions mechanically. In its planning the Presidency may decide to take initiatives on subjects which it finds of special importance and which, for given reasons, it prefers not to leave to the Commission to initiate. Thus the British Presidency announced in 1986 an 'employment initiative'. In fact, every Presidency brings its own input and has its own ideas about the purpose of its work programme. This purpose will show a blend of national and Community interest.

The Presidency therefore sets certain priorities and tries to do so in concert with the Commission. More especially, each Presidency plans for and proposes the decisions to be taken at the European Council meeting which it will host and which will be a media event. Some priorities are more or less dictated to it: business of the Community which is spread over several Presidencies and needs to be kept going by each. To provide some continuity, and to improve Council support for its programme, Presidencies may use the 'troika' system. This brings together the last Presidency, the serving Presidency and the next Presidency. It is used in Political Co-operation and in the Economic Community it is used to overhaul the 'rolling programme' of Council work connected with the realisation of the single market.

When discussion is joined and when difficulties emerge, there is an expectation that the Presidency will bring out a compromise: to the point that this is now regarded as a Presidency duty. The Commission may also propose compromises, but is to an extent inhibited by the fact that a compromise (the noun is used positively) may compromise (the verb is used negatively) its original proposal and any arrangement which it has made with the Parliament to defend the proposal. The Presidency, free of such inhibition (but perhaps having some of its own), may be able to suggest a position to which all can agree. It may also have the technical help of the Commission to get there. If the compromise means changing the Commission's proposal, it will need unanimity. If the Commission is prepared to amend its proposal along the lines of a Presidency compromise which is gaining acceptance ('flying'), a qualified majority may be obtained.

The Presidency represents the Council on a number of occasions. It speaks for the Council in the European Parliament. In certain international negotiations it speaks on some points on which the member states have taken a common position, whilst the Commission speaks on matters within Community competence. The Presidency also receives, on behalf of the Council, personalities and delegations from third countries visiting Brussels and Strasbourg.

Finally, the Presidency takes responsibility, as the Council's memory (via the Council Secretariat) and conscience, for ensuring co-ordination between Councils meeting in different formations, especially where their work converges or overlaps. This helps to give colour to the legal fiction that 'there is only one Council', meaning that it can never be in contradiction with itself. This fiction does not correspond to some public perceptions, notably the charge that the agriculture ministers, being like-minded, combine to best the finance ministers, irrespective of who won the domestic argument about the scale of agricultural support.

In exercising the same responsibility of ensuring singleness of purpose, the Presidency is expected to co-ordinate, as necessary, work proceeding within the Community and related extramural activities (for example, in Political Co-operation or in the framework of the meetings of ministers responsible for immigration).

Intragovernmental co-ordination

In order to react to Commission proposals and to the reactions of others, each member state has equipped itself with a European secretariat in some form, a meeting point at which the different advocacies of ministries (and ministers) can be reconciled and a co-ordinated position upheld. The ministries of external affairs and of agriculture and the economic ministries are core members. These interministerial forums prepare or commission the telexes which are sent to the countries' Brussels representatives, or taken (as briefs) by visiting delegates. The return telexes, reporting the discussion and possibly making proposals for the 'line to take' at the next stage, flow back to capitals and the traffic continues for the next meeting. Permanent representation staff, especially at the top levels, travel regularly to their capitals for the interministerial meetings which discuss Community affairs. When ministers come to Brussels and Luxembourg the permanent representative and his or her staff become their local advisers. In a minister's absence the permanent representative stands in for him or her. (In any formal vote the representative would give the minister's proxy to another minister present, making up the quorum of six. A minister can accept only one proxy. Rigorously formal votes are rare and proxies are almost unknown.)

The chair who is taking a meeting, at ministerial or official level, usually calls for a preparatory briefing session with his or her own people and with the Council Secretariat (both of whom will have provided written briefs) and sometimes also with the Commission. Three bureaucracies are consequently involved in Community work. The Commission 'services' participate in all meetings at official level and support their Commissioner at Council meetings. The Council Secretariat is at the service of delegations and particularly the Presidency. The national bureaucracy instructs its representative and prepares (and usually accompanies) its minister.

The European Parliament

The European Parliament elected by direct universal free suffrage since 1979 is, according to the treaties, advisory and supervisory. The treaties did not envisage that the Parliament should be a legislature; that was the preserve of the Council. Both before and after the direct elections, Parliament has sought to acquire, or *de facto* to exercise, greater power.

In the treaty revisions of 1970 and 1975 Parliament became one-half of the budgetary authority. The directly elected Parliament celebrated its advent by rejecting the draft budget of 1980 and requiring the Commission and Council to produce a new one. The budgetary role and power of the Parliament are discussed fully below and in Chapter 3.

Parliament strengthened its advisory role in the isoglucose case in 1979. In the interval between the last meeting of the outgoing Parliament and the arrival of its successor, the Council adopted a regulation, within the common organisation of the sugar market, imposing a levy on isoglucose. It did so without having had an opinion from the European Parliament, which had been statutorily consulted. The regulation, challenged in the European Court of Justice, was annulled: the Council had not 'exhausted the possibilities' of obtaining the missing opinion.[13] Parliament gained further ground in 1983 when it took the Council to the Court, with some success, for its failure to produce a common transport policy.[14]

The European Parliament made up a large part of the pressure exercised on the European Council before, at and after its Milan meeting in June 1985, leading to the major reforms incorporated in the Single European Act. The Act fell far short of Parliament's objectives but it did introduce:

- The new 'co-operation procedure' which allows Parliament two interventions into the legislative process, where it applies.

- A new assent procedure for the entry of new member states into the Community (Article 237) and for association agreements (Article 238). In either case a positive vote of more than half the members of Parliament is required. In 1988 such a majority could not be found for new developments in the Association Agreement with Israel, either on a first attempt or on a second, which had to be deferred; it was found at the third try (October 1988).

The Inter-Institutional Agreement of June 1988 on budgetary procedures and objectives marked another reinforcement of Parliament's influence. The medium-term spending plan which it incorporated cannot be modified without Parliament's agreement.

The elections of 1989, like those of 1984 and 1979, were contested on the basis of national political groupings, with some co-ordination at the level of the transnational political families. Mainland Britain was the only state which did not practise proportionality: apart from one successful Scottish National Party candidate, only Labour and Conservative members 'passed the post' despite 2.3 million votes for the Greens. The proportional representation system in Northern Ireland was maintained (see Chapter 5).

The European elections which took place in June 1989 caused major changes in the political composition of the Parliament when it met at the end of July. The Socialist Group remained the largest single faction and within it the British Labour component, which had previously ranked equal with the German Socialists, became the largest national subgroup. The traditional Centre-Right majority was replaced by a Left majority of 265 (out of 518), (if everything not Centre, Right or Independent is counted as Left). The Rainbow Group, which had included German and Belgian Greens, lost them to a new 'Greens' group, which included the influx of French Greens. The former Communist group disappeared. Two new groups to the left of the Socialist Group emerged: the European United Left (mainly Italian and Spanish), and the Coalition of the Left (of which French members made up half).

The European Democratic Group lost thirteen seats to Labour candidates and also lost its Spanish members. Its strength fell from 66 to 34 making it the fourth largest group instead of third. The ED made overtures to the PPE but did not merge with it. The European Democratic Alliance (French, Irish and one Greek) lost ten seats. Its Scottish National member transferred to the Rainbow Group.

Some 250 members did not return either because they did not stand again or because they were not elected. The latter group included the last two Conservative members from Scottish constituencies. Among the British members two are also members of the House of Lords, two (from Northern Ireland) are also members of the House of Commons, and three are former Members of Parliament.

Tables 2.2 and 2.3 show the composition of the European Parliament before and after the 1989 elections.

The European Parliament works by means of committees which

Table 2.2 Political groups in the European Parliament (6 June 1989)

	B	Dk	D	EL	E	F	Irl	I	L	NL	P	UK	Total
Soc	8	3	33	10	29	20	—	12	2	9	7	33	166
EPP	6	1	41	8	1	8	6	27	3	7	4	—	112
ED	—	4	—	—	17	—	—	—	—	—	—	45	66
COM	—	2	—	4	3	10	—	26	—	—	3	—	48
LDR	5	2	—	—	2	13	1	6	1	5	10	—	45
EDA	—	—	—	1	—	20	8	—	—	—	—	1	30
RBW	4	4	7	—	1	—	—	2	—	2	—	—	20
ER	—	—	—	1	—	9	—	5	—	—	—	1	16
Ind	1	—	—	—	7	1	—	3	—	2	—	1	15
Total	24	16	81	24	60	81	15	81	6	25	24	81	518

Table 2.3 Political groups in the European Parliament following the 1989 elections

Country	B	Dk	D	EL	E	F	Irl	I	L	NL	P	UK	Total
Soc	8	4	31	9	27	22	1	14	2	8	8	46	180
EPP	7	2	32	10	16	6	4	27	3	10	3	1	121
LDR	4	3	4	—	6	13	2	4	1	4	9	—	50
ED	—	2	—	—	—	—	—	—	—	—	—	32	34
Greens	3	—	8	—	1	8	—	7	—	2	1	—	30
EUL	—	1	—	1	4	—	—	22	—	—	—	—	28
EDA	—	—	—	1	—	13	6	—	—	—	—	—	20
ER	1	—	6	—	—	10	—	—	—	—	—	—	17
CL	—	—	—	3	—	7	1	—	—	—	3	—	14
RBW	1	4	—	—	2	1	1	3	—	—	—	1	13
Ind	—	—	—	—	4	1	1	4	—	1	—	1	11
Totals	24	16	81	24	60	81	15	81	6	25	24	81	518

KEY. Soc Socialist Group; EPP European People's Party; DR Liberal Democratic and Reformist Group; ED European Democratic Group; COM Communist and allied Group; EUL European United Left; EDA European Democratic Alliance; ER European Right; CL Coalition of the Left; RBW Rainbow Group; Ind Non-attached; B Belgium; DK Denmark; D Germany; El Greece; E Spain; F France; Irl Ireland; I Italy; L Luxembourg; NL Netherlands; P Portugal.

report to plenary sessions and submit draft resolutions. The system is generally the same whether the committee is working on exogenous material, such as Commission proposals or Council common positions, or on internally generated ideas, known as 'own initiative' reports. There are currently eighteen committees: Agriculture, Fisheries and Food; Budgetary Control; Budgets; Economic and Monetary Affairs and Industrial Policy; Energy Research and Technology; Environmental, Health and Consumer; External Economic Relations (REX); Institutional Affairs; Legal Affairs and Citizens' Rights; Overseas Development; Petitions; Political Affairs; Regional Policy and Planning; Rules of Procedure and Verification of Credentials and Immunities; Social Affairs and Employment; Transport; Women's Rights; and Youth, Culture, Education, Information and Sport. There are also twenty-four interparliamentary delegations for joint meetings with parliamentarians in other countries.

Outside the formal committee structure there are a number of interparty groups, such as Kangaroo, which covers the internal market, and Animal Welfare. When required, Parliament has also appointed Committees of Enquiry, for example into drug trafficking, alleged irregularities at a nuclear power station and trade in cattle illegally dosed with hormones.[15]

Members join committees according to their interests. The committee chair is the general custodian of the committee. Chairs have an informal group to prepare forward work programmes which should avoid conflict among them for parliamentary time. For each subject handled the committee appoints a rapporteur (draftsman, but the English word is rarely used) who writes the report and draft resolution. When approved by the committee (by simple majority vote, and amended by the same) they are sent forward to the plenary for inclusion in an agenda, debate and vote on the resolution. In some committees the rapporteur works with 'co-ordinators' who are the representatives in the committee of their group interests.

Administrative questions are discussed and decided by the Bureau. This consists of the President, the fourteen Vice-Presidents and the five Quaestors (administrative managers). The Enlarged Bureau consists of the Bureau plus nine group leaders, and, attending by invitation, the doyen-cum-spokesman of the committee chairs. The Commission and Council are represented at Enlarged Bureau meetings for selected items, especially the drawing-up of future sessional agendas. The other duty of vice-presidents, along with the president, is to preside at sittings of the House, at the monthly week-long (Monday evening to Friday lunch-time) part-sessions.

The Parliament has a General Secretariat including interpreters, translators and technical services. Under a secretary general this consists of a Legal Service and seven Directorates General. There is at present little inter-institutional recruitment but there is some co-operation between the Parliament and the Commission. Each political group also has a secretariat. Although graded and remunerated on the Community model, the members of group secretariats are personal appointees of the group – although they may also be seconded from the General Secretariat. They number some 500. Many members also employ personal assistants; these are also personal appointees.

Each political group caucuses before and during a part-session to decide on how its members will vote on draft resolutions and amendments. Group leaders, co-ordinators and group secretariats negotiate with each other to find compromises and composite resolutions. Group secretariats prepare voting lists which guide members during voting periods.

Except when voting for the office bearers of the House, members vote by show of hands, or if that is visually inconclusive or if enough members wish insistently enough, electronically. The scoreboards show total votes cast, for, against and abstentions. This is particularly important when the majority is narrow or when a certain minimum participation is required, as in budget votes and the co-operation and assent procedures. With electronic voting and shows of hands the House can despatch very large numbers of votes in a relatively short stretch. In a budget debate there can be 500 votes in the course of an afternoon sitting. The quorum is one-third of the members, but this becomes material only if at least thirteen members join forces in a quorum call, or if the president announces that there are fewer than thirteen members in place.

Parliament's relations with the Council are conflictual but it wishes to engage in dialogue and concertation and various provisions have been made for exchanges between the two institutions. At every session the Council answers oral questions for an hour (and the same minister answers for Political Co-operation for thirty minutes). The president of the European Council attends a parliamentary session after the meeting over which he presided in order to give an account of it. This often coincides with the appearance of the president of the Foreign Affairs Council who gives a report on his country's Presidency (and who, at the beginning of his term also appeared to talk about his Presidency's programme). Council ministerial representatives also take part in debates in plenary sessions, either at their own request, or to answer questions which have been put down to them and been included in the subject matter of the debate. At least once and often twice during each Presidency, the president of every Council attends the specialised committees meeting which shadows the Council and talks about the Council's programme. This can run to thirty or more such appearances in a year.

In 1975, when the Parliament increased its budgetary responsibilities, it was agreed that for certain matters having budgetary implications there should be conciliation (in French, *concertation*) between Parliament and Council before the latter took a decision if it was likely to diverge from Parliament's opinion (Joint Declaration of 4 March 1975). The stated objective of conciliation is to reach agreement. By about 1980 the conciliation procedure had become discredited especially in Parliament's eyes because it considered that the Council had already exhausted its flexibility in its internal negotiations. During the conference on the Single Act, the member states shied away from revising the conciliation procedure. They also declined to incorporate a mediation phase in the new co-operation procedure: that is, they did not favour the idea that where Parliament and Council diverge there should be an attempt at around the table negotiations to reach agreement. The Parliament, for its part, wants there to be a mediation phase, and remains dissatisfied with the conciliation procedure. In its internal rules, and departing from the agreed nature of conciliation, Parliament describes the procedure as applicable to any major question. This has led to tension when the Council has declined to conciliate in cases to which the procedure does not apply in terms of the Joint Declaration.

In the budgetary field there is dialogue between the Council and a parliamentary delegation prior to the meetings at which the Council reads the draft budget for the first and second times. This is not conciliation: it is not stated that the object of the dialogue is to reach agreement. Without any formal or informal understanding, a custom has developed for the Council to gather in Strasbourg in December for negotiations (usually conducted for the Council by its president) towards an agreement before Parliament takes its final (second reading) budgetary vote.

Out of the budgetary dialogue emerged, in 1981, the Trilogue. This brings together the President of the Budget Council, the President of the Commission usually with the Commissioner responsible for the budget, and the President of Parliament usually with the President of the Committee on Budgets. The Trilogue scored a notable success in the summer of 1988 when it negotiated the Inter-Institutional Budgetary Agreement which was subsequently approved by the three institutions. The Trilogue has so far not been used outside the budgetary field as a way of resolving disputes among the institutions.

The Commission and Parliament, which both stand for the supranational aspect of the Community, are in some sense natural allies *vis-à-vis* the Council. The President of the Commission presents an annual programme to the Parliament. The vote which Parliament takes after the ensuing debate is regarded as a mark of confidence in the Commission. The Commission President and his or her colleagues attend plenary sessions – the Commission then holds its weekly meeting in Strasbourg – participate in debates, answer oral questions and give a monthly account of the action they have or have not taken on parliamentary resolutions.

The Parliament has sought to strengthen its influence with the Commission – and thereby to obtain a foothold in the legislative process – by being ready not to give opinions. This thereby blocks the process unless the Commission accepts Parliament's amendments, and undertakes to amend its original proposal accordingly and subsequently to defend the amended proposal in the Council discussion at which the Commission is present.[16] The Commission and Parliament also agree on an annual legislative programme, covering the content of proposals and the approximate time at which the Commission will bring them forward. The Council – the Community's legislator – does not participate in the preparation of this programme but is under pressure to join in and thus contribute to well-based forward planning. In response to this pressure, Presidencies have begun to draw up 'indications' of what Council agendas will be over the six months of the Presidency.

In 1986 Parliament held twelve sessions (none in August, two in October), all in Strasbourg. It passed 135 resolutions giving opinions on consultations and 340 other resolutions, including 110 on own initiative reports, which were therefore almost as significant quantitatively as the opinions. It produced 2,199 working documents. Members tabled 3,023 written questions (2,671 to the Commission, 195 to the Council and 157 to Political Co-operation) and 1,277 oral questions (800 to the Commission, 290 to the Council and 187 to Political Co-operation). Parliamentary committees met 407 times.

Parliament's budgetary powers and activities are described in Chapter 3.

The Economic and Social Committee

The Economic and Social Committee, which sometimes calls itself a consultative assembly, is representative of three groups: employers, workpeople and independents. It consists of 189 members, evenly divided among the three groups, and divided among the member states as follows: Belgium 12, Denmark 9, Germany 24, Greece 12, Spain 21, France 24, Ireland 9, Italy 24, Luxembourg 6, Netherlands 12, Portugal 12, UK 24. The members are appointed by the Council on the basis of member states' nominations. The four-year term is renewable. The chair rotates between groups and nationalities and, with two posts of vice-chair, is decided by the members.

The Committee is organised in sections (that is, committees). Under Article 197 of the EEC Treaty there must be sections for Agriculture and Transport. There are, in addition, sections for Economic Affairs, Social Affairs, Environment, Industry, Regional Development, Energy, and External Relations. The sections appoint for each referral a rapporteur, whose report and draft opinion are debated and voted upon by the Committee at its monthly meetings.

Numerous treaty articles require the Committee to be consulted by the Council and the latter also consults the Committee optionally. Opinions are not binding on the Council and it can, if it considers it necessary, impose a time limit beyond which the absence of an opinion does not prevent the Council from proceeding (in practice the Council virtually never finds a time limit necessary). The Committee also undertakes reports on its own initiative. In 1986 the Committee held nine plenary sessions.

Unlike the other bodies of the Community, the Economic and Social Committee field is confined to the EEC and Euratom Treaties. An Advisory Committee under Article 18 of the ECSC Treaty has similar functions *vis-à-vis* the High Authority (Commission). Its members, not more than ninety-six and not less than seventy-two in number, are equally divided among producers, workpeople and consumers, and dealers. They are appointed by the Council. The ECSC Consultative Committee meets about six times a year. It is serviced by the Commission.

European Court of Justice

The European Communities have created a new and distinctive legal order. Their judicial organs are the Court of Justice, situated in Luxembourg, and national courts. To national courts, Community law is not foreign law in the technical legal sense of that term (that is, matter of fact obtained from expert evidence) but part of the law which they apply. In its publication *The ABC of Community Law*, the Commission shows the sources of Community law presented in Figure 2.1.

In the Community of Twelve, there are thirteen judges in the European Court of Justice: an odd number avoids tied judgments (although dissenting judgments are not delivered). Judges are appointed for six years, renewable and six or seven appointments expire every three years. The judges select their own president. There are also six advocates general, who assist the bench by analysing the arguments of the parties, applying Community law to the case and giving an opinion on it. The opinion is not binding on the Court and advocates general do not take part in the deliberations of the judges. For each case the president appoints a judge-rapporteur, who takes the lead in the deliberations. The Court may work in plenary or in chambers. There are four chambers of three judges and two chambers of six judges. The chambers do not specialise in particular legal questions or in particular subjects. The full Court must consider cases brought by a member state or by a Community institution. The staff of the Court is headed by the registrar, who is appointed by the Court.

In 1986, 382 cases were brought before the Court. It gave 197 judgments (including forty-two in cases brought by Community staff against their employers). The types of action which come before the Court are the following:

- Action for annulment, aimed at obtaining the cancellation of binding legal acts. These actions can be brought by the Council, the Commission or a member state. They can be brought by individual citizens if the act complained of is addressed to them or, if addressed to another individual, is of direct and individual concern to them. Individual citizens cannot seek the annulment of regulations and directives.

- Action for failure to act. These actions can be brought by Community institutions or member states. Individual citizens may bring

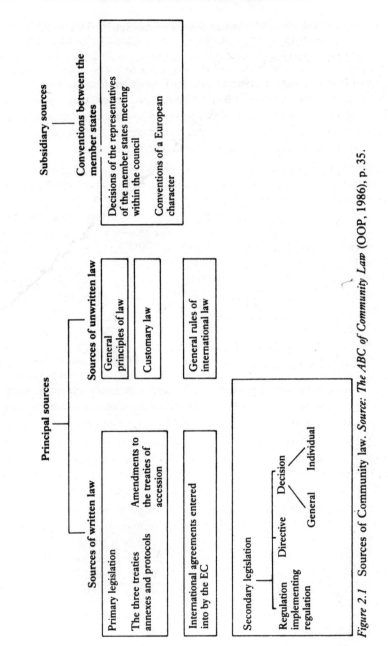

Figure 2.1 Sources of Community law. *Source: The ABC of Community Law* (OOP, 1986), p. 35.

actions to demand that a decision should be addressed to them, but cannot demand the adoption of directives or regulations, or of opinions and recommendations, which have no legal force.

- Actions for infringement of the EEC and Euratom Treaties. These actions can be brought by the Commission or by member states (for example, against each other). In the ECSC the Commission determines whether a member state has infringed the ECSC Treaty and the member state can appeal to the Court.

- Preliminary rulings. A national court may make a reference to the Court of Justice for a ruling on a point of Community law at issue in proceedings before the national court. The national court decides for itself whether to seek a preliminary ruling. The parties in the case cannot compel it to do so. A national tribunal must also refer to the European Court of Justice if the tribunal considers that an act adopted by a Community institution is invalid.[17] In Euratom and the EEC the request for a ruling may concern the validity of an act and how the treaties should be interpreted. In the ECSC only the validity of acts can be questioned. The preliminary ruling of the Court is binding on the national court in the case concerned. There are differing views on whether it has wider application but generally speaking this is a legal nicety.

- Action for damages resulting (by a clear causal link) from illegal actions or, in principle but rarely successfully in practice, from damages caused by (properly adopted) legislative measures.

- Actions brought by members or prospective members of staff seeking application of the Staff Regulations. This can include such matters as allegations that a staff report is biased or that the day fixed for an examination is a holiday in the religion practised by the examinee.

The Council, the Commission or a member state may ask the Court for an Opinion on whether an international agreement that the Community is minded to conclude is compatible with the EEC Treaty or whether agreements negotiated by member states or private persons in the nuclear field are compatible with the Euratom Treaty. If the Court gives an unfavourable Opinion the agreement or draft agreement concerned must be revised to have effect.

In view of the increase in the Court's workload (see Figure 2.2), the member states agreed to provide in the Single European Act (new

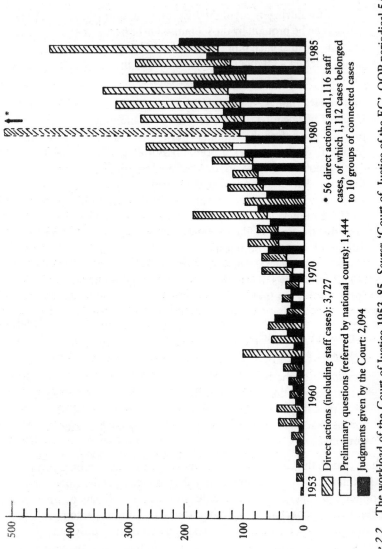

* 56 direct actions and 1,116 staff cases, of which 1,112 cases belonged to 10 groups of connected cases

Direct actions (including staff cases): 3,727

Preliminary questions (referred by national courts): 1,444

Judgments given by the Court: 2,094

Figure 2.2   The workload of the Court of Justice 1953–85. *Source:* 'Court of Justice of the EC', OOP periodical 5/86.

Article 168A of the EEC Treaty) for a Court of First Instance to decide on points of law in certain fields, excluding actions brought by a Community institution or by a member state or referrals for preliminary rulings. The subjects which have been assigned to the Court of First Instance are ECSC matters, competition cases and actions brought by staff (Council decision 88/591/ECSC, EEC, Euratom of 24 October 1988).

There are differences of nomenclature as between the legal instruments which are adopted under the different treaties. The vocabulary and equivalence is as follows:[18]

ECSC (Article 14)		EEC (Article 189)		Euratom (Article 161)
decision (general)	=	regulation	=	regulation
recommendation	=	directive	=	directive
decision (individual)	=	recommendation	=	recommendation
opinion	=	opinion	=	opinion

(ABC of Community Law, Office of Publications of the EC, 1986, p. 29.)

In the EEC/Euratom system, a *regulation* is binding in its entirety and directly applicable in all member states. A *directive* is binding as to the results to be achieved, but leaves the choice of form and method to the member states' authorities. Recommendations and opinions are not binding.

Written constitutions might be expected to contain an affirmation of the fundamental rights of the persons who have accepted the particular form of government. There is no such enumeration in the constituent treaties.[19] The draftsmen seem to have taken the view that the three treaties were such that they could not violate fundamental rights. From 1969 onwards, however, the Court was led towards recognising that fundamental rights, even if not exhaustively enumerated, are part of the bedrock of the Communities' legal order. It did so in such pronouncements as 'the protection of such rights, whilst inspired by the constitutional traditions common to the Member States, must be ensured within the framework of the structure and objectives of the Community' (Case 11/70 *Internationale Handelsgesellschaft*). Later the Court concluded that the European Convention for the Protection of Human Rights and Fundamental Freedoms, 1950, which all member states had ratified by 1976, gives guidelines which must be followed in Community law.

In 1977 the Parliament, Council and Commission adopted a Joint Declaration on the protection of human rights and fundamental freedoms, and declared that in the exercise of their powers and in pursuance of the aims of the European Communities they respect and will continue to respect these rights. It remains the case, however, that definitions of human rights must be looked for elsewhere than in the treaties. It has been suggested – by the Commission and by the European Parliament – that the European Convention should be incorporated directly and *en bloc* into Community law, but there is no consensus among the member states to do so.

National and Community law are in principle complementary. Strictly speaking, there can be no conflict between them because Community law has primacy, and is in part directly applicable: that is to say, it does not require for its validity to be passed into national law by the action of a national law-making body. The rights and obligations accrue directly to the citizens. This effect may or may not have been foreseen by the authors of the treaties, but it has been successfully upheld by the Court and is no longer under legal challenge.

Most regulations are directly applicable, but the test is not what the instrument is called but what it does. If it is complete in itself, so that its implementation and validity do not require any intervention by the Commission or by the member states, then it is directly applicable. On this principle, some provisions of the EEC Treaty itself have been judged to be directly applicable – for example, Article 48 conferring freedom of circulation on workers. Whereas it used to be held that directives being addressed to member states (and not to their citizens) were not directly applicable, the Court has held otherwise in a series of cases since 1970. Direct applicability is one of the distinguishing factors of the European Communities. It turns freedoms into rights which citizens can demand to be vouchsafed to them and it brings the transactions between governments down to the citizens without any further say or choice for the government.

If ultimately there is a conflict between a piece of national law and a piece of Community law, something has to give – and it is national law. The Court uttered this principle in the landmark judgment it gave on 15 July 1964 in *Costa* v. *ENEL* ([1964] CMLR 425) (in which a Milanese shareholder in an electricity enterprise which had been nationalised refused to pay the full amount of his electricity bill because he considered that wrong had been done to him). The Courts said (Case 6/64):

The integration into the laws of each Member State of provisions which derive from the Community, and more generally the terms and the spirit of the Treaty, make it impossible for the States, as a corollary, to accord precedence to a unilateral and subsequent measure over a legal system accepted by them on a basis of reciprocity. Such a measure cannot therefore be inconsistent with that legal system. The executive force of Community law cannot vary from one State to another in deference to subsequent domestic laws, without jeopardizing the attainment of the objectives of the Treaty set out in Article 5(2) and giving rise to the discrimination prohibited by Article 7.

The obligations undertaken under the Treaty establishing the Community would not be unconditional, but merely contingent, if they could be called in question by subsequent legislative acts of the signatories . . .

The precedence of Community law is confirmed by Article 189 . . . This provision, which is subject to no reservation, would be quite meaningless if a State could unilaterally nullify its effects by means of a legislative measure which could prevail over Community law.

It follows from all these observations that the law stemming from the Treaty, an independent source of law, could not, because of its special and original nature, be overridden by domestic legal provisions, however framed, without being deprived of its character as Community law and without the legal basis of the Community itself being called into question.

The Court upheld this principle in a further series of cases. Along with direct applicability, the primacy of Community law is a distinctive and distinguishing feature of Community law. In England it was expressed by Mr Justice Graham in *Aero Zipp Fasteners* v. *YKK Fasteners (UK) Ltd* ([1973] CMLR 819): 'This [European Communities] Act to put it very shortly enacted that relevant Common Market Law should be applied in this country and should, where there is a conflict, override English Law.' The principle is a legal and political milestone and is at the heart of the continuing political controversy over the status of the United Kingdom Parliament, which in the nineteenth century, but not consistently earlier, was held to be 'sovereign' in the sense that its powers were unlimited and incapable of being curbed.[20]

The Court of Auditors

The Court of Auditors, with its seat in Luxembourg, is the Community institution responsible for controlling the Communities' financial regularity. It consists of twelve members, appointed by the Council after consultation of the Parliament. The members choose their president. The Court's staff audit the accounts of the Community institutions and the Court publishes a general report and special reports. The general report is discussed by the ECOFIN Council and in Parliament is debated in the framework of the discharge which Parliament gives to the Commission's accounts. The special reports examine particular branches or problems of expenditure. In the early 1980s the Court gave early warning of the developing financial crisis and exposed the measures of creative accountancy which were being used to put off the evil day. In 1989 it revealed cases of large-scale fraud in several member states and documented the cases. This greatly alarmed the European Parliament and several member states, notably Britain.

The interactions

The ways of the Communities are often regarded as Byzantine, if not impenetrable. In Britain the derogatory word 'legalistic' is often directed at the Communities, independently of the actual and often controversial content of the policies which they adopt. However, the basic constitutional rule, which continues to evolve is straightforward.

The Commission proposes, and generally speaking has the monopoly of the power to propose. It also executes agreed policies, and in doing so collaborates with national agencies (although, for example, there is a single customs tariff, the customs officers are national civil servants). It enforces obligations as 'guardian of the treaties'. Between 1953 and 1985 it brought actions against the ten member states as follows: Belgium 71, Denmark 11, Germany 33, Greece 16, France 76, Ireland 22, Italy 140, Luxembourg 20, Netherlands 20, UK 21 (total 430).

The Council decides, and in doing so uses a variety of tools. The Council also adopts resolutions and makes recommendations (usually to the member states) but these do not have legal force. The members of the General Affairs Council are also the ministers who meet in Political Co-operation.

The Parliament advises but has some decision-making power over Community budgets and has the power to assent (or to refuse to assent) to the entry of new member states into the Community or to the conclusion of new association agreements.

Information

The amount of published information about the activities of the Communities is torrential. Economic interests have made their arrangements to establish contact points. Lobbying, especially for dealings with the Commission and Parliament, has become a major industry. Since virtually all Commission proposals are published, and are regarded more as White Papers than as bills, and since Parliament debates in public both in plenary and in committee, the system is transparent, with one major qualification. Under Article 18 of its Rules of Procedure, the Council's deliberations are secret. The world knows what goes into a Council discussion – the published Commission proposal – and the world learns what comes out – the published decision – but it does not know what is happening in the Council's working groups, in the Committee of Permanent Representatives, and around the Council table. The Council does not have to account to the European Parliament for its decision, although individual Council members are accountable to their democratically elected national parliaments. There has been a move towards openness. When it sends its draft budget to Parliament the Council annexes an Explanatory Memorandum in which it explains why it departed from the Commission's proposals. Under the cooperation procedure the Council sends to the Parliament, along with its 'common position', a statement of the reasons which have led it to adopt the common position.[21] But for many parliamentarians, especially British Conservatives, this amount of *glasnost* is far from enough and there is constant attack on the Communities' 'democratic deficit'.

The outside observers

A group of extramural participants play an important role in the functioning of the Communities. The media are strongly represented internationally in Brussels. The quality press and BBC radio have resident correspondents and the agencies are also present. There are several Commission press conferences each week, and after each Council meeting the president gives a press conference. The European Parliament gives out press releases, as do its political groups. Apart from the general press there are specialised publications, with a reputation for hard inside information. The daily *Agence Europe* published by Emanuele Gazzo, a doughty federalist and tireless leader writer, is almost essential morning reading and is usually impeccably informed. There are numerous other newsletters, in many languages. The proceedings of the plenary meetings of the European Parliament are televised. UK stations do not take the feed regularly.

The media thus make available a large flow of information about what is being discussed, and scoops about what the Commission is likely to propose shortly. Unfortunately, sub-editors freely confuse 'Commission' and 'Community' and sometimes present a proposal as a *fait accompli*. Many Brussels journalists are long-serving and experienced commentators whose factual (and slanted) reporting is a significant input into the process. The Commission (and the European Parliament) maintain information offices in all member states and in some third countries, providing publicity material in the national media.

Another group of Euro-watchers consists of the Brussels offices of organisations which wish to be closely informed and to have a relationship which enables them to intervene. Some major companies have 'EEC affairs' offices under different names. Some major national trade associations, such as the Milk Marketing Board or the Confederation of British Industry have Brussels representatives who keep their ears close to the ground. Some sectors of commerce and industry have set up international trade associations with premises and staff in Brussels: UNICE representing the national employer organisations, COPA representing farmers' unions, and countless others. Normally such organisations seek to become accredited with the Commission, which gives them standing to pursue their search for pertinent information and to feed into the Commission, and to the members of the European Parliament, material about developments which their organisations favour or oppose.[22]

Lobbying

In British English usage 'lobbying' is regarded as something ungentlemanly. It is not so in American English and private intervention in public affairs is an accepted fact in most European countries. The Commissioners, their staff and members of the European Parliament expect to be lobbied. It is almost impossible to lobby the Council collectively because it is corporate only during its meetings, and it is then not available to outsiders. Council members are, however, lobbied by their national interest groups at home.

A profession of lobbyists exists in Brussels. It may run to a dozen or more partners or associates covering the necessary disciplines, especially law and economics, who may be more report writers than gladhanders. There are also freelance consultants with particular expertise and access, usually looking after the affairs of several clients. They are part of the network of information exchanges, forecasting and intervention which is essential to making the machine work.

Distinct from the lobbyists are the law firms established in Brussels, advising clients and general lawyers on Community law and pleading in the Court of Justice in Luxembourg for interests in member states or in third countries.[23]

By the standards of Whitehall, Brussels is an open information arena, where what British traditions would regard as indiscretions abound. But a particular skill is needed for Euro-watchers to find their way through the system in order to obtain hard information, to identify in the timetables the crucial moment for intervention, and to build up the contacts which they and their clients need.

The other Europe

The 'Community method' of decision-making is characterised by several features:

- The Commission has the sole right of initiative. Unless it has made a proposal, it is difficult for the member states to discuss the problem concerned.
- The European Parliament must usually be consulted. Where significant expenditure is involved, it can call for a meeting or meetings with the Council for conciliation.
- The decision, when taken, has legal force, subject to various possibilities for agreeing on 'best endeavours'.
- In making a proposal the Commission is also affirming that the Community possesses the competence to decide and act.
- All the member states must accept the decision. Any derogations must be motivated and temporary.

- Expenditure must be entered in the Community budget, where the Parliament has powers of co-decision (including veto). The execution is examined by the Court of Auditors.
- The Commission is responsible for ensuring that member states fulfil their obligations.
- The Court of Justice rules on complaints.
- There is no provision for withdrawing from membership.

This is quite different from intergovernmental co-operation, of the kind which leads to Memoranda of Understanding or Conventions where the negotiating parties are under no obligation, except moral, to accept limitations on their freedom of action. They can then decide not to accept the conclusions, or to qualify them by national reservations. Any financing is *ad hoc*. There is no accountability to central organs. Any participant can make proposals, and participants can obtain permanent exemptions from activities in which they do not want to participate. They can usually also withdraw from the agreement, using a denunciation procedure.

When the Luxembourg Government organised the signing ceremony for the Single European Act on 17 February 1986, the Luxembourg minister, Robert Goebbels asked why it had been necessary to amend the treaty. He gave two reasons:

the Treaties, particularly in the manner of their implementation, were being imperceptibly but inexorably eroded by a trend back towards classical forms of intergovernmental co-operation, accompanied by a weakening of the institutions and the abandonment of genuine Community procedures;

what were termed the 'new policies' were becoming increasingly likely to fall outside the Community framework proper, thus leading to a kind of European integration which was very different from that originally conceived and from that which European Union was designed to achieve.[24]

Goebbels was drawing attention to the fact that in a number of fields the member states of the Community have decided not to use the classic Community method to obtain an objective common to all or confined to some. The organisations and structures to which these decisions give rise are varied and it is difficult to see in them any clear pattern except that they do not adhere to the 'Community method'.

There are three foundations discharging functions which could, with the relevant organisational changes, equally be discharged by the Commission; indeed the Commission counts as its own the staff employed in the two which are already in operation. The European Centre for the Development of Professional Training, with its seat in Berlin, and the European Foundation for the Improvement of Living and Working Conditions, with its seat in Dublin, are structurally similar. They each have between fifty and sixty staff and cost upwards of 5 million ECUs each a year to run. They carry out research, publish reports, organise seminars and publish a periodical bulletin. Each was set up under a Council Regulation in 1975. The European Foundation, which does not yet exist, rests on an intergovernmental agreement signed on 29 March 1982. The Commission had proposed and the Parliament had supported Article 235 of the EEC Treaty as the legal base. The Foundation is to be financed from the Community budget and from private and public donations. Its task will be to promote mutual understanding, understanding also of European integration and greater awareness of the European cultural heritage. For the time being the steam has gone out of the Foundation. The Commission is itself carrying out missionary work in the cultural field in the context of 'People's Europe'.

Two banking operations are also wholly or partly outside the Community norm. The European Development Fund, which is now in its sixth incarnation, is the financing instrument of the Lomé Convention. Although the Convention is anchored in Article 238 of the EEC Treaty, and although it is a central tenet of financial orthodoxy that all Community expenditure is mediated through the budget, the EDF is not budgetised. The Commission has regularly proposed that it should be, the Parliament has annually insisted that it must be, but the Council has not accepted that it should be. Under the financial package adopted by the Community institutions in the summer of 1988 there is currently no room in the agreed budgetary limits for the next EDF (Lomé IV) to be budgetised.

The European Investment Bank, in Luxembourg, was set up under Title IV of the EEC Treaty. It is autonomous under its governors (the finance ministers) and its Administration Council, consisting of twenty-one officials nominated by the member states and one nominated by the Commission. The bank borrows and lends on: in 1988 9.4 billion ECUs in member states for capital development projects and 700 million ECUs operating outside the Community (especially in Mediterranean and Lomé countries).

The ministers of justice and of the interior (in Britain, the Home Office) of the member states have organised co-operation among themselves outside the treaties and outside, for the most part, the Community method, but with some links in.

In December 1975 the European Council, at the suggestion of James Callaghan, the British Prime Minister, agreed on co-operation in the fight against terrorism and organised crime. This became the Trevi Group, which meets at ministerial and official level, the presidency, secretariat and meeting place being provided by the serving EC Presidency. The Commission is not present.

Separately, but also at the suggestion of the British Government (Douglas Hurd) ministers responsible for immigration began to meet, from October 1986, once in each Presidency. The ministerial meetings are held in the Presidency country. The Commission is present. Secretarial assistance is provided by the Council Secretariat.

The member states co-operate with each other, and with other (not all) members of the Council of Europe, in the Pompidou Group, which is concerned with drugs. The chairing of the Pompidou Group is a matter for its members to decide.

Justice ministers (in Britain, the Law Officers) meet once yearly to discuss co-operation. For part of the time they meet as an intergovernmental conference; otherwise as 'the Council and ministers meeting within the Council', the sign of mixed competence. Part of their work consists of chasing progress on the national ratification of Conventions, some of which are not exclusive Community property whilst others were concluded under Article 220 of the EEC Treaty but also undergo national ratification.

Research, aircraft construction, space exploration and nuclear power generation have called into being many organisations with full or partial membership of the Community's member states, in some cases with outside partners.

The Joint European Torus (JET) at Culham was set up by Council decision to carry out research into nuclear fusion. Sweden and Switzerland are JET members. Expenditure is 80 per cent financed from the Community budget. Within its budget JET is autonomous, managed by its Council, Director, Executive Committee and Scientific Committee.

Eureka was a French brainwave of 1985 and owed part of its inspiration to the realisation that the US Strategic Defense Initiative would have a spin-off in civil science, potentially leaving European research behind. Eureka is not, strictly, part of the European technological community sometimes talked about, but in less formal pronouncements it is often held up as part of the Community's research effort, alongside the purely Community research programmes. In fact, all the member states belong to Eureka, as do Austria, Finland, Iceland, Norway, Sweden, Switzerland and Turkey. The bureaucracy is intentionally light. There is no financing fund. Projects are taken on by governments and private sector firms when multinational projects are set up. The arrangements for initiating these projects, defining their objectives and organising co-operation are in the hands of the enterprises.

COST (Co-operation on Science and Technology) preceded Eureka. It exists to further co-operation between the Community, its member states and the member states of EFTA. COST ventures usually involve national research laboratories. The Commission of the EC co-ordinates and stimulates.

When Euratom opened its doors in 1958, fast-breeder nuclear reactors were high on its agenda. From 1962 onwards it began to conclude development contracts with entities in the member states. As time passed, however, the six member states became dissatisfied with the share-out of contracts (which could be seen as a subsidy for national research) and Euratom slipped into the background. Various groupings of firms in several member states carried on the work: Debene in Germany, Belgium and the Netherlands, Superphénix joining France and Italy and SNR2 being a link between them. The UK joined in one of the Debene projects in 1972. Interest in fast breeders went up and down. It reached a high point in 1984 when a series of agreements were concluded between Belgium, Germany, France, Italy and Britain, envisaging the construction of three fast breeders, later reduced to one. The projects seem subsequently to have gone back into the doldrums.

The construction of modern civil and military aircraft depends on an international market and high-cost research at the frontier of knowledge. The Communities are not concerned with military production, where several co-operative ventures exist (Jaguar, Tornado, European Fighter Aircraft). But when European achievements are related, alongside those like JET or ESPRIT, which belong to the Communities, it is customary to include the Airbus (France, Germany, Britain and Spain) and the space rocket Ariane (of the European Space Agency, to which belong Belgium, Denmark, Germany, Spain, France, Ireland, Italy, the Netherlands, Britain, Austria, Norway, Sweden and Switzerland).[25]

The European Patent Office, in Munich, was created by a Convention of 1973 and was signed by the nine member states of the

Community plus Austria, Greece, Liechtenstein, Monaco, Norway, Sweden and Switzerland. Although the Office did not belong to the Community, the Secretariat General of the Council provided a service generally recognised as essential to the success of the negotiations which led to the Convention. In 1975 a Convention was signed in Luxembourg by the nine member states setting up a Community patent. The Convention has not yet come into force, pending national ratifications. In November 1986 the Commission proposed a Council regulation on a Community Trademark under Article 235 of the EEC Treaty.

Cultural co-operation is a Community activity, an essential part of People's Europe. But alongside what is properly *communautaire*, France has launched two ventures. In 1987, on the thirtieth anniversary of the signature of the EEC and Euratom Treaties, the French Government distributed to the other member states a prospectus in the form of a 'Blue Book' for education and culture. The various programmes which it proposed were not to rest on Community decisions or to require a legally based structure. They were also to be open to other (European) states.

In 1987 also, the French Government convened in Paris a meeting to discuss film co-production. The Commission had made a proposal in this field in 1985, but this had not proceeded. Nine member states showed interest in joining in an arrangement, with Germany, the Netherlands and Britain demurring. Membership was also to be open to other European countries. There is a coded reference to this project in the Conclusions of the European Council meeting in Hanover of June 1988: '[The European Council] feels that urgent considerations should be given to the possibility of creating an [*sic*] Eureka project in the audio-visual sphere'. The meaning here is not a project within Eureka but a project like Eureka. In September 1988 this was followed up by a further French memorandum for a 'Eureka audio-visual programme', open to other European states as well as to member states of the Community.

One feature common to many of these schemes is that they are 'Europe à la carte'. They are not confined to the member states of the Community and they can proceed even if some member states do not join in. This latter aspect touches on the debate about 'graduated integration' – may it be a hindrance to the cause of European integration if the bus cannot leave unless all are aboard? The 'Europe à la carte' models provide a means for like-minded member states to go ahead together, without waiting for the hesitant or the opposing. Also known as 'variable geometry', these arrangements usually imply that the Commission, if present at all, is not exercising its treaty functions as initiator and enforcer, that the European Parliament has no say, and that there is no, or virtually no, Community funding.[26] In the Single European Act, an attempt was made to build a bridge between the Community method and variable geometry. New Articles 130L, M and N, in Title VI, Research and Technological Development, provide for 'supplementary programmes' involving certain member states only, who pay for them subject to a possible Community financial contribution. This possibility has not been taken up.

Goebbels, the Luxembourg minister (p. 84 above) hailed the Single Act as a return to Community orthodoxy. Its R. & D. title gives treaty respectability to research projects 'à la carte'; but two and a half years after this condemnation of '"new policies" . . . becoming increasingly likely to fall outside the Community framework proper', a new one, exactly of that kind, took off (audio-visual). So far nothing that began outside the Community method has been brought within it. European Political Co-operation was given a treaty basis in the Single European Act, but it does not use the Community method (see Chapter 4). Eurocontrol, with responsibilities for air-traffic control in part of the airspace over Europe, is independent of the Community. It has been suggested that it, or a reformed version of it, should become a Community body, but no such proposal is under formal discussion. Eureka, closely linked to the Community and enjoying administrative assistance provided by the Commission, is not set to become a Community body either. In the other direction, organisations which were at first conceived as within the Community have slipped out of it: audio-visual co-production, research and development of fast-breeder reactors, and the European Foundation.

In some eyes these departures from the strict model of Community action weaken progress towards European union because they depend on intergovernmental co-operation. To others they complement the orthodox integration and permit progress which would otherwise take too long, if it happened at all. It will be interesting to see whether a venture which had its beginnings outside the Community, such as Eureka, and establishes its viability is ever taken into the Community fold. After the Single Act it seems less likely that exercises which begin in the Community will pass outside it. Indeed so much was said at the European Council meeting in Rhodes in December 1988 about the audio-visual Eureka that it has acquired the coloration of belonging to the Community, as well as providing for the participation of other European countries, including those of Eastern Europe.

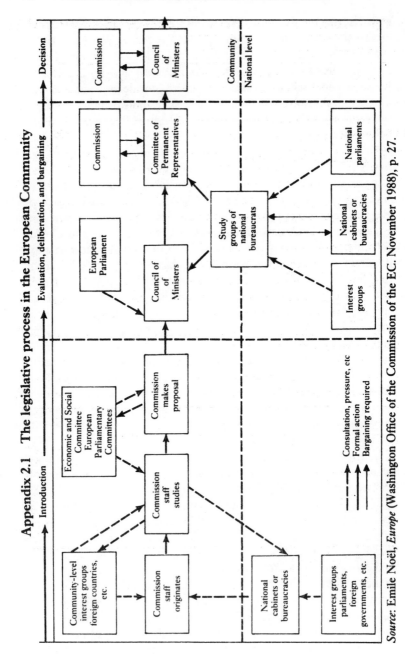

Appendix 2.1   The legislative process in the European Community

Source: Emile Noël, *Europe* (Washington Office of the Commission of the EC. November 1988), p. 27.

Appendix 2.2 Authorised staff and administrative costs 1988

Authorised staff

Institution	No. of authorised posts	
	Permanent	Temporary
Parliament	2,975	430
Council	2,129	1
Economic and Social Committee	485	–
Commission		
Operation	11,823	505
Research and investment	2,584	489
Office for Official Publications	396	–
European Centre for the Development of Vocational Training	57	–
European Foundation for the Improvement of Living and Working Conditions	51	–
Court of Justice	626	46
Court of Auditors	319	56
Total staff	22,972	

Source: 1988 Budget (OOP).

Administrative costs (rounded)

Institution	Cost (ECUs (m))
Commission	1,400
Parliament	400
Council	200
Economic and Social Committee	45
Court of Justice	60
Audit Court	30
Total	2,100

Source: 1988 Budget (OOP).

Notes

1. This 'flagrant violation' of the treaty was attacked by a European parliamentarian in the debates on 16 November 1988.
2. Article 10 of the treaty establishing a single Council and a single Commission of the European Communities.
3. All of the original six have seen one of their nationals appointed as president. The Dutch President – Mr Mansholt – held office for only a brief period when Mr Malfatti of Italy resigned in 1972. Of the new six only the UK has provided a president in Roy (later Lord) Jenkins, 1977–81.
4. For an inside account of the Commission, and its president, at work, see Roy Jenkins, *European Diary 1977–81* (London, Collins, 1989).
5. Article 179 (EEC).
6. Article 13 of the Protocol on the Privileges and Immunities of the European Communities.
7. The work of some councils is shared between the top-level official committees. COREPER I (Deputies) is generally responsible for the internal market and consequently prepares work for ECOFIN on financial services and for the Agricultural Council on veterinary directives.
8. A frequently used gloss is a statement in the Council minutes. In these statements the persons making them say how they interpret a Community decision and what they intend to do about it. The statements may be made by the Council and/or the Commission or by one or more member states. Such statements are not published – although there have been inadvertent publications. Statements in the Council minutes almost certainly do not have legal force.
9. The two Committees of Permanent Representatives are staffed by Brussels residents. The Special Committee for Agriculture is partly resident and partly non-resident. The high-level Article 113 Committee (trade policy) is entirely non-resident.
10. Capital-to-capital contacts are bilateral, except in the tripartite gatherings of the members of Benelux and business meetings in the Troika of the last, current and next Presidency. Gatherings of three or more would normally be frowned upon, as threatening to create an inner circle.
11. The absence of officials from meetings of the European Council is a matter of convention, and was confirmed as the European Council's desired method of work. Officials from member states and from the Commission attend all other Council meetings. In a 'restricted' meeting the number of officials present is reduced to one or two. Very occasionally there are meetings of 'ministers only'. Work usually continues at ministerial lunches, with two officials present: the chair of COREPER and the senior member of the Council Secretariat.
12. The ministerial discussion may establish what is agreed textually or in substance with instructions for a final text to be prepared. The draft on which delegations finally agree is further examined by the Council's 'jurist-linguists' (legal revisers) to ensure that it says the same thing in all languages, and otherwise contains no legal drafting blemishes.
13. Cases 138 and 139/79.
14. Case 13/83, judgment given on 22 May 1985.

15. There have been or are five Committees of Enquiry. They proceed on the distant model of a US Congressional or Senate Committee, but have no powers to compel witnesses to testify. They hold 'hearings' to which they invite interested parties. At least one of them (on the carriage of toxic materials) ministers from some member states spoke. The Committees of Enquiry produce reports, which are their property and cannot be amended in debate on the floor of the House. The Committee of Enquiry usually also produces a draft resolution, which sets out what should be done to remedy a particular evil and on which the House votes. An essentially similar task to that of a Committee of Enquiry can be taken up by a rapporteur within a Standing Committee – for example, the Report on Religious Cults.

16. See W. Nicoll, 'Le dialogue législatif entre le Parlement et la Commission: la procédure de renvoi en commission du parlement européen', *Révue du Marché Commun*, Paris, No. 316, April 1988, pp. 240–2.

17. Case 314/85, judgment given on 22 October 1987.

18. *ABC of Community Law* (OOP, 1986), p. 29.

19. The abortive Draft Treaty of the European (Political) Community took into its third article Part I of the Convention for the Protection of Human Rights and Fundamental Freedoms concluded in Rome on 4 November 1950 and the Protocol signed in Paris on 20 November 1952.

20. Taken from a lecture given by (later Sir) Jean Pierre Warner, then Advocate-General, in Luxembourg, summer 1977: 'Community law from the point of view of the national judge'.

21. From January 1989 common positions adopted by the Council are published in the *Official Journal*. The Explanatory Memorandum on the draft budget and the motivation of common positions in the co-operation procedure are not published in the *Official Journal*. They are distributed to Members of the European Parliament as sessional papers, which do not have a security classification.

22. A convenient list of Euro-Trade Associations is published by Editions Delta, Brussels. See also W. Rogers (ed.), *Government and Industry* (Kluwer, 1986), Ch. 6, Part D.

23. In the summer of 1988 a Brussels-based barrister, Ian Forrester, took silk (that is, became a Queen's Counsel), the first time this had happened outside the courts of the United Kingdom or Commonwealth.

24. *Speeches and Statements Made on the Occasion of the Signing of the Single European Act* (OOP, 1986), p. 18.

25. A Commission proposal to fund aeronautical research from the Community budget 'hit heavy weather', according to the *Financial Times*, 18 November 1988, in the meeting of the Council (Research) the day before. A modified version was later brought within an existing programme.

26. See the articles by B. Langeheine, and U. Weinstock, and by W. Nicoll, in *Journal of Common Market Studies*, Vol. 23, No. 3, March 1985. See also Helen Wallace, *Europe: The Challenge of Diversity* (London, Royal Institute of International Affairs, 1985).

3

The Communities' Budget

The lion's share of Community expenditure is incurred through the General Budget, which applies to the Economic Community and to Euratom. A separate budget covers the Coal and Steel Community.[1] In addition, the Economic Community finances the European Development Fund, providing aid under the Lomé Convention. The borrowing and lending operations of the Community (and of the European Investment Bank) do not constitute budgetary expenditure.

The 1988 total (see Table 3.1) represents less than 1.2 per cent of the gross domestic product of the twelve member states, and less than 4 per cent of the sum of their national budgets. In the member states public sector expenditure can reach 50 per cent of the national product. Thus the Community budget does not have the same economic management functions as a national budget. It exists to pay partly for the running of the Community institutions and partly for the expenditure incurred in the execution of Community policies, especially (60 per cent of budget) its price guarantees.

The Community does not pay the price guarantees directly. Community farmers cultivating produce for which there is a market organisation but who cannot obtain the guaranteed prices on the market, can sell to the intervention agency at the guaranteed price. The intervention agency is, in general terms, financed by the member state concerned. The Community, through the budget, meets the cost of storage and (in part) the interest cost. It also meets the cost of the difference between the price paid by the agency and the price obtained on withdrawal from store – for export at (generally) a price subsidised down to the world level, or for purchase by the Community as food aid, or for distribution at less than the ruling Community price to particular groups of Community citizens.[2] More recently, the Community budget has paid for the depreciation of some of the stocks. There is interesting debate about

Table 3.1   The Community budget 1988 (million ECUs)

General Budget (EEC, Euratom)	43,820
ECSC Budget	562
European Development Fund	837

who are the ultimate owners of intervention stocks, and how much discretion – if any – the member states may have as regards providing the means to enable the intervention agencies to meet the duly verified claims of Community farmers against the Community. However that may be, the advocates of a massive transfer of the Community's surplus food stocks to famine-stricken countries may not be aware that the Community has not paid for the products as long as they remain in store, undepreciated.

The sources of revenue for the Community budget are its (so-called) 'own resources' and miscellaneous other receipts. The own resources are divided into four categories. The first two, sometimes called 'traditional own resources' are the customs duties collected by the member states on imports into the Community and the levies paid on agricultural imports. The third own resource is a (low) percentage of VAT. A 'fourth resource' came into force in 1988. It is for each member state an amount proportional to the country's share in the total gross national product of the member states. This last is to be distinguished from the 'financial contributions' on the basis of which the Community was originally financed (Article 200 of the EEC Treaty). Financial contributions – broadly proportional to GNP – passed through the member states' national budgets. The new fourth resource is Community property – not a contribution offered by the member state, but a right vested in the Community.[3] (See also Appendix 2.)

The composition of the receipts of the 1988 budget is as shown in Table 3.2. The breakdown in percentage shares is given in Table 3.3.

The customs duties element tends not to be buoyant as a revenue source in view of tariff cuts. VAT used to be regarded as a rough barometer of relative prosperity, but from 1988 it is corrected by the more accurate measure of the fourth resource. Various identifiably 'Community' consumption taxes have been discussed – a tax on vegetable oils, a tax on mineral oil, a stamp duty – but have not been adopted.[4]

The division of the financial charge upon the member states, in gross terms, is as shown in Table 3.4. The incidence of each revenue component differs from country to country. The UK provides relatively

Table 3.2   Community budget resources 1988 (million ECUs)

Traditional own resources	11.41
VAT	24.27
Fourth resource	7.11
Financial contribution (Portugal, in place of VAT)	0.21

Table 3.3   Community budget resources 1988 (%)

Customs duties	19.62
Agricultural levies	3.28
Sugar levies	3.16
VAT	54.58
Fourth resource	16.23
Financial contribution	0.48
Balance c/f from 1987	1.14
VAT balances	0.80
Miscellaneous	0.71
	100.00

more VAT than the other member states (80 per cent of its total, compared with 60 per cent for Germany and 65 per cent for France). Belgium and the Netherlands are relatively strong sources of customs duties and agricultural levies: the so-called Rotterdam (or Antwerp) effect of imports which clear customs at entry points but go elsewhere in the Community for consumption.

The net positions are less well documented. The Commission is properly wary of publishing net balances, on the grounds that the figures are misused to measure the total benefit of Community membership, a concept which to it, and to many member states, goes far beyond budgetary outfall. Nevertheless, the problem of 'budgetary imbalance' was a burning issue for most of the 1980s, the UK arguing that it was inequitable that it and not one of the most prosperous member states should be the second largest source after Germany of budgetary finance. This is shown in Table 3.5, culled from a miscellany of sources and showing orders of magnitude rather than a coherent analysis.

Expenditure under the general budget gives spending effect to policies on which the Community has decided. Generally speaking, budgetary expenditure cannot be incurred unless there is a legal basis for it, distinct from the budget itself – a regulation or a directive which has created an object of expenditure.[5]

Table 3.4 Contribution by member states to Community budget 1988 (%)

Belgium	4.4
Denmark	2.2
Germany	27.2
Greece	1.0
Spain	7.3
France	21.7
Ireland	0.8
Italy	15.7
Luxembourg	0.2
Netherlands	6.5
Portugal	1.0
UK	12.0
	100.0

Table 3.5 EC net balances 1983–5 (million ECUs)[1]

	1985 [2]	1984	1983	
Belgium	+ 500 ⎱	+ 690	+ 432	
Luxembourg	+ 300 ⎰			
Denmark[3]	+ 300	+ 460	+ 307	
Germany	−3,500	−3,400	−2,435	
Greece	+1,300	+ 980	+ 923	
France	0	− 760	− 269	
Ireland[4]	+1,100	+ 920	+ 757	
Italy	+ 800	+1,500	+1,140	
Netherlands	+ 400	+ 420	+ 308	
United Kingdom[5]	−1,000	− 810	−1,163	
Spain (1988)[6]	—	—	—	+1,000

[1] For the Ten, after UK budgetary correction.
[2] Per capita figures in sterling, rounded: Belgium +£30, Luxembourg +£600, Denmark +£35, FRG −£35, Greece +£80, France +£0, Ireland +£180, Italy +£10, Netherlands +£15, UK −£10.
[3] Danish national income statistics (converted to million ECUs) give 1983, 160; 1984, 480; 1985, 280; 1986, 365.
[4] In May 1987 the Irish government published the following figures for net receipts (in IR£ m): 1983, 543; 1984, 664.2; 1985, 915.3; 1986, 900.2.
[5] For earlier periods see *The Budget Problem*, Foreign and Commonwealth Office/Central Office of Information, London, 1982.
[6] Spain's Finance Ministry, quoted in *El País*, 20 December 1988 (= ± £15 per capita).
Sources: For 1985, *Economist*, 20 June 1987, p. 25; for 1983 and 1984, press release, Bundesministerium der Finanzen, Bonn, 5 February 1986.

Appropriations which are entered in the budget are labelled to show their characteristics. Non-differentiated appropriations refer to expenditure which is contracted for (or committed) and executed within the budgetary year. Agricultural price guarantee appropriations are non-differentiated. Differentiated appropriations are committed in one budgetary year and may be executed in subsequent years. These appropriations are described as 'commitment' and 'payment' appropriations (CA and PA). In any published budget there are different amounts for CA and PA opposite the budget entry. 'Appropriations for commitments' and 'appropriations for payments' are budgetary sub-totals: the sum of the non-differentiated appropriations and the commitment appropriations; and of the non-differentiated appropriations and the payment appropriations.

Expenditure (both commitments and payments) is classified as compulsory (CE) and non-compulsory (NCE). Among anglophone practitioners these are often given their French abbreviations DO and DNO. Compulsory expenditure is that which flows ineluctably from the treaties or from legislation adopted thereunder. The Community has no choice: price guarantees or amounts of aid which appear in agreements between the Community and third countries, for example, are obligatory. NCE is not so fixed. The Community has discretion over how much it wishes to spend in the Regional Fund and the Social Fund. It is, of course, true that once expenditure under these funds has been committed, then the prospective beneficiaries have an enforceable claim against the budget. But that does not make the expenditure compulsory in treaty language.[6]

In 1988 a new subset of NCE began to be used informally: privileged and non-privileged expenditure. 'Privileged' meant expenditure (in commitment appropriations) which has been included in multiannual sectoral programmes (structural funds, research and development, integrated Mediterranean programmes). This distinction, which does not exist in the Financial Regulations, was repudiated by the European Parliament, since it implied that this expenditure might be cut.

The 'agricultural guideline' is a limit on the year-to-year growth of expenditure under EAGGF Guarantee. The 'maximum rate of growth of NCE', or more familiarly the 'maximum rate', is a limit on the year-to-year growth of NCE, which can be overstepped. The 'maximum rate' is an objective measurement announced by the Commission under Article 203(9) of the EEC Treaty.

The 'preliminary draft budget' is the estimate of expected revenue and required expenditure which the Commission puts forward around mid-June of the year before the budgetary year concerned (Community budgetary years run January–December). The preliminary draft is addressed to the 'budgetary authority', which has two branches: the Council and Parliament. The draft budget is adopted by the Council, ideally in July, and overhauled by the Parliament in October. It then undergoes second reading, at the Council in November and in Parliament in December. If all goes well, it is signed by the President of Parliament, who thus marks the establishment of the budget. If all does not go well, so that the budget does not exist on 1 January, there is a fail-safe mechanism to allow the Community to live financially. Under 'provisional twelfths' the Commission can spend each month one-twelfth of the provision made for that expenditure in the lower of the previous year's budget or the draft budget (if no draft budget exists, in the preliminary draft budget). This system is cumbersome and is intended to bring pressure on all concerned to end it by working for the establishment of a budget.

While the draft budget is pursuing its course, the Commission can by a letter of amendment change its preliminary draft. It can also introduce, during the budgetary year, preliminary draft amending budgets (which do not increase expenditure) or preliminary draft supplementary and amending budgets (which do). These then follow the same procedural path as main budgets. The Council establishes the draft budget (line by line) by qualified majority vote. It can amend the preliminary draft by qualified majority vote – in other words, technically the preliminary draft is not a Commission 'proposal', which the Council could amend only by unanimity. The Parliament can amend the NCE provisions by a majority vote of its members (260 votes). It can also propose to modify the CE by a majority of the votes cast (members present and voting). Examining Parliament's first reading, the Council can, if it has a qualified majority:

- reject any parliamentary proposed modifications of CE which do not increase expenditure;
- accept any parliamentary proposed modifications of CE which increase expenditure;
- modify any parliamentary amendments of NCE.

Examining the outcome of the Council's second reading, the Parliament can:

- by a majority of its members and three-fifths of the votes cast (members present and voting) amend or reject the modifications which the Council made to Parliament's amendments (NCE);

- by a majority of its members and two-thirds of the votes cast reject the draft budget and ask for a new one.

At second reading Parliament cannot:

- further amend NCE, if the Council has not touched it;
- vote further on CE.

These rules of Article 203 of the EEC Treaty bring out the vital operational significance of the classification of expenditure into CE and NCE. In the treaty model, Parliament's interest is in securing NCE classifications. It succeeded in pushing its NCE sphere from the starting point, which was part of the administrative expenditure, out into the structural funds, and has resolved to go further.

The rough rule of thumb is that Parliament has the last word on NCE and the Council on CE. But this is governed by several constraints. First, the total size of the budget may not exceed the own resources available for the year. Strictly speaking, the Community budget cannot be in deficit. In practice, creative accountancy has often been prayed in aid to make a real deficit disappear optically. Second, the Council (and indeed the Community at large) cannot overstep the agricultural guideline. Third, the Parliament in its approach to NCE cannot exceed the maximum rate unless either:

- the Council has already absorbed more than half the rate but not more than the whole of it (the Parliament can always use half: if the maximum rate of increase is 8 per cent and the Council has used 6 per cent, Parliament can still use 8/2 = 4 per cent).
- the Council agrees (by its qualified majority) to increase the rate.

In practice the Treaty model is qualified by the Inter-Institutional Agreement of 1988, which fixes budgetary amounts independently of their classification and stipulates that the amounts cannot be changed without the agreement of either side. The agreement included a five-year expenditure plan, broken down by objectives (see Table 3.6). Unless the Council and the Parliament agree to change it, this plan must be respected in each budgetary round. The figures for 1990–2 are to be adjusted by a price deflator. The plan can be regarded as either disciplining expenditure by containing it (EAGGF Guarantee) or allowing it to grow faster than the maximum rate rule would allow (structural funds). It therefore marks a quantitative change in the budgetary dialogue.

Table 3.6 Financial perspectives (commitment appropriations) (million ECUs at 1988 prices)

	1988	1989	1990	1991	1992
1. EAGGF Guarantee section	27,500	27,700	28,400	29,000	29,600
2. Structural actions	7,790	9,200	10,600	12,100	13,450
3. Integrated Medical programmes and R. & D.	1,210	1,650	1,900	2,150	2,400
4. Other policies	2,103	2,385	2,500	2,700	2,800
of which NCE	1,646	1,801	1,860	1,910	1,970
5. Reimbursement to member states; administration of which stock reduction	1,240	1,400	1,400	1,400	1,400
6. Monetary reserve (for EAGGF Guarantee)	1,000	1,000	1,000	1,000	1,000
Total	45,303	46,885	48,900	50,950	52,800
of which					
CE	33,698	32,607	32,810	32,980	33,400
NCE	11,605	14,278	16,090	17,970	19,400

In the decade between the running-in of the directly elected Parliament and the intensive inter-institutional negotiations which followed the entry into force of the Single European Act, the budgetary process was unsettled by:

- dispute within the Council and later between the Council and the Parliament over whether the UK should be compensated for 'budgetary imbalance' (the net cost to the UK after membership);
- the Council's attempts, with a success which was only partial and which was criticised by Parliament for faintheartedness, to control agricultural spending;
- the Council's attempt, stoutly resisted by the Parliament, to keep the growth of NCE within the maximum rate;
- the secular tendency for expenditure to exceed the resources available, leading to 'phoney' budgets and to the parliamentary rejection (twice, 1980 and 1985) of the Council's draft as inadequate: three times (1984, 1985 and 1988)[7] the budget had to be topped up by national contributions, quite apart from other devices to reduce apparent, but not actual, expenditure.

Table 3.7 Expenditure changes unde the General Budget: 1980, 1985, 1988 (million ECUs)

	1980		1985		1988	
	CA	PA	CA	PA	CA	PA
EAGGF Guarantee	11,485.5	11,485.5	19,955.0	19,955.0	27,500.0	27,500.0
EAGGF Guidance	448.0	317.0	726.0	660.0	1,131.1	1,203.0
Regional policy	1,484.7	722.7	2,588.7	1,697.8	4,022.7	3,211.4
Social policy	972.7	768.8	2,231.3	1,626.2	3,109.0	2,841.2
Energy and industry	443.4	379.5	1,046.9	706.8	1,306.2	1,120.6
Development co-operation	804.0	641.6	1,322.8	1,043.7	1,095.1	892.9
Admin. budgets	938.8	938.8	1,332.6	1,332.6	1,974.1	1,974.1
Totals	17,491.9	16,182.5	30,616.0	28,433.2	45,344.2	43,820.4
Balance (other expenditure)	914.8	928.6	1,412.7	1,411.1	5,206.0	5,077.2

Note: CA Commitment appropriations; PA Payment appropriations.

Expenditure under the General Budget has progressed as shown in Table 3.7. The 1988 budget is the take-off point for the doubling, by 1993, of the Regional and Social Funds, giving budgetary expression to the principle of cohesion which is an ingredient of the Single European Act. In accepting this commitment, the Council also accepted that the growth in NCE over the period could exceed the series of annual maximum rates. The combination of this and the restriction on the growth of EAGGF Guarantee expenditure will bring the share of such expenditure down from its current level of about 60 per cent of budget. The 1988 agreement is also seen as turning a page: in the words of the parliamentary rapporteur on the 1989 budget, the first to which the agreement applies, the subject now moves from conflict to co-operation, and all concerned have to relearn the process. This was borne out when for the first time in five years the 1989 budget was adopted without incident before the budgetary year opened.

Appendix 3.1   The Community budget

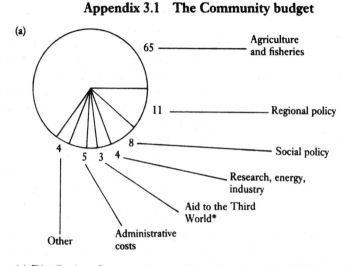

(a) Distribution of community expenditure (as percentage, 1989 commitments).
(* Excluding similar expenditure financed outside the budget by the European
Development Fund.)

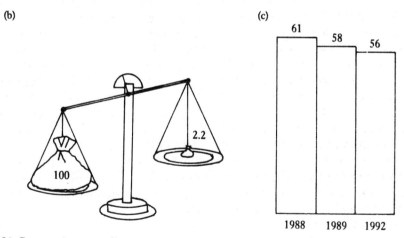

(b) Community expenditure compared with overall expenditure by public
administrations (as a percentage, 1987).

(c) Agricultural guarantee expenditure as a percentage of the Community
budget.

Source: Commission of the EC, *A Community of Twelve: Key Figures* (OOP,
1989), p.29.

In its *Bulletin* No. 2 of 1988 the Commission summarised the agreements which emerged from the European Council in February and
which, when transposed into Community legislation, became known as
the Delors package. The summary of the changes made in 'our
resources' on the receipts side of the budget is as shown in Appendix
3.2.

Notes

1. The budget of the Coal and Steel Community is financed by a levy on Community coal
   and steel production, fixed by the Commission and approved by the European
   Parliament. D. Strasser, *Finances of Europe* (Brussels, Office for Official Publications of
   the European Communities, 1981) 2nd edn, p. 161.
2. These payments, which are the cash flow of the intervention agencies, are based on
   claims submitted to the Commission by the member states. Payments to and by the
   Community pass through accounts in the national central bank. The Commission
   account can go into the red (if the central bank so agrees) when the payments to the
   member states exceed the collections from it and if the Commission does not transfer
   liquidity from another account.
2. The coming into being of the fourth resource signals the end of a controversy over
   Article 200, which financed the early Community: whether (as in the Council's view) it
   is spent although never formally cancelled, or whether (as in Parliament's view) it lives
   on and is a Community way of making good shortfalls in available receipts compared
   with required expenditure. It is spent.
4. A suggestions that part of national VAT rates should be identified to consumers as a tax
   they pay to the Communities has also not been taken up.
5. Sometimes, however, expenditure is for a pilot scheme for which it would be premature
   to establish a legal base. Sometimes Parliament has argued that if it inserts new
   expenditure there is an obligation on the Council, as legislator, to provide a legal base in
   good time for the expenditure to be legally executed (otherwise the provision will be
   nugatory).
6. Needless to say there is a long-running disagreement about the classification of a
   number of budgetary headings, especially within the EAGGF Guidance section.
7. The intergovernmental agreement to provide supplementary finance for the 1988
   budget was a holding measure, pending national ratifications of the decision to
   increase own resources with retroactive effect from 1 January 1988.

Appendix 3.2   Changes to the structure of resources

Present system (VAT ceiling)	Commission proposal (GNP ceiling)	European Council's conclusions (GNP ceiling)
Traditional own resources (about one-third of total resources): (1) agricultural levies (2) customs duties.	Traditional own resources.	Traditional own resources (less 10% collection costs).
VAT: Nominally 1.4% but effectively about 1.25% because UK abatement is financed within the VAT ceiling. Revenue degressive in that high-consumption, low-income member states pay relatively more.	1% VAT effectively.	1.4% VAT, but including UK abatement; hence effective rate of about 1.25%.
	Additional base equal to difference between GNP and VAT. Similar to proportional revenue structure in that when the call-in rate on the additional base approaches 1% the third and fourth resources taken together become GNP finance.	GNP: this implies less proportionality than the Commission's proposal in that VAT is included twice (first as VAT, second as a component of GNP). Therefore:
		Special provision for high-consumption, low-income member states. For those member states whose VAT constitutes more than 55% of GNP, the VAT base is reduced to 55% of GNP and the uniform VAT rate is applied to the reduced base only. The effect of the special provision is to limit the impact of the VAT resource at Community level and consequently to increase the impact of the GNP resource.

4

European Political Co-operation

The earlier chapters have traced the evolution and gradual laying of 'the foundations of an ever closer union among the peoples of Europe', as it is put in the Preamble to the EEC Treaty.[1] They have demonstrated also that the true nature of the Communities and that 'closer union' cannot be understood by a formal, legalistic study of the provisions of the founding treaties alone. It must be located within a wider political environment, full cognisance being given to political developments and aspirations, especially to the recognition that the endeavour to create economic integration was intimately related to the endeavour to achieve political integration, with the creation of a Western European political federation with common foreign and defence policies.

Inherent in the original federal ideal espoused in the late 1940s and early 1950s, for example, was the notion that Europe, or the Europe that came to be embodied in the EC and its constituent member states, would act as a single unit externally in world affairs. Indeed, one important mainspring of the European momentum had been the realisation that in 'a world dominated by political and economic units of continental dimensions, the European nations cannot hope to survive on a basis of political or economic independence'.[2] Europe, which had been the cradle and cauldron of world history for a century or more, had now been devastated by war and its former colonial power was also evaporating. It appeared that European power was now being bypassed in an apparently bipolar world by extra-European powers. Europe was becoming an object of the game of international politics rather than a participant in it. Many came to believe, therefore, that only a united Europe would recover the continent's old greatness, significance and influence, once again giving Europeans an important voice. By the time of the Messina Conference in 1955, the path of unity was regarded as 'indispensable if Europe is to maintain her position in the world, regain her influence and prestige'.[3] The new Europe, then, was to become an actor on the world stage in its own right, and acting as a single unit. This basic aspiration has surfaced on several subsequent occasions, for example in the ill-fated attempt in 1972–3 to define 'the European identity' at least partially on the basis of Europe's position and responsibilities with regard to the rest of the world. In the autumn of 1973 the foreign ministers of the Nine stressed that 'the Nine' intended to 'play an active role in world affairs', to 'progressively define common positions in the sphere of foreign policy', and to seek to act 'as a single entity', bringing out the 'distinct character' of that entity. In sum, in their external relations the ministers agreed 'progressively to undertake the definition of their identity in relation to other countries or groups of countries . . . [for] in so doing they will strengthen their own cohesion and contribute to the framing of a genuinely European foreign policy'.[4]

In November 1959 a meeting of the foreign ministers of the Six discussed the question of foreign policy co-ordination, agreeing to meet quarterly. The whole issue took on a new momentum and importance with the Bonn Declaration of July 1961. In the Bonn Declaration the six foreign ministers agreed to hold:

at regular intervals, meetings whose aim will be to compare their views, to concert their policies and to reach common positions in order to further the political union of Europe thereby strengthening the Atlantic alliance. The necessary practical measures will be taken to prepare these meetings. In addition, the continuation of active co-operation among the Foreign Ministers will contribute to the continuity of the action undertaken in common.

The consequent Fouchet–Cattani talks on a treaty of European political union faltered over perennially disputed issues in European co-operation: whether to move away from supranationality, to circumvent the role of the Commission, and whether to deal with defence outside the NATO context, with the divergence of view being between the French and the Five.[5] The breakdown of these talks in April 1962, however, did not mean the end of the issue, and at the end of the decade this and related issues were back on the agenda.

The Hague summit in December 1969, as was seen in Chapter 1, agreed amongst other things to pave the way for the enlargement of the Community, to instruct the foreign ministers to report on 'the best way of achieving progress in the matter of political unification, within the context of enlargement', and to pave 'the way for a united Europe capable of assuming its responsibilities in the world of tomorrow and of making a contribution commensurate with its traditions and its mission'. Both the Hague meeting and the subsequent foreign ministers' report agreed, as the former put it, that applicant states must 'accept the treaties and their political finality'.[6] The foreign ministers stressed 'the correlation between membership of the European Communities and participation in activities making for progress towards political unification'. In addition they made clear that such progress was most likely to be achieved by a decision 'to cooperate in the field of foreign policy'. In drawing up their proposals the foreign ministers acknowledged that they were heavily influenced by their belief that:

- conformity with the preambles of the founding treaties required 'tangible form should be given to the will for a political union';
- the evolution of common policies 'requires corresponding developments in the specifically political sphere';
- 'Europe must prepare itself to discharge the imperative world duties entailed by its greater cohesion and increasing role'.

Current developments within the Community were regarded as making it necessary to step up 'political co-operation' and as an initial step 'to provide . . . ways and means of harmonizing their views in the field of international politics'. Bringing all these considerations together, the foreign ministers 'felt that foreign policy concertation should be the object of the first practical endeavours to demonstrate to all that Europe has a political vocation'. This co-operation was to have two objectives: firstly, to engender 'greater mutual understanding' on international issues 'by exchanging information and consulting regularly', and secondly, to 'increase their solidarity by working for a harmonization of views, concertation of attitudes and joint action when it appears feasible and desirable'. The scope of consultation was 'all major questions of foreign policy' and states could propose any topic for discussion.[7]

The procedural proposals of the foreign ministers were based upon a report drawn up by the heads of the political departments of the member states under the chairmanship of Vicomte Davignon (the Belgian Political Director), and the mechanism for carrying out what became known as European Political Co-operation (EPC) used to be referred to as the Davignon procedure. The initial basic system comprised the following elements: a meeting of foreign ministers at least twice a year; these meetings to be prepared by a Political Committee, comprising the heads of the political departments, which would meet at least four times a year; the ability of that committee to set up working parties for special tasks, and panels of experts; and the appointment by each state of an official to act as 'correspondent' with his or her counterparts in other states.

Crucially, as can be seen, this system was to operate separately from the Community system *per se*, in that it was outside any treaty framework. The Commission had no integral role, merely being 'consulted if the activities of the European Communities are affected by the work of the Ministers', and there was no question of voting – every decision was to be through consensus. In addition, the work of EPC was to be chaired by the state occupying the Presidency of the Council of the European Communities, that state also hosting the meetings and being responsible for providing 'secretarial service and . . . the practical organization of the meetings'.[8]

This EPC or Davignon system was avowedly intergovernmental and was to run in parallel with the treaty system and framework. Some, like Ralf Dahrendorf, initially saw this as a source of great potential strength, recognising the reality of interaction between sovereign states,[9] whilst others, including the Commission, saw the avoidance of existing institutions as a retreat from Community to intergovernmental action. But a common policy, as distinct from co-operation in foreign policy, remained only a long-term objective. Almost immediately after its founding the EPC system began to evolve, with the Paris summit of October 1972 of the heads of state or government of the Community not only asserting the goal of European Union, but also agreeing to redefine EPC. The process of consultation was to be intensified, with foreign ministers meeting quarterly, and the aim of co-operation was now to be regarded as not just to consult on current problems but 'as far as possible to work out joint medium and long-term positions bearing in mind the implications and effects in the field of international policy of Community policies in preparation'. The foreign ministers were asked to report by June 1973 on methods for improving EPC.[10]

A few weeks later than scheduled that report appeared, and was made official at the Copenhagen meeting of September 1973. The report regarded the initial experience as very satisfactory, arguing that on many matters states had been able to decide matters jointly and 'make common political action possible. This habit has also led to the "reflex" of coordination' among the states, so that this 'collegiate sense in Europe is becoming a real force in international relations'. In phrases that have been repeated over the years, 'the characteristically pragmatic mechanisms' of EPC were praised, as were their 'flexibility'. The

ministers were confident that there was a growing belief in the useful-
ness of concerted action, but did feel there ought to be a greater
emphasis upon making an original contribution to world politics rather
than simply reacting to the initiatives of others. They decided to meet
quarterly instead of twice a year, noted that the Political Committee was
meeting as often as necessary (usually monthly), and formally set up the
Group of 'Correspondents', which had in fact already been meeting.
The members of this group were charged with the implementation of
political co-operation as well as with preparation of the work of their
more senior colleagues and political masters. The system of working
parties was also formalised rather more. As part of this process of
greater intensity of consultation, the COREU system was also established, namely a telex liaison system between the departments of foreign
affairs. The Copenhagen Report outlined more clearly the role of the
Presidency and accepted that it imposed a heavy administrative burden.
Importantly, it reaffirmed that 'the purpose of the consultation is to seek
common policies on practical problems'. In the report each state now
agreed 'as a general rule not to take up final positions without prior
consultation with its partners' within the framework of EPC. Perhaps
indicative of certain tensions that had arisen, the report allocated a
specific section to the relationship between EPC and the work of the EC
per se. This acknowledged the intergovernmental nature of EPC as
compared to the juridical commitments involved in the treaties, but was
rather vague as to the distinctiveness of subject matter in each context. It
did, however, acknowledge that the Commission could, as it had been
doing, make its views known on activities which had 'an incidence on
Community activities'. Additionally, the Council was to be informed,
through the president of COREPER, of the agreed conclusions obtained in Political Co-operation, where these conclusions had an
interest for the work of the Community.[11]

The problem of the discrepancies between EPC and the EC system
became glaring in November 1973, when in the morning the foreign
ministers met in Copenhagen as the 'Conference of Foreign Ministers'
only to have to travel to Brussels in the afternoon for an EC Council
meeting. This did, however, demonstrate the absurdity of the position.
These problems were exacerbated by the fact that the meetings had to
deal with the newly assertive Arab states who, after the Arab–Israeli
Yom Kippur War of October 1973, began to use oil as a diplomatic
weapon and to insist upon a linkage between trade and political
questions. Also crucial in the evolution of EPC was the change to a more

'pro-European' president in France, as Valéry Giscard d'Estaing replaced Georges Pompidou in 1974 and the former French insistence on the separation of political from economic questions became somewhat muted. As a result it became possible to avoid the fiasco of twin-sited meetings and to blur the clearly artificial distinctions which had been created and maintained. By the summer of 1974 the system was introduced of holding political co-operation discussions 'within the margin' of Council meetings and at the same place.

That year also saw other significant developments in the area of political co-operation, namely the initiation of the so-called *Gymnich* meetings. In April 1974 an informal meeting of foreign ministers without officials took place in a convivial atmosphere allowing wide-ranging but informal exchanges of view and attitudes. These now biannual meetings have become a fully fledged part of Political Co-operation, and contribute to the creation of a good atmosphere between ministers. A further development was the evolution of the 'troika' arrangement *vis-à-vis* the Presidency, namely that the incumbent Presidency responsible for the EPC would be aided by its predecessor and would have representation from its successor in order to maintain continuity. Perhaps more important as a portent for the future was the decision of the Paris summit of 1974 to create the European Council, as an institutionalisation of the previous periodic summits and a mechanism whereby at the very highest level EC and EPC matters could be discussed together. The European Council was also meant to provide momentum for integration by the injection of political will at the very highest level.

This activity and interest in the early 1970s, accompanied by rhetoric about European identity and European union, was belied by the absence of the political will to move forward in a fundamental way. That absence was both caused by and symptomatic of the uncertain environment in international politics and economics generated by the Arab–Israeli conflict of 1973 and the energy crisis of the 1970s. Contrary to expectations that exogenous crisis might stimulate centripetal behaviour patterns, it instead produced centrifugal pressures for each state to seek to arrange its own deal to its own best advantage. In addition, of course, the enlargement of January 1973 had hardly had time to settle when a sceptical government came to power in London in 1974.

In this climate it was perhaps not surprising that the promised definition of the 'European Identity' in the document published in Copenhagen in December 1973 proved to be somewhat disappointing.

Although there was apparent rhetorical agreement that the states had 'the political will to succeed in the construction of a United Europe', and to 'progressively . . . undertake the definition of their identity' so as to 'strengthen their own cohesion and contribute to the framing of a genuinely European foreign policy', the rhetoric was overtaken by events, and the enthusiasm of the early 1970s died away.[12] Indeed, the lukewarm response to the wave of reports on 'European union' which reached their climax with a report on the subject by the Belgian Prime Minister, Tindemans, in December 1975[13] shows that conditions were not right for decisive progress on the major question of the political and economic future of Europe, nor indeed for significant development of EPC. The second half of the 1970s saw a period of disenchantment, and the report of the 'three wise men' (Biesheuvel, Dell and Marjolin) made at the request of the European Council in 1979 agreed that the 'present time seems to us ill-suited to futuristic visions which presuppose a profound and rapid transformation of attitudes within the Community. The chance of such transformation in the next few years seems to be exceedingly slight.'[14]

None the less, progress had been made in EPC in the 1970s, especially significant being the accumulated habit of working together and the embryonic reflex of co-ordinated action. Perhaps most importantly, by the end of the decade the various states had begun to take the system for granted and to recognise and accept that there were common European interests. On the other hand, in 1979 Philippe de Schoutheete, the Belgian Political Director, could argue 'we have reached a plateau, as it were. We can continue more or less with what we are already doing, but it is difficult to do much more on the basis of present data and structures.'[15]

Despite this inauspicious background, the new decade of the 1980s brought a bout of renewed activity. The renewal arose from a variety of factors, including an increasing disillusionment with the United States as the leader of the Western world and a consequent acceptance of the need for greater European consultation and greater autonomy from American leadership. In addition, there was the pervasive concern to reinforce Europe's capacity to act as a single entity in world affairs, particularly the perceived need to allow the Ten to be more positive and to take a longer-term view, instead of merely reacting to world events as had tended to be the case. There was, perhaps, also something of a sense that the batterings that the European idea had received in the 1970s had demonstrated the dangers of simply living on a plateau. Moreover, the inept and delayed response to the Soviet invasion of Afghanistan in December 1979 had revealed that all was not well with the machinery, whilst the calls for action over the American hostage crisis in Tehran and the Afghan and Polish crises re-emphasised the artificial nature of the distinctions being drawn between economic, political and security issues, especially when consideration began to be given to the imposition of sanctions against the Soviet Union and Iran.

In the winter of 1980–1 a series of initiatives began to appear, partly to breathe new life into EPC and to enable it to respond to crises, but also partly to relaunch the movement towards European union. The British Foreign Secretary, Lord Carrington, was associated with the first; the German and Italian ministers, Genscher and Colombo, with the second. The Carrington initiative resulted in the London Report on EPC of October 1981, whilst the Genscher–Colombo initiative resulted in the Solemn Declaration on European Union of June 1983. Both had a significance for the Single European Act. In any event the initiatives overlapped.[16]

It was at Venlo in May 1981 that the EPC dimension of the question was discussed, and it became controversial because of the desire of the Germans to include defence questions in the ambit of EPC. Whilst this was ruled out, it was agreed that broad aspects of security could be discussed, as indeed they had been for several years. At Venlo four options with regard to EPC were discussed: (i) to maintain the present system as it was; (ii) to make minor administrative and procedural modifications to the present system, whilst retaining its present aims and features; (iii) to draw up a new report which would change the nature and expand the scope of political co-operation; and (iv) to draw up a formal treaty of political co-operation. It was agreed to ask the political directors to examine options (ii) and (iii), and the final compromise was between options (ii) and (iii) since it maintained the existing basic features but added new ones as well. The other contentious matter was the scope of political co-operation, particularly whether it included the military as well as the political aspects of security. Given the role of non-alliance member Ireland, and with help from other states, the narrow interpretation was maintained in the formal London Report – that is, EPC was identified with the political aspects of security, although it was quite clear that the distinctions between the political, economic and military aspects of security were difficult, if not impossible, to maintain. The London Report reaffirmed the agreement that 'having regard to the different situations of the Member States' (which Dublin interpreted as a nod in the direction of their apparent neutrality), the ministers had agreed 'to maintain the flexible and pragmatic approach which has made it possible to discuss in political cooperation certain important foreign policy questions bearing on the political aspects of security'. The reports of 1970 and 1973 were endorsed and emphasis was put on a 'commitment to consult partners before adopting final positions' or taking foreign policy initiatives, on taking full account of the views of the other members, and on giving 'due weight to the desirability of achieving a common position'. They agreed it was increasingly possible for them 'to speak with one voice in international affairs', and that the objective was 'not merely a common attitude but joint action'. The London Report also contained some organisational points:

- a desire to lighten the burden of detailed work at foreign ministers' meetings;
- a reaffirmation of the informal character of *Gymnich*-type meetings, reasserting the lack of a formal agenda and the absence of officials;
- an emphasis on the co-ordinating and directing role of the Political Committee *vis-à-vis* subservient groups;
- a desire to avoid the situation where 'most of the efforts of political cooperation are devoted to reacting to world events as they occur', as was currently the case, and to take instead 'a longer-term approach to certain problems', a hope which, as has been seen, had been expressed before;
- an emphasis upon the centrality of confidentiality to EPC;
- a recognition that the interests of continuity and the pressure of work required that the Presidency 'be assisted by a small team of officials seconded from preceding and succeeding presidencies', and that the president could delegate certain tasks to its predecessor and successor;
- a clearer recognition of the need for 'discussion of the Community and political cooperation aspects of certain questions', to be co-ordinated 'if the subject-matter requires this';
- a revamping of crises procedures.[17]

In the London Report there was a shift to greater political, if not legal, commitment and, if not a move towards a secretariat, at least a reinforcement of the troika. EPC, however, still remained neither merged nor juridically linked with the EC institutions proper, although the rather closer involvement of the Commission was acknowledged. In essence, the London Report provided the foundation of Article 30 of the Single European Act.

Wider questions of institutional reform remained on the agenda given the Genscher–Colombo initiative, and some of these proposed reforms touched upon EPC. The Solemn Declaration on European Union made in Stuttgart in 1983, for example, expanded the scope of EPC discussion to 'the political and economic aspects of security', as well as reiterating the commitment to prior consultation and the aspiration to 'joint action'. It ducked the questions raised by Genscher and Colombo of a single Council of Ministers responsible both for EC and EPC matters, and of a small secretariat for EPC. Some states clearly still wished to maintain the intergovernmental–juridical division between EPC and EC and interestingly, whilst the issue of EPC–EC relations was broached with a call for 'greater coherence and close coordination between the existing structures . . . so that comprehensive and consistent action, can be taken to achieve European Union', the declaration again flinched from how this was to be achieved. Moreover, the declaration could hardly resolve the dilemma, since whilst 'solemn' it was not law.[18]

The debate about EC institutional reform and political and economic development, and about the enhancement and extension of EPC, did not, however, lapse after 1983. That the initiative was maintained owed much to the veteran Italian campaigner, Altiero Spinelli. After direct elections to the European Parliament in 1979, Spinelli and others began to agitate for institutional reform, and in 1981 the Parliament created an Institutional Committee with Spinelli as a 'co-ordinating rapporteur'. This in turn produced the Draft Treaty Establishing the European Union, which is fully discussed in Chapter 1. The draft treaty incorporated the notion that EPC and EC concerns be brought together within a single Community framework, but acknowledged that, whilst the former would remain a matter of 'co-operation', and thus presumably consensus, the latter would remain within a legal framework and be open to majority voting.[19] At the very least the efforts of the European Parliament kept the momentum going after the disappointing Solemn Declaration, and had an effect on the European Council meeting at Fontainebleau in June 1984.

The Fontainebleau Council agreed to create 'an *ad hoc* Committee consisting of personal representatives of the Heads of State and of Government . . . to make suggestions for the improvement of the operation of European cooperation *in both the Community field and that of political, or any other cooperation*.[20] It was to be modelled on the Spaak Committee of 1955–6, which followed the Messina Conference of June 1955.[21] The new committee, the Ad Hoc Committee on/for Institutional Affairs, known as the Dooge Committee after its chairman, had the task in practice of reviewing progress and the multiplicity of proposals now existing.

The Dooge Committee examined socioeconomic issues, institutional reform and 'the search for an external identity', namely the enhancement of EPC by amongst other things the inclusion of 'security and defence'. Many passages of the report had specific reserves attached to them by governmental representatives, thus the Danes and Greeks entered reserves on identity, and Dooge himself on 'security and defence'. As a way forward the Dooge Committee proposed an 'intergovernmental conference to negotiate a draft treaty of European Union, based on the "*acquis communautaire*", the Stuttgart Solemn Declaration and the Dooge Report itself, and to be guided by the "spirit and method" of the Parliament's Draft Treaty'.[22] However, there was a split on this matter between the 'maximalists' and 'minimalists', a division which continued through to the European Council of June 1985 which discussed the report and beyond. The maximalists, led by Italy, wanted real progress towards European union, whilst the minimalists, led by the UK, were opposed to treaty changes and challenges to sovereignty, favouring the pragmatism of functional co-operation and countenancing only procedural changes and perhaps some new policies. This division led at Milan to a vote over the holding of an intergovernmental conference, with Britain, Greece and Denmark being in the minority.

In the event the recalcitrants did not obstruct the convening of the conference in July 1985, although they reserved their position. One of the bones of contention was whether EC matters should be treated separately from EPC matters, and this was only resolved right at the end of the Luxembourg Intergovernmental Conference of December 1985 which produced the *Single* European Act. Between July and December there were two principal working parties, the political directors prepared the draft on EPC and a group comprised largely of the permanent representatives of the member states to the EC dealt with questions of treaty reform. These groups reported to foreign ministers on six occasions, but the main issues were only settled by the heads of state or government at Luxembourg. In general, whilst there was some agreement regarding the 'extension of the *scope* of the Community', there was general resistance on 'the *level* of integration'.[23]

Alongside what it had to say about the Communities, the Single European Act provided for the codification of political co-operation, the provision of a legal base for it, and the creation of a secretariat for EPC to help the Presidency and to provide continuity.[24] In the negotiations on EPC there was some broad agreement, namely that the objective should be to reiterate and reinforce existing structures whilst introducing some small changes. There was disagreement as to the nature and size of the secretariat, an echo of the Fouchet debates nearly twenty-five years earlier. The French and Germans envisaged a secretary general being appointed for four years by a European Council, and heading a secretariat. The Italians and Dutch were suspicious of this as a putative rival to the Commission and favoured, along with the British, a small secretariat in arrangement with the pre-existing Council Secretariat in Brussels. The final agreement regarding EPC was contained in Title III of the Single European Act, headed 'Provisions on European cooperation in the sphere of foreign policy' (this title consisted of one article, Article 30), and in the Preamble and Title I, 'Common provisions'.

Although brought together in the Single European Act, the distinction between EPC and EC was not removed. Article 3 reasserts the distinctive juridical base of the two systems, as does the Preamble, although Article 30.5 does make the explicit point that the 'external policies of the European Community and the policies agreed in European Political Cooperation must be consistent'. Whilst not having the same juridical base as EC matters, EPC was at last provided with a legal basis by the Single European Act, although the terminology encompassed in Article 30 would clearly be difficult to enforce, and it can be argued that in practice the commitments remain political rather than legal, if only in the sense that there is no way of enforcing them. After all, how are commitments to 'endeavour jointly to formulate and implement a European foreign policy', to 'inform and consult', to 'take full account of the positions of the other partners' and to give 'due consideration to the desirability of adopting and implementing common European positions' to be legally judged or enforced?[25] On the other hand, the Irish Supreme Court took a much more stringent view of the obligations involved when asked in an action initiated by Raymond Crotty to determine whether Title III was compatible with the Irish Constitution's stress upon sovereignty and independence. It took the view that 'although the approach to the ultimate aim of European Union is to be reached by a pathway of gradualism, each member state will immediately cede portion of its sovereignty and freedom of action in matters of foreign policy'. It further argued that what had been an aspiration had now passed 'into a realm of solemnly covenanted commitment to the conduct of foreign policy in a way that will lead to European Political Union, at least in the sphere of foreign policy'. The Court argued that to suggest that all that was involved was a mere formalisation of existing practices underestimated the true nature in international law of a treaty, and that the Single European Act meant that Ireland 'would be bound in international law to engage actively in a programme which would trench progressively on Ireland's independence and sovereignty in the conduct of foreign policy'. It concluded that for these reasons the Single European Act was incompatible with the Constitution as it stood and that, if Ireland wished to ratify it, it would need to amend the Constitution by referendum. The Irish people did so in May 1987.[26]

It may be fairly assumed that most of the governments would have been surprised at the interpretation accorded by the Irish Supreme Court to Title III. What the governments were less united about was the scope of their agreement 'to coordinate . . . positions more closely on the political and economic aspects of security'.[27] Security was among the last points to be settled in the negotiations. The Italians favoured the creation of a mechanism for consultation between EPC and the Western European Union, and for EPC to discuss a number of security issues. The UK, and to some extent the French, Germans and Dutch, favoured primarily using NATO and the WEU. This subject caused difficulties for the Danes and Greeks, but most particularly for the Irish, given their non-adherence to NATO or the WEU and their rhetorical neutrality. Indeed, the apparent threat to their 'neutrality' was one of the factors motivating Mr Raymond Crotty in his action against the Irish Government.

The Single European Act acknowledged the need for greater coordination on the political and economic aspects of security to promote 'a European identity in external policy matters', as well as the need 'to maintain the technological and industrial conditions necessary for . . . security', albeit within the framework of existing competent institutions. In addition, those who wished were to be free to pursue 'closer cooperation in the field of security . . . within the framework of the Western European Union or the Atlantic Alliance'.[28] Given the atmosphere generated by their Supreme Court decision and the referendum, on submitting their ratification the Irish Government deposited a Declaration which affirmed its view that Title III did not affect

'Ireland's long established policy of military neutrality'.[29]

The debate about security raised questions of definition since, for example, it is clear that the EPC system worked quite well in the periodic meetings of the Conference on Security and Co-operation in Europe (CSCE), which dealt with, amongst other things, confidence-building measures. The history of the EC and EPC shows quite clearly that it is not possible to draw rigid demarcation lines between the political, economic and military aspects of security, or indeed between the EC and EPC systems. Although the latter has formally caused problems, in 1981 Commissioner Christopher Tugendhat argued that 'in practical terms the distinction between political cooperation and discussion in the Council of Ministers . . . is not . . . rigid. Already, we have seen the dividing line between the two become blurred.'[30] With regard to both the former and the latter, the difficulties can be illustrated by the agreements of the Community states to issue statements condemning the Soviet invasion of Afghanistan and to ensure that Community products did not substitute for the grain sales cut off by the USA. In connection with Iran, there was Community action which included the withholding of arms sales and other sanctions. As Tugendhat commented, the 'Community was able without anyone nit-picking over the precise framework within which discussion was taking place, to take decisions on these issues'.[31]

It has not all been plain sailing as there was nit-picking in April–June 1982 over the question of sanctions against Argentina after the attack on the Falklands. However, the Community decision to embargo imports from the Argentine did for the first time refer in its preamble to the agreement reached in Political Co-operation on the taking of economic measures.[32] The Single European Act nevertheless makes clear that far-reaching changes in EPC were rejected by the member states and asserts that, in addition to the developments outlined in Title III, EPC will 'confirm and supplement the procedures agreed in the reports of Luxembourg (1970), Copenhagen (1973), London (1981), the Solemn Declaration on European Union (1983) and the practices gradually established among the Member States'.[33]

One advance was contained in Article 30.10(g) which created a secretariat, to be based in Brussels, to 'assist the Presidency in preparing and implementing the activities of European Political Cooperation and in administrative matters. It shall carry out its duties under the authority of the Presidency.'[34] This ended the 25-year argument about the structure and location of such a secretariat, and after the European

Council meeting in the summer of 1986 the arrangements for the secretariat were determined and it has now become operational.

As for the rest of the organisational scheme, Title III (or Article 30) confirmed the existing practice: the central role of the Presidency; the (at least) quarterly meetings of foreign ministers; the innovative, preparatory and pivotal role of the Political Committee; the responsibility of the European Correspondents' Group for monitoring the system and studying organisational issues and the role of the working groups on specific matters under the direction of the Political Committee. The arrangements outlined in Title III were to be reviewed after five years, but they do provide the current basis of EPC.

The Single European Act, which came into operation in the summer of 1987 after ratification in the twelve member states, represents the current state of play on the issues of institutional reform, the socio-economic objectives to be pursued over the next five years, the attitude to European union and the development of EPC. Not all member states were happy with the outcome. The Italians, for example, felt that it did not go far enough towards the European Parliament's draft treaty. The British, as will be seen in the next chapter, had mixed feelings. The Danes suffered the embarrassment of their Parliament, the Folketing, originally narrowly rejecting the reforms and demanding a renegotiation of the package, an attitude echoing some of the original and continuing Danish distrust of the EC and its impact upon Danish sovereignty. Renegotiation was ruled out by a majority of Community members (only the UK favouring such action). In a second vote, a week after the first, the Folketing called for a national referendum on the issue. In the February 1986 referendum, 56.2 per cent of those voting accepted the package of EC reforms, in a turnout of 75 per cent. After the Irish hiccup was overcome, the Single European Act began life on 1 July 1987.

Any assessment of these developments, and of the Community generally, must take into account the question of perspective. The member states of the Community have been 'increasingly viewed by third countries as a coherent force in international relations', acting as a 'caucus in international conferences',[35] there being little doubt that on many issues Community states 'clearly form an important diplomatic "bloc" '.[36] It may also be argued that 'the various collective actions' of the states 'gradually constitute a policy line from which it is difficult to depart'[37] and that, as the London Report of 1981 put it, political co-operation has become 'a central element in the foreign policies of all member states'.[38] Other reports on Community behaviour are replete with references to the states adopting 'common positions', achieving 'coordination of their positions' or having found it 'possible to harmonise successfully the various attitudes', leading to the pursuit of 'an agreed policy' or even on occasion 'a common foreign policy'.[39] These tendencies have, perhaps, been most pronounced at the UN, where the Presidency has now routinely spoken for the Twelve in major debates and in delivering explanations of votes. The Twelve have sought to act together to resolve common problems on such issues as the Middle East.

Perhaps a major step forward for EPC and the statement of a distinctive European position was the formulation of a common position on the Middle East in the form of the Venice Declaration at the end of May 1980. In the Venice Declaration, nine European states with historically widely disparate interests and views on the Middle East question managed to agree a common position. This position revolved around 'the two principles universally accepted by the international community: the right to existence and to security of all the States in the region, including Israel, and justice for all the peoples, which implies the recognition of the legitimate rights of the Palestinian people'. The Nine furthermore recognised that the PLO would have to be 'associated' with the negotiations, that there should be no 'unilateral initiative to change the status of Jerusalem, that the continued occupation of the occupied territories was unacceptable and that the renunciation of violence by all was crucial to the creation of the necessary confidence for peace'.[40] Other successes have been the relatively concerted behaviour at the UN and a variety of other international forums, especially at the original and subsequent review meetings of the Conference on Security and Co-operation in Europe (CSCE) where, despite a number of pressures, the Community states have managed to operate as an identifiable caucus.[41]

Success in EPC has stemmed from the habit of consultation producing a 'European reflex', allowing them to see the 'collective dimension' of issues, and making it 'normal' to search 'for consensus'.[42] Indeed, the EPC, especially *vis-à-vis* the officials involved, can be characterised as exhibiting a tendency towards 'groupthink', in that those involved have tended to develop an *ésprit de corps* and to take a convergent view.[43] Reinforcing this has been the situation described by Wallace and Allen, to the effect that in all major states there has been a bureaucratic contest over the control of Community affairs. In this 'bureaucratic politics' struggle EPC has been a clear, undisputed sphere of influence for the foreign ministries.[44]

Most important, however, have been the exogenous and indigenous pressures relating to the perceived need for the Community states to play a wider, more coherent world role. Exogenous factors such as the Community being the world's largest trading unit and its relationship with the African, Caribbean and Pacific countries have made it a force to be reckoned with in the world. It has thus faced the problem that Brandt identified for the Federal Republic of Germany twenty years ago, namely being an economic giant but a political dwarf. It has learnt that giants cannot happily be dwarfs. The external world expects it to have a coherent view, and friends such as the United States are exasperated when it does not, as became clear during Kissinger's ill-fated 'Year of Europe' in 1973 when the USA lost patience with a divided Europe and yearned for a single, clear, united European voice. Equally exasperating was the inability of the Europeans to produce a single focus point for the discussion of a myriad of issues and negotiations. Kissinger's belief in linkage between economic, political and defence issues ran into the problem of the Europeans having different organisations for each.

Equally important was the indigenous pressure on the EC states to play a wider world role: after all one of the underlying imperatives for integration was the desire for a united Europe to play a major role in the world. As noted earlier, as early as the Messina Conference there was agreement that unity was 'indispensable if Europe is to maintain her position in the world, regain her influence and prestige'.[45] As the USA and USSR have surged forward in power, but as somewhat paradoxically the sources and centres of power have become more diffuse, so the Europeans have had to come to terms with the fact that, in general, they have more influence when acting together. It is also true, of course, that several internal EC policies, particularly on agriculture, have external repercussions and that the development of internal policies can be undertaken only with cognisance of the external dimension.

Despite all of these successes and imperatives, it must be concluded that the record on EPC is at best mixed, that there is really no common European foreign policy since, whilst 'a pattern of solidarity has been reached, it is by no means complete or wholly predictable'.[46] A number of states have fairly consistently maintained their freedom of manoeuvre, with France initially being particularly independent and Greece later taking over this role. More broadly, if one examines issues at the UN which are put to a vote, as against including resolutions which all UN members supported, then Community states all vote the same way in only about half the votes, although it should be noted that it is increasingly rare for the Community to 'split for or against a resolution'. Rosemary Foot has argued that an analysis of Community states' voting at the UN tends 'to reduce the credibility of the claim that the Community has become recognised as a united political force at the UN'. Furthermore, the issues they disagreed upon were 'the major ones'.[47]

One area of particular difficulty has been southern Africa and especially, in recent years, South Africa. In 1976 the EC states made their first collective statement on South Africa, and in 1977 they agreed a Code of Conduct for EC firms operating in South Africa, relating especially to the firms' employment practices there, although the Code was applicable only on a voluntary basis. The change in circumstances generated by the escalation of civil unrest which began in September 1981 and the imposition of a state of emergency in July 1985 led to new pressures upon the EC states. Since that time the Twelve have found common action difficult to agree, a divergence reaching its height in 1986 when at The Hague European Council meeting there was a deep split between those who would have liked to decide upon sanctions there and then and those who wanted only a declaration of intent. There was, and continues to be, prevarication over both the nature of measures and the timing of their introduction.[48]

A notorious example of failure to agree was in relation to the response of the Community states in EPC to the shooting down of the South Korean Boeing 747 (KAL–007) in 1983 by the Soviets. Despite repeated efforts at official and ministerial level to agree a statement condemning the Soviet Union, no such statement could be agreed because the Greeks refused to join in any such condemnation.

That divisions occur on such issues is not surprising. Roger Morgan noted perspicaciously many years ago that the development of a common foreign policy was likely to be hampered by the legacies that the member states brought with them to EPC, especially their centuries of distinctive experience. He identified four distinct problems, namely: (i) the states in the Community were far from agreement on many aspects of their internal arrangements, and some of these disputes had external repercussions; (ii) the inevitably divisive factor of straightforward commercial competition; (iii) the differing geographical perspectives from which they viewed the outside world, a factor specifically relating to the varying but long-standing historical traditions of each country's view of its place in the world; and (iv) the different substantive interests of the EC members in the international system as a whole, and in both economics and strategy.[49] These problems have been exacerbated, of course, by the adhesion of Greece, Spain and Portugal since he wrote.

This legacy of which Morgan writes reflects, for example, the different experiences of colonialism undergone by Britain, France and Ireland; the differing wartime experiences of Britain, Ireland and the continental states; and the profoundly differing post-war political experiences of Spain, Portugal and Greece compared to the Nine of 1973. The diversity engendered by this type of input into national political cultures has not unnaturally led to divergences in perceived national interests on a range of issues within EPC, and the EPC policy-making system is not always able to cope given the requirement of consensus and unanimity. The colonial experience seems to have been particularly significant, with divisions in EPC appearing on Namibia, Rhodesia, apartheid and sanctions, decolonisation, and Third World issues, especially the New International Economic Order, although the nuclear powers have also diverged on questions of disarmament.[50]

To some extent the divergences are submerged because of the highly declaratory nature of EPC, the fact that it consists largely of statements and has few other instruments. This is coupled with a tendency for the participants to unite 'behind a common position sufficiently loosely defined to allow each to add his own interpretation, so producing some forward movement without confronting the major obstacles ahead'.[51] This makes assessment of the success of EPC difficult. It is clear that the record of co-ordinating policy is patchy and that the impact on third parties can be exaggerated; on the other hand, it exists and its existence is no longer a matter of debate. Indeed, with the Single European Act coming into force in 1987, it has even acquired a certain legitimacy.

Notes

1. Preamble, Treaty Establishing the Eurpoean Economic Community, Rome, 25 March 1957.
2. Declaration of Political Principles of European Union, approved by the International Council of the European Movement at Brussels, 28 February 1949. Reproduced in Richard Vaughan, *Postwar Integration in Europe* (London, Edward Arnold, 1976), pp. 37–9.
3. The Messina Resolution is reproduced in Miriam Camps, *Britain and the European Community* (London, Oxford University Press, 1964), pp. 520–2.
4. *Bulletin of the European Communities*, 12–1973, pp. 118–22.

5. A. Silj, *Europe's Political Puzzle: A Study of the Fouchet Negotiations and the 1963 Veto*, Occasional Papers in International Affairs No. 17 (Harvard, Harvard Center for International Affairs, 1967).

6. Communiqué of the Conference of the Heads of State and Government of the European Community's Member States, 2 December 1969, The Hague, *Bulletin of the European Communities*, 1–1970, pp. 11–18.

7. Report by the Foreign Ministers of the Member States on the Problems of Political Unification, *Bulletin of the European Communities*, 11–1970, pp. 9–14.

8. Ibid.

9. See Ralf Dahrendorf, 'A new goal for Europe', in M. Hodges, (ed.), *European Integration*, (Harmondsworth, Penguin, 1972), pp. 74–87.

10. Communiqué issued by heads of state or government, 19–20 October 1972, Paris, *Bulletin of the European Communities*, 10–1972, pp. 9–26.

11. Second Report of the Ministers for Foreign Affairs, Copenhagen, September 1973, *Bulletin of the European Communities*, 9–1973, pp. 12–21.

12. The European Identity, issued during Conference of Heads of State or Government, Copenhagen, 14 December 1973, *Bulletin of the European Communities*, 12–1973, pp. 118–22.

13. Report on European Union by Leo Tindemans, December 1975, *Bulletin Supplement*, 1/76.

14. Report on European Institutions presented by the Committee of Three to the European Council ('Report of the Three Wise Men'), Luxembourg, 1980.

15. Phillippe de Schouteete, 'European political cooperation: achievements and prospects', *European Documents*, No. 1061, Agence Europe, Brussels, 3 July 1979.

16. For these developments see also Chapter 1 above.

17. Report on European Political Cooperation, London, 13 October 1981, *Bulletin Supplement*, 3/81, pp. 14–17.

18. The plan set out to create an 'Act' and evolved as a Solemn Declaration. See Gianni Bonvicini, 'The Genscher–Colombo plan' and the 'Solemn Declaration on European Union' (1981–83) in R. Pryce (ed.), *The Dynamics of European Union* (London, Croom Helm, 1987), pp. 174–87.

19. Otto Schmuck, 'The European Parliament's Draft Treaty Establishing the European Union (1979–84)' in Pryce, op. cit., pp. 188–216; see also Chapter 1 above.

20. Fontainebleau European Council, 25–6 June 1984 (emphasis added). See also Patrick Keatinge and Anna Murphy, 'The European Council; Ad Hoc Committee on Institutional Affairs (1984–85)' in Pryce, op. cit., pp. 217–37.

21. But as shown in Chapter 1 there were differences.

22. Ad Hoc Committee on Institutional Affairs Report to the European Council, Brussels, 29–30 March 1985; see also Keatinge and Murphy, op. cit., p. 228.

23. Richard Corbett, 'The 1985 Intergovernmental Conference and the Single European Act' in Pryce, op. cit., p. 244 (emphasis in original).

24. Ibid., pp. 245–59; Single European Act, *Bulletin Supplement*, 2/86.

25. Single European Act, op. cit.

26. Judgment of the Irish Supreme Court, 9 April 1987. The Irish people voted in a referendum on 26 May 1987: 69.9 per cent of those voting were in favour of the proposed amendment and 30.1 per cent were against, with a turnout of 44 per cent. For a fuller account see Trevor C. Salmon, *Unneutral Ireland: An Ambivalent and Unique Security Policy* (Oxford, Clarendon Press, 1989), Conclusion *passim*.

27. Single European Act, op. cit., Article 30.6 (a).
28. Ibid., Article 30.6 (a), (b), (c).
29. For the Declaration by the Government of Ireland see *Ireland Today: Bulletin of the Department of Foreign Affairs*, No. 1037, May/June 1987. Ireland deposited its ratification on 24 June 1987. The Declaration reads: 'the provisions of Title III do not affect Ireland's long established policy of military neutrality and that coordination of positions on the political and economic aspects of security does not include the military aspects of security or procurement for military purposes and does not affect Ireland's right to act or refrain from acting in any way which might affect Ireland's international status of military neutrality'. Incidentally, in December 1985 the Danes made a reservation concerning their desire to continue participating in Nordic co-operation.
30. Christopher Tugendhat, Vice-President of the European Commission, First Annual Shell Lecture, St Andrews University, 14 May 1981, in a speech which evoked a bitter reaction from the Irish Commissioner, Michael O'Kennedy.
31. Ibid.
32. *Official Journal*, L102/1, 16 April 1982.
33. Single European Act, op. cit., Article 1.
34. Ibid., Article 30.10(g).
35. Brigid Laffan, 'The consequences for Irish foreign policy', in David Coombes (ed.), *Ireland and the European Communities: Ten Years of Membership* (Dublin, Gill and Macmillan, 1983), pp. 96 and 104.
36. Patrick Keatinge, 'The Europeanisation of Irish foreign policy', in P. J. Drudy and Dermot McAlease, *Ireland and the European Community: Irish Studies 3* (Cambridge, Cambridge University Press, 1983), p. 45.
37. Translation from Phillippe de Schoutheete, *La Cooperation Politique Européenne* (Paris, Fernand Nathan, 1980), pp. 118–19.
38. London Report, see n. 17 above.
39. These statements are from *Developments in the European Communities: Second Report*, pp. 7–8, *Third Report*, p. 12, *Fourth Report*, p. 13, and *Fifth Report*, p. 17, published by Stationery Office in Dublin for the Irish Government, 1973, 1974 and 1975.
40. Declaration on the Middle East issued by Venice meeting of heads of state or government, 12–13 June 1980, *Bulletin of the European Communities*, 6–1980, pp. 10–11.
41. For reviews of EPC see William Wallace, 'Political cooperation: integration through intergovernmentalism', in H. Wallace, W. Wallace and C. Webb (eds), *Policy-Making in the European Communities* (Chichester, John Wiley, 1983) 2nd edn, pp. 373–402; C. Hill (ed.), *National Foreign Policies and European Political Cooperation* (London, Allan and Unwin, 1983); David Allen, Reignhardt Rummel and Wolfgang Wessels, *European Political Cooperation* (London, Butterworths, 1982); de Schoutheete, *La Cooperation Politique Européene*, op. cit.; and P. Ifestos, *Contemporary European Diplomacy: National or Supra-National? The EEC's European Political Cooperation* (Aldershot, Gower, 1987). On the Middle East see David Allen and Alfred Pijpers (eds), *European Policy-Making and the Arab–Israeli Conflict* (The Hague, Martinus Nijhoff, 1984).
42. Translation of de Schoutheete, *La Cooperation Politique Européene*, op. cit., pp. 118–19.
43. Christopher Hill, 'National interests: the insuperable obstacles' in Hill, op. cit., p. 189.

44. William Wallace and David Allen, 'Political cooperation: procedure as substitute for policy', in Wallace, Wallace and Webb (eds), *Policy-Making in the European Communities* (Chichester, John Wiley, 1977), 1st edn, pp. 227–47.
45. Camps, op. cit., pp. 520–2.
46. Keatinge, op. cit., p. 47.
47. Rosemary Foot, 'The European Community's voting behaviour at the United Nations General Assembly', *Journal of Common Market Studies*, Vol. 18, No. 4 (June 1979), pp. 350–60.
48. See M. Holland, 'The EEC Code for South Africa: a reassessment', *The World Today* (January 1985), pp. 12–14; M. Holland, 'The European Community and South Africa: economic reality or political rhetoric?', *Political Studies* Vol. 33, No. 3 (1985), pp. 399–417; M. Holland, 'Three approaches for understanding European Political Cooperation', *Journal of Common Market Studies*, Vol. 25, No. 4 (July 1987) pp. 295–314.
49. Roger Morgan, *High Politics, Low Politics: Towards a Foreign Policy for Western Europe* (The Washington Papers No. 11, Center for Strategic and International Studies, Georgetown University; London, Sage Publications, 1973), pp. 21–25.
50. See Foot, op. cit., *passim*.
51. William Wallace, 'Cooperation and convergence in European foreign policy', in Hill, op. cit., p. 10.

5

The Political Background in the United Kingdom

Pre-entry debates and developments

Frequent suggestions have been made that the United Kingdom should join a federation on the continent of Europe. This is something which we know, in our bones, we cannot do. We know that if we were to attempt it, we should relax the springs of our action in the Western democratic cause and in the Atlantic association which is the expression of that cause. For Britain's story and her interests lie far beyond the Continent of Europe. Our thoughts move across the seas to the many communities in which our people play their part, in every corner of the world. These are our family ties. That is our life: without it we should be no more than some millions of people living on an island off the coast of Europe, in which nobody wants to take any particular interest.[1]

This view of Sir Anthony Eden, the British Foreign Secretary in 1952, epitomises the prevailing British sentiment to European federation and the European movement in the decade after the war – and perhaps it still captures something of the heart of the British position towards Europe. There has been a 'time-lag in political psychology'[2] as the British government and people have adjusted, or rather failed to adjust, to the profound changes in the British position in the world over a period of years. There has been a significant secular trend. In the mid-nineteenth century Britain 'produced about two-thirds of the world's coal, about half its iron, five-sevenths of its steel, two-fifths of its hardware and about half its commercial cotton cloth'. Indeed, at that time 'over 40 per cent of the entire world output of traded manufactured goods' was produced within the United Kingdom.[3] One-third of the total exports of all other countries came to Britain in the 1840s. Not surprisingly, Paul Kennedy concludes that 'Britain had probably reached its true zenith as a world power and may be imagined like some ball or shell at the height of its trajectory before it begins its slow, steady descent',[4] this descent being perhaps the most critical element of the environment within which British policy was made, although there was a significant perceptual problem in adjusting to that changing environment. The difficulty in adjustment is understandable in that, even a hundred years after reaching its zenith, the British still remained a massive imperial power, had apparently proved themselves capable of winning two world wars against great continental coalitions, had enormous military power compared to all but two other powers in the world, and appeared to be relatively economically strong.

In British policy there has thus been a pervasive belief in British greatness, almost in the right of Britain to have a major influence over events. Moreover, this has been coupled with a degree of paternalism towards Europe, a paternalism evidenced in Churchill's famous speech in Zurich in September 1946, when it was explained that Britain and its Commonwealth, along with the United States and perhaps the Soviet Union, were to be 'the friends and sponsors of the new Europe' but not, it would seem, although this point initially eluded many in Europe, an integral part of it.[5] In 1953, speaking in the House of Commons, Churchill made clear that Britain's relationship with Europe 'can be expressed by prepositions, but the preposition "with" but not "of" – we are with them, but not of them'.[6]

This attitude was coupled with the continuing reality of geopolitics. Britain's geographical position provided a certain insularity, if not detachment, from European developments. Whilst British proximity to Europe led to a recognition that Britain required to be alert, to be continually aware of European developments and of the evolution of potential challenges to its own position, there was also the Channel which allowed Britain to play a balance of power role in Europe. This involved judiciously throwing British influence on the side of those opposing the strongest and most threatening power or powers of the day. This policy additionally suited a state whose dependence on trade and the international economy gave it a vested interest in the maintenance of international peace and stability in Europe and elsewhere.

Given this background, there was a certain British coolness towards schemes for closer European co-operation even before 1945. The British opposed the creation of a Supreme Allied Command in the First World War. They opposed French suggestions that the post-war League of Nations should have united military and naval forces. Later, Britain played an important part in the failure of the proposals made by

Aristide Briand, the French statesman, to the Tenth General Assembly of the League in September 1929. It was also antipathetic to more general proposals.

A jolt to British policy came in 1940 when it appeared that a threatening power was on the verge of capturing control of most of continental Europe. This 'most fateful moment in the history of the modern world' led to the Declaration of Anglo-French Union on 16 June 1940. The proposal, involving 'joint organs of defence, foreign, financial, and economic policies . . . a single War Cabinet . . . [with] all the forces of Britain and France . . . under its direction',[7] was overtaken by events, and was in any case a specific idea to meet a very specific problem – that is, keeping the French in the war. It was an aberration from the more traditional patterns of British policy.

When European peace came in May 1945, Britain perceived itself to be a world power. Indeed, the victory seemed to confirm that fact. Britain had 'won' the war. Moreover, because of its lone stand following the defeat of most Western European states in the summer of 1940, it had a unique status, having been present at the top table throughout the great wartime conferences which decided the future destiny of Europe and the nature of the post-war settlement. Britain was perceived to have the influence of a victor, and this status appeared to be confirmed by Article 23 of the United Nations Charter which named Britain as one of the five permanent members of the Security Council, and by Article 27 which gave those permanent members a veto power. Also in the summer of 1945 there was the Commonwealth and Empire, with Britain still possessing the largest empire the world had ever seen, approximately a fifth of the world's population, including some four hundred million on the Indian subcontinent. The combination of victory, UN role and Commonwealth, in addition to continuing involvement in the world economy, meant that Britain perceived itself as having a global role and responsibility rather than being a mere regional actor. Others might think almost exclusively in terms of European reconstruction and influence, but Britain had other, equally important, considerations on its mind. As Clement Attlee put it in May 1948, 'we are not solely a European Power'.[8] These other considerations, often involving pressing and important decisions, added fuel to a traditional scepticism of apparently visionary plans.

These, then, were the factors shaping British attitudes towards schemes for tying the European states more closely together in the post-war period. There was at least one other important specifically post-war ingredient: the gradual emergence of the antagonism betweeen the former wartime allies. Its perceptions of Soviet behaviour led the post-war Labour Government, particularly its Foreign Secretary, Ernest Bevin, to be anxious to involve the United States in the defence of Western Europe against the threat posed by the Soviets. A key element in British thinking, therefore, was to see itself as a sort of bridge between the Americans and the Europeans, an interlocutor between different cultures and, perhaps, interests. Following the awful destruction in the war, Europe was perceived as too weak to stand alone against the threat. Europe, therefore, needed US support and involvement and part of the British mission was to bring that about.

The difficulty with this basis of British policy was that it was fundamentally untenable because of an acceleration in the secular trends in economic power. Whilst at the end of the war Britain gave an appearance of world power, the war had in fact accelerated the deterior-ation in the British position, with the new Labour Government inherit-ing a 'bankrupt estate', the war effort having 'cost about a quarter of the country's national wealth'.[9] Particularly significant, perhaps, was the changed position in trade. In 1938 exports had totalled £471 million, but by 1945 this total had dropped to £258 million; on the other hand, over the same period imports had grown from £858 million to £1,299 million.[10] Overseas debts increased fivefold and Britain became the world's largest debtor. The various economic traumas of the Labour Government were signs of the problem. The decision in 1947 that Greece and Turkey could no longer be supported owing to financial stringency and the devaluation of sterling in the summer of 1949 from $4.03 to $2.80 (30 per cent) were open admissions of the malaise.

Other things were changing too, most notably the relationship with the USA and the Commonwealth. The 'special relationship' with the USA was perhaps never so special as the UK thought, and as British power declined so American power and assertiveness increased. There was the danger that Britain would become, for the Americans, just one of several European states with which it did business, although remain-ing for a while *primus inter pares*. Perhaps the real watershed was the débâcle in Anglo-American relations precipitated by the Suez crisis of 1956. The British felt betrayed by the Americans, having initially perceived American support for action. Exacerbating matters was the realization that such support was necessary: that Britain, even with France and Israel, could not otherwise achieve its objectives *vis-à-vis* Egypt. On the other hand, the Americans were rather dismayed by the ineptness of British policy and the inability to impose British will. The rift was healed and perhaps too much significance can be attached to it. None the less, the relationship had to some extent depended upon myth, and after the smash Humpty Dumpty could not be put together again.

Suez was also a contributing factor in the changing relationship with the Commonwealth, for it showed that the UK no longer had the strength to enforce its will, even in an area which had traditionally been regarded as vital to British security and national interest. More generally, there was the secular trend of decolonisation, a process initiated by the withdrawal from the Indian subcontinent in August 1947, leaving it partitioned between two sovereign states, India and Pakistan. A series of factors came into play on the decolonisation issue, but the end result was a position in which those that became newly independent wished to emphasise their new status by adopting starkly independent positions. This was partly achieved by attacking British policy in some areas, a tendency exacerbated by the situations in southern Africa.

A Britain that had initially been antipathetic to close links with Europe slowly had to begin to adjust its position. It is important to note, however, that Britain had not been opposed to all European involvement. It was a founding member of the Organisation for European Economic Co-operation (OEEC) in April 1948 – changed into the Organisation for Economic Co-operation and Development (OECD) in 1960, then including the USA and Canada – and the Council of Europe in May 1949. In the military field it had signed the Treaty of Dunkirk in 1947, binding it and France to resist any German aggression, and in March 1948 it had signed the Brussels Treaty with Belgium, France, Luxembourg, and the Netherlands – this being subsequently expanded to the Western European Union (WEU) in 1954, following the Paris Agreements of that year which allowed the Federal Republic of Germany and Italy to accede to the Brussels Treaty. It is worth noting that in Article 4 of the Brussels Treaty the signatories bound themselves 'If any of the High Contracting Parties should be the object of an armed attack in Europe . . . [to] afford the Party so attacked all the military and other aid and assistance in their power.'[11] The treaty also contained some provisions on socioeconomic co-operation. In addition, of course, on 4 April 1949 the British signed the North Atlantic Treaty, which committed the United States to take such action 'as it deems necessary' to help any party to the treaty which was attacked.[12] On 4 January 1960 Her Majesty's Government also signed the Convention of Stockholm establishing the European Free

Trade Association (EFTA). The question, of course, is why such involvement was regarded as acceptable whilst other types of involvement were shunned.

The fundamental position of the Labour Government of 1945–51 and most members of its Conservative successor was that federalism in Europe should not be encouraged and that the federalist momentum would in any case blow itself out in time. No British government was 'prepared to transfer control of the British economy, or other aspects of policy, from the British Government to a European body, either through the delegation of power or the acceptance of majority voting'.[13] The war experience had much to do with this, enhancing as it did British confidence in themselves and scepticism about Europeans, and also relevant was the vexed issue of sovereignty. Whilst the first majority Labour government may have had a particular interest in retaining its newly acquired control over the British economy, it did not have a monopoly of such concern, Harold Macmillan, then in opposition, declaring in 1950, 'Our people will not hand over to a supranational authority the right to close down our pits and our steel works'.[14] In particular, there was objection to those parts of the Schuman proposal of May 1950 which would have allowed the new Coal and Steel Community to bind member states without their consent, and decisions to be binding upon people and firms without their government's direct involvement. As Attlee put it, 'We . . . are not prepared to accept the principle that the most vital economic forces of this country should be handed over to an authority that is utterly undemocratic and is responsible to nobody.'[15] The preferred model was strictly intergovernmental co-operation in limited fields, especially economic and defence, and schemes in which it was clear that Her Majesty's Government had to acquiesce before decisions affecting the United Kingdom could be agreed. The power of decision was to remain in British hands, and this was so in all the organisations in which the British became involved. This attitude had a damaging effect partly because 'there has never been much real understanding in the United Kingdom of the depth of the drive towards real unity, as distinct from intergovernmental co-operation, on the continent'.[16]

To some extent it was the gradual realisation of the depth of this drive, in addition to other developments discussed in this chapter, which ultimately led to the change in British policy, if not completely in attitudes, towards European integration. A significant contribution to the greater British understanding of the strength of commitment on the continent was the failure of the so-called Maudling negotiations held under the auspices of the OEEC. Reginald Maudling, the British Paymaster-General, chaired a committee in 1957–8 which investigated possible forms of association between the customs union proposed by the founding Six of the European Economic Community and the other OEEC countries, particularly the possibility of creating a free trade area between them. These negotiations failed and ended in 1958 fundamentally because the Six, and especially France, were unwilling to link the new common market with a free trade area that gave comparable advantages in trade to the participants but without the commitment to common tariffs, policies and harmonisation implicit in the experiment of the Six. Part of the argument was that the proposed free trade area was a British device not only to gain advantages but also to water down the aspirations and programme of the Six.

The British clearly were hostile to the evolution of the Six in the form and manner in which it was happening. In June 1958 the Prime Minister, Macmillan, wrote his Foreign Secretary and Chancellor a personal minute giving vent to his feelings about 'Little Europe'. He argued that Britain:

ought to make it quite clear to our European friends that if Little Europe is formed without a parallel development of a Free Trade Area we shall have to reconsider the whole of our political and economic attitude towards Europe. I doubt if we could remain in Nato. We should certainly put on highly protective tariffs and quotas to counteract what Little Europe was doing to us. In other words, we should not allow ourselves to be destroyed little by little.

We would fight back with every weapon in our armoury. We would take our troops out of Europe. We would withdraw from Nato. We would adopt a policy of isolationism. We would surround ourselves with rockets and we would say to the Germans, the French and all the rest of them: 'Look after yourselves'.[17]

Macmillan was inclined to make his attitude clear to the Europeans, and a few days later he did tell President de Gaulle of France that failure to reach a free trade agreement between the EEC countries and Britain could spell the end of NATO. In fact, Britain did not succeed in altering the commitment of the Six. It was British policy that had to adjust and it did so in a rather different way than Macmillan proposed in 1958. In the short term the two sides went their own ways. The British Government proceeded to negotiate with the other non-EEC OEEC states and these negotiations led to the formation of EFTA in 1960. The Six proceeded with their plans, introducing their first intra-EEC tariff reductions on 1 January 1959.

EFTA represented the British belief in purely intergovernmental limited co-operation, without trespassing into the area of sovereignty. It also appeared to offer the advantage of an alternative to the EEC, without closing the door on new negotiations between the EEC and EFTA. Crucially, it was still believed that some kind of link could be negotiated between the Six and the EFTA seven. During 1960, however, this assumption began to come under fire in Britain, it gradually being realised that if there were any negotiations then the Six were likely to insist on a customs union. This raised the question of whether Britain would be better off joining the Community as it stood. Working in the same direction were:

- The recognition that the Community endeavour was no mere vision, but that it was becoming a reality.

- The realisation of dangers to the British trading position as the Six began and accelerated tariff reductions, so that by the beginning of 1961 these reductions totalled 30 per cent since January 1958. In addition, there was growing recognition that EFTA was no real alternative market to the population of the Six, and that Empire and Commonwealth were for the most part too impoverished.

- Despite the 1959 general election, 'You've never had it so good' and the apparent arrival of the British 'affluent society', concern about the 'stop–go' pattern of the British economy, with periods of booming activity being followed by a government financial squeeze. It began to be questioned whether plunging the British economy into the competitive EEC market might not break this stop–go pattern and introduce new vitality.

- A greater awareness of the deterioration in Britain's international position. After Suez it was clear the Commonwealth could not be counted on, whilst in March 1961 South Africa left the Commonwealth. A further portent of the future was the bilateral meeting between Khrushchev and Kennedy in Vienna in June 1961, a break in the pattern from previous four-power meetings including Britain and France, the abortive Paris summit of May 1960 being the last when Khrushchev attacked President Eisenhower over the U–2 spy plane incident.

With its decisive election victory of October 1959 it became easier for the Government to begin to think about these issues, and to resolve to mend fences with Europe. These adjustments, however, were not decided upon suddenly, nor was the conclusion that there was a need for adjustment in policy reached simultaneously by all policy makers, whether ministers or officials. The case for reconsideration and perhaps applying to join the EEC had many strands; some arguments were always accorded greater weight than others, and some caused more problems than others. To most people the political arguments were stronger than the economic, and in the Government's decision political considerations appeared to predominate. Caution needs to be exercised, however, over claims that the decision 'to negotiate . . . in terms of joining the European Economic Community represented a radical change in British policy'.[18] It is better regarded as a case of making the best out of a bad job, of other avenues for progress, prosperity and influence being closed or downgraded.

The decision, moreover, was the result of a gradual process of adjustment as the reality of Britain's position began to sink in. After the election, attempts were made to restore relations with the Europeans and to still suspicions that the British had destructive motives towards Europe, a charge that the British Foreign Secretary, Selwyn Lloyd, explicitly denied in a speech to the Consultative Assembly of the Council of Europe on 21 January 1960.[19] In the winter of 1959–60 and the following spring and summer there was a continuing re-examination of British policy towards Europe. Particularly influential was an inter-departmental committee of senior civil servants, the Economic Steering Committee. This re-examined the options open to Britain in its relation with the Six, and covered both political and economic questions. The conclusion was in favour of British membership on political grounds.

There were two different types of concern. On the political question, there was now a fear that recent upheavals in France, with de Gaulle coming to power, might lead to continuing instability in France, which could have as a corollary the disintegration of the EEC and a concomitant weakening of the Western cause. Equally unattractive for Britain was the prospect that a successful Community would prove to be more of a magnet to third parties especially the United States, than a singular Britain. If Britain joined, it could contribute to a real Atlantic partnership. On the economic side, the arguments relating to competition and scale of market appeared decisive. This report influenced Prime Minister Macmillan, but did not convince all of his colleagues, and for a while the preference appeared to be for an arrangement short of membership. None the less, a review of the implications of membership was undertaken by all departments in the spring of 1960 and by the summer the matter was subject to wide press speculation.

The Cabinet returned to the matter in the summer of 1960 and, according to Miriam Camps, was given material the gist of which was that (i) in the longer term Britain should give higher priority to Europe than it had previously, (ii) joining the EEC might be the only solution to the problem of how to attain a sufficiently close relationship, (iii) joining was, subject to some modifications in the Community's arrangements, technically feasible, and (iv) the political case was stronger than the economic.[20] The Government was not united on its position, although crucially Macmillan seems to have been convinced of the case. It was agreed that whilst the ground might be prepared there was no urgency and that a series of further consultations were in order, particularly with the Commonwealth, EFTA members, the USA and, not least, the six member states of the Community. During this phase Macmillan, exercising prime ministerial prerogatives, began to set the climate for a decision on negotiating entry – for example, he shuffled ministers so as to influence the outcome of the decision. After much internal and external negotiation and consultation, Macmillan announced to the House of Commons on 31 July 1961 that the Government had 'come to the conclusion that it would be right for Britain to make a formal application . . . for negotiations with a view to joining the Community if satisfactory arrangements can be made to meet the special needs of the United Kingdom, of the Commonwealth and of the European Free Trade Association', it being added there was 'no guarantee of success'.[21] On 10 August 1961 Britain made its formal application.

All of the considerations discussed above were relevant to the Government decision. A key factor appears to have been the realisation that in the 1960s there was 'a tendency towards larger groups of nations acting together in the common interest', and that Britain would have 'no influence' in Europe if on the outside, this also being an argument against association rather than membership.[22] Although this was clearly a serious endeavour, the Commons was told that it would make the final decision and that there could be a situation in which potential gains were outweighed by potential losses, especially if the Commonwealth relationship were disrupted. Both Macmillan and Hugh Gaitskell, Leader of the Opposition, emphasised their antipathy towards federal developments; in Gaitskell's words, 'there is no question whatever of Britain entering into a federal Europe now'. Tory opponents of the decision tended to focus on the federalist objectives of the Six, which they believed should be taken seriously, and the blow to the links with the 'old' Commonwealth which, after all, had stood by Britain in the recent war. Labour wished to make entry conditional upon Commonwealth and EFTA agreement and tabled an amendment along those lines. They abstained, however, on the main motion. Over a year later, the Labour National Executive Committee laid down five conditions that needed to be satisfied:

1.   Strong and binding safeguards for the trade and other interests of our friends and partners in the Commonwealth.
2.   Freedom as at present to pursue our own foreign policy.
3.   Fulfilment of the Government's pledge to our associates in the European Free Trade Area.
4.   The right to plan our own economy.
5.   Guarantees to safeguard the position of British agriculture.

It wished the actual terms to be known, rather than passing 'judgment on the abstract question' of whether Britain should join.[23]

Actual negotiations commenced on 10 October. The leader of the UK negotiating team was Edward Heath, appointed Lord Privy Seal but also acting as a Foreign Office minister. Strictly speaking, the UK objective was to see what terms were on offer and then to decide, but in all other respects the negotiations were for membership. The negotiators had a difficult hand to play: to uphold domestic interests, especially on the food and agriculture front, to obtain concessions for Commonwealth countries, and to seek arrangements to meet the legitimate interests of all the members of EFTA (the 'London Agreement' of June 1961). Not unnaturally, given past suspicions, Heath initially tried to show British commitment, although even here a word of caution was entered about the importance of the Commonwealth interest. Heath did make it clear that the UK accepted the objectives laid down in the Treaty of Rome and then raised the more major issues: Commonwealth, agriculture and EFTA.[24]

In the negotiations the main problems were to find agreement on the transitional period, which the UK wished to be long, and to obtain market access for the less developed and developed Commonwealth in place of Commonwealth preference in the UK. As negotiations proceeded, agreements of varying firmness were reached on common customs tariff adjustments for particular products, on the possibility of association for African countries (the Six were simultaneously considering the renewal of the first Yaoundé Agreement), on the intention to negotiate long-term commodity agreements helpful to India and Pakistan, which did not wish to become associates, and on the adoption by the UK of the mechanisms of the Common Agricultural Policy, which themselves were being elaborated – indeed, the negotiations were a stimulus to the Six to be able to speak with one voice on agriculture. By the end of 1962 prospects for a successful conclusion to the negotiations remained uncertain.

The negotiations effectively came to a conclusion on 14 January 1963 when President de Gaulle of France made clear his opposition to British membership. Having commented on Britain's insularity, its earlier refusal to participate, the problems posed by its agriculture, and its attitude to the Commonwealth, he argued that Britain was not yet ready for full-hearted commitment and that its membership would give the United States too much influence. The French President made his views known shortly after the Rambouillet meeting with Macmillan, but more particularly after the Nassau agreement on Polaris between Macmillan and President Kennedy. An unspoken French argument was the fear that the UK might have represented a challenge to French leadership of the Community, with de Gaulle at that time exercising great influence over the German leader, Adenauer.

In February 1963 the EEC Commission, in response to a request from the European Parliament, produced a report on the state of negotiations between Britain and the Six as of January 1963. It suggested, in conformity with the views of the Five and Britain, that substantial progress had been made and that, contrary to French assertions, Britain had demonstrated a willingness to accept the Rome Treaty. The report implied that the negotiations eventually might have succeeded if allowed to proceed, and that it was possible to envisage solutions to the major unresolved issues: agriculture, arrangements for New Zealand lamb and dairy produce, and arrangements for EFTA and Commonwealth countries.[25] Following the breakdown, the British attempted to continue to pursue links with the Six but the January 1963 blow and the continued presence of de Gaulle resulted in little progress.

In October 1964 the Labour Party, led by Harold Wilson, won the general election in Britain. On 'reading the books' the Government concluded that it had inherited a crisis and introduced a package of drastic measures. These included a 15 per cent import surcharge, which threw EFTA into disarray. Several months were needed to repair the fences. So far as relations with the EEC were concerned, the new British Government at first pursued traditional 'bridge-building' policies. These were discussed at an EFTA meeting at head of government level in Vienna on 24 May 1965, at which Wilson, changing the metaphor, spoke of the two sides coming out of their fortresses. In so far as this meeting produced any overtures, they were disregarded by the Six, who did not reply to the message sent to them.

In November 1966 Wilson announced the British intention to seek membership again, the Government clearly having begun to prepare the ground earlier in the year. He announced that a deep and searching review of the issues had been conducted and made the point that there was support for such a move 'provided the right conditions . . . are established'.[26] Wilson and the Foreign Secretary, George Brown, then toured Europe both preparing the ground and seeking support. They took with them proposals, worded in general terms, for a technological community, to which the UK would be able to contribute its lead in such fields as jet engines, nuclear reactors and computers. Very early experiences in the closing weeks of 1964, when the new Government had had to cancel three new aircraft projects, also showed that in high technology the UK could not go it alone. The option of joining with – and being overwhelmed by – the USA could not be entertained. The Commonwealth connection was strained by the Commonwealth Prime Ministers' Conference in London in September 1966 which, dealing virtually only with Rhodesia, was a 'nightmare' for its British hosts and cast doubt on the capacity of the Commonwealth to endure.

On 2 May 1967 Wilson announced formally that Britain would reapply for full membership, and a new application was lodged on 11 May. Whilst there had been a growing awareness of the need to renew the application, there were still hesitations. In February 1967, for example, 107 Labour MPs tabled a motion recalling their party's stiff conditions for entry. Whilst Wilson won a clear Parliamentary Labour Party majority for his position after a series of PLP meetings, in the crucial Commons vote on 10 May, after a three-day debate, some thirty-four Labour MPs voted against the resolution supporting the Government's decision, and a further fifty abstained. On 11 May seven rebel Labour parliamentary private secretaries (PPSs) were sacked because of their failure to support the decision, and Richard Crossman has suggested that whilst there were no resignations he calculated that only ten out of twenty-one Cabinet members were really in favour, seven were hostile and four were 'possible' supporters.[27] The Labour critics, including Michael Foot, argued that entry would injure the Commonwealth and EFTA, retard trade growth in non-EEC areas, injure the

Labour Government's regional policies and exacerbate the balance of payments problem. Despite this, the vote in favour of 488 to 62 was the 'biggest majority on a contested vote on a matter of public policy for almost a century',[28] and did suggest both a shift in attitudes since 1961 and something like bipartisan agreement about going into Europe.

The decision to apply did not mean that all the proponents of entry were enthusiastic, or were convinced of the necessity of membership. A detailed civil service analysis of the issue again appears to have concluded that 'the economic arguments were finely balanced; it was the political arguments which might be seen as compelling'.[29] Even on the political side, Wilson only a few months earlier had clearly still been hankering after a global role. But the pressures of the economic situation were to produce substantial defence reviews which involved clear limitations on a global role. The 1967 Defence White Paper, for example, focused on economies and envisaged the reduction of commitments in the Far East, the Persian Gulf and Aden. In addition, since the Cuban missile crisis of 1962 there was increasing evidence of Soviet–American bilateralism, whilst in September 1965 two Commonwealth members, India and Pakistan, resumed their intermittent war, a conflict terminated by Soviet rather than British mediation. The Rhodesian Unilateral Declaration of Independence of November 1965 had further exacerbated British relations with the Commonwealth. No wonder it was observed that Wilson, his senior colleagues and most of the civil service had concluded that there was 'no greatness outside' the Community.[30] Wilson addressed the political dimension in the Commons, seeing the possibility of Europe moving forward 'in political unity', a unity in which Britain must play its 'full part'. Also relevant, although not mentioned, was a growing realisation that the federalist aspirations of the original Community had run out of steam, a point brought out initially by the EDC failure and then reinforced a decade later by the veto crisis of 1965–6.

On the economic side, as the defence reviews illustrated, there were clear problems with the British economy as growth was significantly less than anticipated. Furthermore, the traditional 'stop–go' pattern had reasserted itself with a severe squeeze in July 1966, and devaluation by 14.3 per cent was only a few months away after the May decision. By 1967, moreover, it was increasingly clear that a modern, technologically oriented Britain needed large markets within which to sell its goods. Wilson, indeed, referred to the 'long-term potential' presented to both Britain and Europe by a single market of 300 million people, a market which allowed 'enormous possibilities' of integrated technology on a 'truly continental scale'. More problematical were what Wilson saw as the small number of crucial issues to be resolved by negotiation: agriculture, especially the financial arrangements associated with it; the Commonwealth dimension, especially New Zealand agriculture and the interests of sugar-producing countries; and the freedom of a Labour government to ensure industrial and social development in the less-favoured UK regions.[31]

If Labour were divided, not all Conservatives were happy either: twenty-six Conservative MPs voted against the 10 May proposal. One, R. H. Turton, tabled an amendment deploring the apparent willingness to commit the UK to entry before there was any clear view of the consequences. His amendment drew attention to Commonwealth and EFTA anxieties, and expressed concern at 'the probability of injurious repercussions on British sovereignty and the rule of law, on the price of food, on the balance of payments and on the role of sterling in the world'.[32] None the less, in 1965 Edward Heath had been elected leader of the Conservative Party and he seems to have worked hard to gain support within the party for his view that, whilst the terms should be carefully scrutinized, the negotiations should be pursued to a successful conclusion. It can be argued, however, that as in 1961 there was little enthusiasm and the commitment had only a shallow root within the party as a whole.

Given the overwhelming support of the Commons, the Government proceeded to apply for membership and towards the end of May Lord Chalfont, Minister of State for Foreign Affairs, was given responsibility for the day-to-day negotiations. The second application, however, met the same fate as the first, de Gaulle again exercising a unilateral veto. In another press conference, on 27 November 1967, de Gaulle again traced the history of British scepticism towards Europe and commented on the need for a 'very vast and deep mutation to be effected' in British attitudes before Britain could 'really make fast to the continent'. He referred to specific issues as well – for example, his belief in the incompatability of the Common Agricultural Policy with Britain's relations with the Commonwealth – and following devaluation on 18 November was able to focus on Britain's economic weakness. He appeared to feel that British membership presented a threat to the very existence of the Community.[33]

If de Gaulle was the bulwark against British membership, the atmosphere changed radically following his resignation from the French

Presidency in April 1969. The events in France in 1968 weakened not only de Gaulle's position but also that of France internationally. Also in 1969 there was a shift in German attitudes following the electoral victory of the Social Democratic Party in the autumn elections. This was important because, coupled with developments in France, it marked a changed relationship between Bonn and Paris, with Bonn being less willing to follow the French lead. Given these and other developments, the meeting of the Six in The Hague in December 1969 agreed that if applicants accepted the treaties, their political finality and decisions taken under the treaties since they came into force the Six would agree to an opening of negotiations. Furthermore, it was agreed that preparatory work should take place as a matter of urgency and that the Six would enter the effort in a most positive spirit.

On 10 February 1970 the Labour Government published a new White Paper, an 'economic assessment' of Community membership, which was generally objective but reaffirmed the Government's commitment to reaching a successful conclusion:

This White Paper demonstrates the need for negotiations to determine the conditions on which the opportunity for entry could be seized. Failure to reach agreement in these negotiations would not necessarily condemn Britain or the European Communities to political or economic sterility. But Europe would have lost another historic opportunity to develop its full economic potential in the interests of the welfare and security of its citizens.

The White Paper emphasised the 'necessarily extremely speculative' nature of the calculations it contained, but was rather gloomy about the impact on the cost of living and the balance of payments.[34] In the Commons, Wilson stressed that the White Paper did not allow for what it was hoped to achieve in the negotiations, nor did it estimate the costs of alternatives – for example, the status quo. He emphasised that Britain would be negotiating from a much stronger position than previously, given improved economic performance. Wilson felt that 'on fair terms we can stand and profit' by entry but he warned that, 'should the negotiations not lead to acceptable terms for entry, Britain is and will be strong enough to stand on her own feet outside'.[35]

Whilst George Thomson, Chancellor of the Duchy of Lancaster, was appointed to lead the negotiations, little happened before the general election of June 1970 intervened. In its manifesto Labour expressed 'a determination' to join if Commonwealth interests were safeguarded. Moreover, it argued that the improved economic position meant that

Britain would be negotiating from a position of strength and could stand on its own feet if the terms were unsatisfactory.[36] The Conservatives similarly expressed the view that entry would be the best solution, although 'obviously there is a price we would not be prepared to pay'.[37] The party's sole commitment was to negotiate, and no unequal or unfair settlement would be recommended. The Liberals were more positive, speaking of the Community as 'an exciting experiment'.[38] In general, there was a bipartisan view, with some significant discussion in both major parties, that Britain should join if the terms were right. The debate over the next few years revolved around that issue. Immediately after the election, for example, backbenchers from both parties were tabling motions in the Commons urging the Conservative Government to insist on satisfactory safeguards for British sovereignty, food prices and the cost of living, the balance of payments, and Commonwealth and EFTA trade. These were also themes of the Common Market Safeguards Campaign formed in February 1970, headed by Douglas Jay (President of the Board of Trade 1964–7 in the Labour Government) and with all-party representation.

The negotiations were conducted by the Heath Government. Heath, a convinced European, had made his maiden speech in the Commons in June 1950, in which he welcomed the Schuman plan. He had also headed the British negotiating team in 1961–3. The negotiations were formally opened at a special meeting in Luxembourg on 30 June 1970, with Britain represented by Anthony Barber, Chancellor of the Duchy of Lancaster. He stressed British support for a united and prosperous Europe, and its acceptance of the treaties and the decisions which had flowed from them. The main issues to be negotiated from a British perspective remained the same: agricultural policy, budgetary contribution, Commonwealth sugar exports, New Zealand, and certain other Commonwealth issues. Before substantial negotiations could commence, Barber became Chancellor of the Exchequer following the death of Iain Macleod in July. Geoffrey Rippon replaced Barber as the minister with responsibility for negotiations, and detailed discussions began. During the negotiations the Labour Party argued that it could determine its position only when the package agreement was available. None the less, in January 1971 about 100 Labour MPs signed a motion expressing the belief that 'entry into the EEC on the terms so far envisaged would be against the interests of this country'.[39]

The main phase of the negotiations was concluded in June 1971, and in July the Government issued a White Paper, 'The United Kingdom and the European Communities'. This argued that for ten years governments had felt the interests of British 'security and prosperity' would 'best be served by British accession'. It maintained that events over that decade had raised the question of 'whether our influence . . . will be greater if we are members of the European Communities than if we remain outside them'. The political case was that the 'joint strength' of the whole European Community 'can be so much greater than that of its individual members', and it was argued that the Kennedy Round of the 1963–7 GATT tariff reduction negotiations, in which the Community fared well, had demonstrated this. Membership would provide influence from within on Community decisions. The White Paper addressed the sovereignty question by stressing that the Community was no federation and that on 'vital national interests . . . it is established that the decision should be unanimous'. More generally, 'what is proposed is a sharing and an enlargement of individual national sovereignties in the general interest'. The White Paper dismissed various alternatives to membership such as a North Atlantic Free Trade Area and the Commonwealth.

On the economic issue, the White Paper began by focusing on the relatively disappointing performance of the British economy in comparison to European economies, and saw entry as a stimulus to improvement, although the improvement would not be automatic and there would be costs. On agriculture Britain accepted the CAP. This meant that British retail food prices would rise by about 15 per cent over the six-year transition period, a rise of 3 per cent in the cost of living. The budgetary contribution was subject to a complex mathematical formula but it was expected to be around £300 million per annum. Some transitional arrangements were made for New Zealand but by 1977 its cheese exports to the Community would be reduced by 80 per cent. In effect, the question of Commonwealth sugar was postponed, while association with the European Communities was envisaged for the independent Commonwealth countries in Africa, the Pacific, the Caribbean and the Indian Ocean. Again, some questions were to be resolved later – for example, the arrangements for trade with India, Pakistan, Ceylon, Malaysia and Singapore – whilst special arrangements were to reduce the impact upon Australia and Canada.[40]

Between 21 and 26 July 1971 the Commons held a debate on the White Paper, with the main debate on entry taking place between 21 and 28 October. During the summer the argument was carried on in the country as positions were adopted on both the principle of entry and the terms negotiated. At its conference the Conservative Party not unnaturally supported the Government's position by a majority of about eight to one. Conservatives against, including Derek Walker-Smith and Enoch Powell, tended to argue against the loss of Commonwealth preference, the budgetary arrangements, the agricultural settlement, and the loss of sovereignty. Powell argued that membership was incompatible with national independence and that some European non-members had prospered. The Liberals approved entry by a substantial majority.

The Labour Party position was to prove more complicated. A special one-day conference was held in July, but no vote taken. The speakers, however, divided about half and half in favour and against entry. The opponents argued that the deal ended a 150-year policy of cheap food and increased the cost of living. Moreover, Jay argued that the Conservatives had abandoned the 1961 and 1967 conditions and that this was especially damaging regarding the reactionary agricultural policy and the balance of payments. Wilson himself argued that the terms negotiated failed to meet four essential conditions: (i) the size of the burden on balance of payments; (ii) the control of capital movements; (iii) Commonwealth sugar safeguards, and (iv) New Zealand's needs. Embarrassingly for Labour, its Deputy Leader, Roy Jenkins, told the PLP that he felt his 'own personal conviction [is] that a Labour Cabinet would have accepted these terms by a large majority', a view endorsed by George Thomson.[41] Labour's NEC recommended to the party conference that entry be opposed on the terms negotiated, and that the deal be submitted to the democratic judgement of the people through an election. The conference carried this by a majority of five to one, the TUC conference having earlier decided without a vote to declare against entry.

In the decisive Commons vote after the debate of 21–8 October 1971, Conservatives were allowed a free vote but Labour imposed a three-line whip. The motion was 'That this House approves her Majesty's Government's decision on principle to join the European Communities on the basis of the arrangements which have been negotiated'. The result was 356 in support to 244 against, a majority of 112. The Lords approved a similar motion by an even bigger margin. In the Commons, despite the three-line Labour whip, 69 Labour MPs voted for the Government motion, as did 5 Liberals, whilst 39 Conservatives and 1 Liberal voted against. Most of the views expressed repeated familiar refrains, but a common theme among Labour speakers was the lack of consultation with the British people, a fact contrasted with referendums in Denmark, Ireland and Norway. In his contribution, perhaps partly to attempt to lay foundations for party unity, Wilson focused on this question of consultation and also said that a future Labour government 'would . . . immediately . . . give notice that we could not accept the terms negotiated', especially the CAP burden, the blow to the Commonwealth and the threat to regional policy. If the Community refused to negotiate, or negotiations failed, Labour would seek an amicable settlement, making it clear that all Community actions would be dictated by a British determination to achieve its aims.[42] For the moment Wilson was able to keep the disagreements within bounds and Roy Jenkins, for example, despite voting against the three-line whip, was the following month re-elected as Deputy Leader by the PLP. Things became more strained subsequently.

The next major hurdle for the Government was the passage of the European Communities Bill, which was given a second reading in February 1972. The bill gave domestic effect to the Treaty of Accession, which had been signed in Brussels on 22 January 1972. Again, previous arguments tended to be repeated. On this occasion the majority was reduced to a mere eight, and that included five Liberal votes. Labour united against; fifteen Conservatives voted against the Government and another four abstained. This changed voting pattern reflected concern at the particular nature of the bill rather than a shift in attitudes to the principle of membership. The bill had a tortuous progress through the Commons, being debated exhaustively, but it emerged unscathed and without amendment. During its passage Labour opponents proposed an amendment calling for an election and the 'express consent' of the British people before the bill came into force. Six Conservatives agreed, but asked for a 'consultative advisory referendum' to be held. Both amendments were defeated.[43]

It was the tabling of this latter amendment that was the catalyst for more formal division in the Labour Party. When the rebel Conservative amendment was tabled, the Labour Shadow Cabinet decided that the PLP should support it, reversing an earlier decision the same month that the PLP should oppose a referendum. The new decision brought to a head the dissatisfaction of the pro-marketeers within the party and three members of the Shadow Cabinet resigned: Roy Jenkins, who also resigned as Deputy Leader of the party, George Thomson and Harold Lever. All opposed the principle of a referendum, whilst Jenkins expressed additional concern that the party was moving from opposition to the terms of entry to a position of opposition in principle. Wilson argued that the Shadow Cabinet had moved to support a referendum because an election had been refused. The final vote on the bill, the third reading, saw a Government majority of seventeen, with some Conservatives still voting against. Notwithstanding these traumas, the United Kingdom became a member of the European Communities on 1 January 1973, with the issue still causing division in the parties.

Thus the decision was made, but equally significant was the lingering feeling that, Heath and a few others apart, there was no deep enthusiasm for the experiment of uniting Europe, a feeling only reinforced by the party divisions on the issue. Northedge's comment reflects accurately that the British sojourn to Europe was motivated not by enthusiasm, but by the lack of visible alternatives:

[The] important thing about Britain's entry into the EEC was that it had every appearance of being a policy of last resort, adopted, one might almost say, when all other expedients had failed. There was no suggestion of it being hailed as a brilliant success . . . the impression remained that it was brought about in humiliating circumstances and when other options in foreign policy had lost their convincingness.[44]

This set the tone for British attitudes and policies towards the Community in the years that followed entry.

Post-entry debates and developments

Entry did not, of course, resolve the issue of the nature of Britain's relationship with Western Europe. A little over a year after entry, a general election was fought with the major parties offering fundamentally opposed views on Community membership. Labour in its manifesto for the February 1974 election argued that entry on the Heath terms was a profound political mistake, as was entry without the consent of the people. It called for a renegotiation of the terms, in particular, for (i) major changes in the CAP, so that cheap food could still be imported into Britain; (ii) new methods of financing the Community; and (iii) Parliament's retention of power over regional, industrial and fiscal policies. If the renegotiation succeeded, the British people would be asked to express their verdict through either a general election or a consultative referendum. If the result was positive, Labour would play its full part in the new Europe. If renegotiations did not succeed, 'we shall not regard the treaty obligations as binding upon us'.[45] The Conservative manifesto contended that it was too soon to attempt a complete assessment of entry but that it was 'already clear that we are better able to secure our interests, both economic and political, within the Community than would have been possible had we remained outside',[46] a view the Liberals supported, although they argued for more power for the European Parliament and a less protectionist CAP.[47] A significant element in the campaign, in which it must be said the Community was not a key issue, was the intervention of Enoch Powell, former Conservative Cabinet minister, who announced that he would not stand for re-election. Powell took this view because this was:

the first and last election at which the British people can be sure of an opportunity to decide whether their country is to remain a democratic nation, governed by the will of its own electorate expressed in its own Parliament, or whether it will become one province in a new European super-State under institutions which know nothing of the political rights and liberties that we have so long taken for granted.

By implication, he appealed to voters to vote Labour, since it was committed to 'submission to the electorate' of the issue, and he disclosed that he had voted Labour.[48] Powell's intervention revealed that the Tory objectors had not been won over. The result of the election was a minority Labour Government.

The demand for renegotiation was formally lodged on 1 April, although the Foreign Secretary, James Callaghan, had to admit that the new Government was still reviewing a number of the issues. Concern was, however, expressed about economic and monetary union and European union as goals, and about the CAP, the question of trade with the Commonwealth and developing countries, the Community budget, and certain regional and industrial policies. The reaction of the other member states was generally reserved but it was clear that there was no support for a fundamental revision of the Community as it had developed. The other member states baulked at the idea of renegotiation: a treaty had been signed and *pacta sunt servanda*. Its minority status also deprived the British Government of authority. A more detailed British submission was made by Callaghan on 4 June, and by the Minister for Agriculture on 18 June.

A further British election was called in October 1974, as a result of which Labour returned with an overall majority of three. Labour argued in its manifesto of September that it alone was committed to allowing the British people to make their own decision on the Community, Labour guaranteeing consultation with the people within twelve months of the election. It also warned against the danger of the Community becoming a protectionist bloc.[49] The Conservatives reiterated that the terms were acceptable, indeed would have been accepted by a Labour government, and warned of the dangers of withdrawal, giving the advantage of the enlarged home market and 'membership of the biggest trading block in the world'. Withdrawal would lead to the loss of economic and political allies, the loss of jobs and the loss of influence. The best results were to be gained from positive and ongoing negotiation from within.[50] The Liberals too wished to see continued membership.[51]

The Labour Government pursued the renegotiation over the autumn and winter, and this process culminated at the first European Council meeting in Dublin in March 1975. On 18 March Wilson announced to the Commons that the Cabinet had decided to recommend that Britain should continue to be a member on the renegotiated terms. In general, Wilson claimed progress on all major items. On agriculture it was claimed that price increases had been kept below cost, reinforcing the downward trend in CAP prices, which it was felt would also contribute to reducing surpluses. Credit was also claimed for improving the position of Commonwealth sugar producers and of New Zealand. A new corrective mechanism for adjusting British budgetary contributions was also agreed (although it never operated and was soon forgotten) and European monetary union had been tacitly abandoned, and was unlikely in the foreseeable future. Wilson claimed to have received reassurances about regional policy and regional and national aids. He was also reassured on industrial policy matters, and seems to have concluded that other member states had coped with the problems in ways compatible with the treaty. Wilson then claimed that the Lomé Convention of 1975 between the Community and the African, Caribbean and Pacific countries met a number of Labour's previous objections, indeed that the affected countries wished Britain to remain a member. Given this progress, Wilson maintained that 'our renegotiation objectives have been substantially, though not completely achieved', although he admitted that some of the reduced problems were the result of passage of time rather than renegotiation.[52]

Not all the Cabinet agreed, and Michael Foot, Eric Varley, Barbara Castle, Tony Benn, Peter Shore, Willie Ross and John Silkin all availed themselves of the opportunity, provided by the suspension of collective responsibility for the referendum, to make their dissent known. They felt that agriculture would remain protectionist and food dear, that the Community budget remained unfair, that there would be an appalling trade deficit, and that little had been done for Asian countries. Even more fundamentally, they pointed to the threat to British democracy posed by the subordination of the British Parliament and people to Brussels. The UK had not taken back the power of decision over a range of issues, including certain areas of taxation and control of the economy.

These matters were aired in a three-day Commons debate in early April 1975 which concluded with a 396 to 170 vote in favour of the recommendation supporting continued membership. On this occasion it was a free vote. More Labour MPs voted against the motion than for – an odd position for a government to find itself in. Indeed, seven Cabinet members voted against, as did thirty other ministers.[53] This was allowed only because Wilson had decided, given the 'unique circumstances' of the referendum, to allow ministers to dissent and even to campaign for their view in the country. However, this freedom was not extended to parliamentary or official business and consequently Wilson sacked Eric Heffer, Minister of State for Industry, for having spoken in the Commons debate in defiance of these guidelines. Equally embarrassing for the Government, a special Labour Party conference on 26 April voted by 3,724,000 to 1,986,000 that Britain should leave the Community, although Wilson and Callaghan both spoke in favour of continued membership. As a consequence, and a compromise position, the Labour Party mounted no national election-style campaign. Dissenting members were allowed to campaign for their views.

The Conservatives overwhelmingly supported the Government motion in April, with 249 in favour and only 7 against, and in general tended to regard the renegotiation as a side issue to the main question – Britain's continued membership. Their new leader, Margaret Thatcher, argued that Community membership allowed Britain to have the advantages of being in a larger, more influential grouping whilst retaining national identity. In addition, the Community contributed to peace and security and was a secure source of food supplies. Membership provided a world role for Britain, whilst withdrawal would be a leap in the dark. If Britain were to leave it would have no idea what its trading conditions would be, or what would happen to sterling – it was not a genuine alternative. Heath argued that the fundamental issues remained as they had been, the fundamental political purposes of the Community, with the objective of a peaceful, strong and free Europe.[54]

For the referendum on 5 June, the first ever in mainland Britain, the Referendum Act allowed £125,000 each to two umbrella organisations, Britain in Europe (pro-membership) and the National Referendum Campaign (anti-membership), although one of the features of the campaign was the disproportion of resources in favour of Britain in Europe. The referendum question was: 'Do you think that the UK should stay in the European Community (Common Market)?' Three pamphlets, paid for by the Government, were circulated to each household, one from each umbrella organisation and the Government's own 'Britain's New Deal in Europe'. This backed up the Government's own recommendation, but also made it clear that the Government would accept the result of the referendum. It reviewed the renegotiation, making the same sort of points that Wilson had made earlier, and sought to reassure the public on sovereignty, arguing that medium powers like Britain 'are more and more subject to economic and political forces which we cannot control on our own', whilst membership meant that no new policy could be decided in Brussels unless Britain agreed. In addition, it asserted that Parliament retained the final right to repeal the Act which made Britain a member. A 'No' vote would mean uncertainty and being on the outside of the Community tariff wall, with a risk to employment and prices. It would mean that Britain had no say in Community decisions. A 'Yes' vote was no panacea, but meant being inside the world's most powerful trade bloc, having access to food, and enjoying opportunities for attracting Community funds, like the Social and new Regional Fund.[55]

The National Referendum Campaign, the disparate umbrella group opposed to membership, included Labour, Conservative and Liberal anti-Market groups and the Welsh and Scottish Nationalists, as well as Ulster Unionists. Its chairman was a Conservative MP, Neil Marten. It argued that renegotiation had failed to achieve 'fundamental' changes and that there was already evidence that pre-entry promises of greater investment, productivity and employment, a rise in the standard of living, and a trade surplus with the Common Market had not been fulfilled. It made much of the loss to the British of their right to rule themselves, claiming that laws would increasingly be made not by Parliament, but by unelected Commissioners in Brussels. Specifically, it saw membership as involving 'still higher food prices', a loss of jobs in peripheral areas of Britain, a threat to the coal and steel industries, and a mounting trade deficit. It claimed that there was an alternative, namely continued involvement in the free trade area already existing between the Community and EFTA, which allowed for free entry of EFTA's industrial exports but no involvement with the CAP. Why be scared in any case when the precious asset of North Sea oil would soon be on tap?[56]

Britain in Europe argued that continued membership was good for jobs, prosperity, peace and the Commonwealth. It sought to demonstrate that the Commonwealth supported membership and that it was now impossible to go it alone, that that kind of sovereignty was a chimera. It allayed fears about British 'traditions' and argued that membership had saved money on food in 1973 and 1974, the food of the Community also being important for a country that could not feed itself. As to alternatives, these were ridiculed, it being emphasised that opponents of entry spanned many shades of opinion from a 'siege economy' view to reliance on the Commonwealth.[57] Roy Jenkins was the President of Britain in Europe, whilst Edward Heath and Jo Grimond, the Liberal ex-leader, were also involved. It had the overt support of the National Farmers' Union and the Confederation of British Industry, as well as other professional and business organisations.

The overall result of the referendum was 'Yes': 17,378,581 (67.2 per cent); 'No': 8,470,073 (32.8 per cent). The turnout was about 64 per cent, which compares with an average 75 per cent for general elections. The voting showed a pattern of greater support in the south of the country and more doubts in the north. Of the sixty-eight counties and regions on which counting was based, only two returned a negative verdict. The Western Isles voted 70.5 per cent 'No', whilst the Shetland's voted 56.3 per cent 'No'. The Government felt that the result was decisive for the country as a whole, especially because of the generally consistent pattern of voting across the country, and Harold Wilson claimed that the 'debate is now over' and the 'historic decision has been made', and called for past divisions to be laid aside. He also called for a positive attitude in Community matters.[58]

As is now well known, the referendum did not resolve the issue of British membership and this was particularly true in Wilson's own party. Whilst a slight majority in the party had voted 'Yes' in the referendum, many in the party refused to accept the result, believing 'If ever there was a cooked referendum, that was it . . . In that referendum there was ten times as much money spent on putting the case for as on putting the case against.'[59] In addition, of course, important power centres in the party, those in which activists were influential, had opposed continued membership. After initial demoralisation at the result they began to campaign once more against the Community, and against the disloyal leadership. Community membership thus became an issue in the internal Labour debate about who controlled policy decisions within the party. Exacerbating this was the demand of some of these opponents for an alternative economic strategy, particularly relevant being the call for import controls, which would have been incompatible with Community membership. The IMF crisis of 1976, and the consequent deflationary measures, strengthened the critics' position within the party, and by the winter of 1976–7 the increase in strength of anti-Community feeling was apparent. The pro-Community case was weakened in the party by the departure of Roy Jenkins in September 1976 in preparation for his translation to Brussels as President of the Commission.

A complicating factor for the Government was the loss of its majority. In April 1976 Callaghan replaced Wilson as leader of the party and as Prime Minister, and a year later he entered into the 'Lib–Lab pact' in order to ensure the survival of the Government. As part of the deal the Liberals were allowed something of a veto over Government proposals before their first reading in the Commons. Part of the arrangement was a Liberal demand that legislation for direct election to the European Parliament should be put to the British Parliament in the summer of 1977, the Labour Government having previously shown no serious commitment on the issue and having been at least partly responsible for the postponement from the originally planned 1978 date for the elections to 1979, this delay having been partly caused by the wish of the Government to avoid splitting the party.

The initial proposal of the Government, published in February 1976 in a Green Paper 'Direct elections to the European Assembly', said nothing about alternative electoral systems, and argued for the West-minster model.[60] By the spring of 1977, as part of the Lib–Lab pact, it was agreed that there should be a free vote on proportional represen-tation, and the European Assembly Elections Bill published in June 1977 did say that the British elections would be by the 'regional list system such that each elector has a single vote' for a named candidate, with proportional representation within the region, unless Parliament decided to use the traditional system in Great Britain. Given the Northern Ireland problem it was agreed to use the single transferable vote (STV) system there in order to ensure minority representation. In December 1977 the Commons voted by 319 to 222 for the traditional British system except in Ulster. The regional list system was supported by 147 Labour MPs, partly to honour the Lib–Lab pact, whilst 115 voted against and 49 abstained. The Conservatives were against the regional list by three to one, although some influential figures voted for. Also indicative of the evolving Labour attitude was a significant amendment to the bill. Reflecting Labour distrust of the Community, concern over federal tendencies and the loss of sovereignty, backbenchers forced through the provision, Section 6 of the Act, that 'No treaty which provides for any increase in the powers of the Assembly shall be ratified by the United Kingdom unless it has been approved by an Act of Parliament'. The Act became law in May 1978.[61]

This did not resolve the problem for Labour as there was still the question of its attitude to direct elections, with some arguing that Labour should not participate as participation would afford the European Parliament and Community a legitimacy that critics wished to deny them. In 1976 the party conference had opposed the holding of direct elections partly on these grounds, and partly on the grounds of sovereignty and the British people's need to have democratic control over their own destiny. Despite this, the party subsequently had to come to terms with the reality of elections. In the autumn of 1977 the National Executive Committee (NEC) was asked to choose between boycotting the elections and reluctantly taking part so that dissatisfaction with membership could be aired and represented. It prevaricated until April, when it agreed that, if elections took place which it opposed in principle, it would none the less recommend Labour participation. Even so a campaign to undermine this decision continued afterwards.

One way in which the NEC achieved revenge was by asserting control over the manifesto for direct elections. The party Constitution, Clause 5, specifies that a national general election manifesto shall be drawn up jointly by the NEC and the Parliamentary Labour Party (PLP) leadership, in fact the latter having *de facto* predominance. Direct elections to the European Parliament were a new phenomenon, and not clearly covered by the Constitution. Moreover, they were not constitutionally the concern of the PLP at Westminster. The NEC determined to fill the vacuum. This meant that the manifesto was more hostile to the Community than it might otherwise have been, a difference reflected somewhat in the tone of the Labour manifestos for the May 1979 general election and for the 7 June direct elections to the European Parliament. In the manifesto for the May general election, Labour called for 'fundamental and much-needed reform' of the Community. It welcomed enlargement as 'an opportunity to create a wider and looser grouping of European states, thus reducing the dangers of an

over-centralized and over-bureaucratic EEC'. Europe was to be democratic and socialist, but equally important each people and national
parliament was to be sovereign. This theme of national control perme-
ated the attitude to trade, industry, economics and finance questions.
There was an attack on dear food and agricultural surpluses, and a claim
that Britain was 'now providing a net subsidy to some of the other EEC
countries amounting to £900 million a year'.[62] The manifesto published
for the June European elections made the same points but in a more
strident manner, for example calling the CAP 'an expensive farce' and
advocating a right of Westminster to reject, alter or repeal any Community legislation of which it disapproved, the Treaty of Rome being
altered to encompass this. Significantly, it also argued that the British
people had been 'deeply disillusioned by the experience of EEC
membership'. If 'fundamental reforms' were not achieved 'within a
reasonable period of time', the Labour Party 'would have to consider
very seriously whether continued EEC membership was in the best
interests of the British people'.[63]

The Conservative Party, whilst not united on all aspects of policy
towards Europe, had broadly united behind the referendum result.
Whilst having to be careful not to be less concerned about the British
dimension than Labour, it was much more positive in its attitude,
stressing that honest and genuine co-operation with Community partners was the best way forward. Despite the need to change some
Community policies, the Community in the Conservative view had not
failed Britain. Conservatives felt Labour's negative attitude to Europe
had prevented the UK from taking full advantage of the benefits of
membership. None the less, as a harbinger of things to come, stress was
laid upon the need for a 'common-sense Community which resists
bureaucracy and unnecessary harmonization proposals, holding to the
principles of free enterprise which inspired its original founders'. The
CAP was to be reformed and 'National payments into the budget should
be more closely related to ability to pay'. There was opposition to any
European Parliament unilateral expansion of powers.[64]

The Liberals supported an extension of the European Parliament's
powers, in line with their continuing belief in the need for a more
democratic Community. They acknowledged that their long-term aim
was 'a federal Europe' with more equitable socioeconomic policies.[65]
The nationalist parties sought either fairer treatment for the nations of
the Community or withdrawal.

The European elections were overshadowed in Britain by other

Table 5.1   UK European election results (June 1979)

	Seats	Votes
Conservative	60	6,508,512
Labour	17	4,253,117
Liberal	0	1,690,598
Scottish National	1	219,142
Plaid Cymru	0	83,399

significant events in the earlier part of the year. In March there had been referendums on Scottish and Welsh devolution, and this issue was the catalyst which brought down the Callaghan Labour Government at the end of the month. On 3 May a general election was held, an event which in effect inhibited publicity for the direct European elections and postponed the debate about European attitudes. Whilst the turnout in the Community as a whole averaged 61 per cent, in Britain it was 32.1 per cent, some 15 per cent below that achieved by the next lowest, Denmark, and below the average turnout for local elections in Britain. Of those voting, about one-third were against membership and two-thirds for, proportions nearly reversed amongst non-voters. Conservative Party supporters were much more in favour of membership than Labour supporters, by a ratio of about two to one. Reasons for not voting included ignorance about the issues and opposition to the idea of membership and to according the Community system legitimacy. The results were as shown in Table 5.1. In Ulster the Democratic Unionist Party, the Official Ulster Unionist Party and the Social Democratic and Labour Party each won one seat, 7 June being the first time since 1918 that the people on the island of Ireland had voted on the same day for the same parliament using the same electoral system.

These results did nothing to endear the Community to the Labour Party, out of office after the general election. The Community issue was again caught up in the struggle for control of the party, with the leadership being blamed for the 1979 defeats on the grounds of not projecting the democratically determined positions of the wider party. This struggle was evident in calls for NEC control over the manifesto, changes in the electoral system for the leader, and the reselection of MPs. Furthermore, following the defeat James Callaghan resigned as leader and was replaced by Michael Foot, an inveterate campaigner against membership who had been one of the Cabinet dissidents in

1975. Given these developments, perhaps not surprisingly, the Labour manifesto for the June 1983 general election baldly stated that 'British withdrawal from the Community is the right policy for Britain': this to be achieved within the next five years. The principal grounds for this policy was the view that membership was a 'serious obstacle' to 'radical socialist policies'. The party claimed that it would seek withdrawal in an 'amicable' manner so as not to prejudice employment in the short term and co-operation with the Community in the longer term, as the party remained 'internationalist' and committed to co-operation 'with the whole of Europe'. It was not withdrawal from 'Europe' but extrication from the burdens of Community membership. The decision on withdrawal was to be made by Parliament, on the basis that a vote for Labour in 1983 was to be regarded as a vote for withdrawal.[66]

A year later, in the manifesto for the second round of direct elections, most of the 1983 themes were repeated, except that the party somewhat moderated its position on withdrawal, arguing now that 'Britain, like all member states, must retain the option of withdrawal from the Communities' but also pointing out that by the end of the life of that UK parliament, 1988, Britain would have been a Community member for fifteen years and that 'this will be reflected in our pattern of trade, the way our economy works and our political relations overseas'.[67] The new leader, Neil Kinnock, played a part in this move, which was one aspect of a general reshaping of party policy. Fundamentally, the party was coming to the pragmatic view that membership was rather like an escalator – the longer the time involved, the greater the pain and dislocation of jumping off, so that there could be a point, perhaps somewhat indeterminate, at which the pain and dislocation became too great. In 1984, although not all the party was happy, there were signs that a greater consensus was emerging on this issue. By 1987 the Labour Party was no longer committed to withdrawal, but rather focused on working constructively with Community partners 'to promote economic expansion and combat unemployment', whilst standing up for British interests and working for the reform of the CAP.[68] The June 1989 direct election campaign set the seal on Labour's conversion to support for the Community, with the party focusing on the need for the use of Europe's combined strength to tackle common problems. At the end of the 1980s Labour saw the advantages of the social dimension of the Community, and saw Europe as a vehicle for progress on the environment. The party still preferred, however, close co-operation rather than any attempt to create a united states of Europe, and was wary of full-scale monetary union and the harmonisation of VAT rates.

This gradual evolution of Labour policy rather mirrors the general British evolution in the post-war period and illustrates the validity of Northedge's insight quoted earlier in the chapter. Labour were 'reluctant Europeans'.[69]

It appeared to many that, given the adversarial nature of British politics, if one party were opposed to or equivocal about membership then the other should be more committed. The conduct of British policy towards the Community has been in the hands of that other party since the May 1979 election, and it is interesting to see how even in this other party there has been something less than enthusiasm for full-hearted commitment. The decade since 1979, with British policy under the direction of the Conservative Government of Margaret Thatcher, has seen a continuation of the predominantly suspicious British attitude to European integration and the European Community, coupled with an acceptance of the fact that the question of membership was now closed. The pervasive concern, therefore, has been the attempt to remodel the Community in the British image, that image reflecting certain features common to both major parties and to traditional British post-war policy.

Initially the endeavour to remould the Community was somewhat hampered by the focus upon the problem of the British contribution to the Communities' budget, an issue which dominated British policy towards the Community in the period 1979–84. The issue was raised at Mrs Thatcher's first European Council in Strasbourg in June 1979, when the British case was rebuffed. Five years of often acrimonious debate and negotiation followed. Part of the difficulty was the sense of *déjà vu* among the other member states given previous British concern on the issue, and part was the tone set by Mrs Thatcher's expressed determination at her second European Council meeting, in Dublin, to 'get our money back'.[70]

The details of the budgetary issue and the budget have been discussed in Chapters 1 and 3 and will not be repeated here. It is important to note, however, how important this issue was to the Conservative Government and how by 1981 'the persistent debate about the financial and agricultural problems of the Community [had] left the British government in a very exposed position but still failing to convince its partners that the problems went far deeper than an attempt to engineer special British pleading'.[71] One reason it was regarded as special pleading was the repeated emphasis put by the British upon the fact that only they and West Germany were not net beneficiaries and that the budget took no account of prosperity, indeed it seemed rather to benefit the more prosperous at the expense of the less prosperous.

Year by year, grudging and hard-won progress was made on the issue with a series of measures. In Dublin in 1979 agreement was reached on a series of 'complementary measures' – the use of projects in the Social and Regional Funds to redress the budgetary balance. Then came agreements to have *ad hoc* refunds in the UK's favour for 1983, for a new correcting mechanism in 1984 and for a general solution to the British element of the problem. A key turning point appears to have been the gradual realisation that the problems did go far deeper than British selfishness. This process was aided by the need of the Community to raise more money as the budget was approaching the limit of available resources. Reform needed the support of all and gradually linkage was established between an increase in resources, the reform of the Common Agricultural Policy, budgetary discipline and a permanent formula for resolving the problem of budget imbalances – the British problem.

Exacerbating the tension between Britain and its partners during these years was the British negotiating tactic of linking the resolution of its budget demands to the fixing of prices for the Common Agricultural Policy. Although initially successful, this tactic came unstuck on 18 May 1982 when seven members forced through sixty-two regulations to increase farm prices by about 11 per cent. Britain sought to veto this, arguing that it would oppose any increase in farm prices until it had a satisfactory solution to the budget rebate problem. This was seen as a tactical linkage by other states, but the British argued that the two issues of farm prices and budgetary imbalance were related since the farm price increases would add nearly £90 million to Britain's contribution. The decision to ignore the veto and push through a qualified majority vote was resisted only by Britain, Denmark and Greece and the farm price increases were approved. This issue fuelled Britain's concerns about sovereignty and its sense of betrayal, given the previous understandings about the veto which had been in operation since 1966. Part of the explanation for the vote may have been that many in the Community were irritated by British persistence over the budget and also felt that Britain was offering little in return for the support the Community offered to it during the Falklands War.

There was a general perception that the British attitude to the budget was only part of the problem, that the real issue was whether Britain was willing to become more *communautaire* in orientation and policy. Mrs Thatcher, for example, had continued her predecessor's policy of not paticipating in the exchange rate mechanism of the European Monetary System (EMS), although Britain does contribute to the European Monetary Co-operation Fund and the pound forms part of the Community currency basket, the ECU. Those who support non-participation in the exchange rate mechanism argue that such participation would involve losing control over the money supply, which has been a key tenet of the Government's economic strategy, and that there is no need for any sort of exchange rate policy, the preference being for free-floating rates. Critics may dispute the validity of the case but the key point is that Britain has not formally become involved in the exchange rate mechanism, although senior figures in the Government, like the Chancellor, Nigel Lawson, and his predecessor, Sir Geoffrey Howe, are believed to be in favour of such a move. At the end of the 1980s the debate still continues over the principle and timing of membership. The Prime Minister seems set against membership and this may stem in part from the traditional British concern with 'sovereignty' over such sensitive matters. Non-membership is indeed seen by many as a further indication of Britain's approach to European integration. Interestingly, in 1983 a House of Lords Select Committee observed that 'Belonging to it would be an indication of a wider and more fundamental commitment to Europe; an attitude which may help explain the value which present members place on their participation in the system.'[72]

The Common Agricultural Policy (see Chapter 6) also caused discord between Britain and most of its partners. In addition, it exacerbated the budgetary issue and provided fuel for the domestic critics of membership. In part Britain and its partners had different perspectives on the need to reform the CAP because of basic differences in their economies: Britain is a net food importer, it has a small but efficient farming sector and it also has a much smaller farming population than its partners. Partly as a consequence Britain receives less than 10 per cent of Community agricultural expenditure, whereas that expenditure consumes over 60 per cent of the Communities' budget. Britain has, therefore, focused on limiting the apparently open-ended commitment to agricultural expenditure, on reducing the relative size of the agricultural budget, and on limiting surpluses and overproduction by holding down prices for those products. The endeavour to make progress in these areas has been problematical because of the central importance of agriculture to the economies of other member states. However, in 1988 significant progress was made which, although falling somewhat short of Mrs Thatcher's persistent demands, went some way towards the British position. For the first time, and reflecting also the British drive for budgetary discipline, there was agreement to a legally binding ceiling on annual CAP expenditure, it being kept within a fixed limit which was to grow at substantially less than the rest of the budget, increasing annually at a maximum of 74 per cent of the rate of increase in the Community's GNP. There was also agreement on a system of production ceilings for all farm products by means of 'stabilisers' – price cuts, taxes on farmers or reduced buying of surpluses.

As particular problems for the British have been resolved or ameliorated, especially the budget issue, there has been a growing view that there has been 'a marked change both in British policy and in the attitudes of Britain's partner governments and of people working in Community institutions towards the United Kingdom'.[73] There is some truth in this but there has remained a general lack of British enthusiasm for some of the proposals for institutional reform and development in the 1980s, as well as for the proposals on European union which have been made from time to time. As the question of membership came to rest and some of the disagreements over particulars were resolved, the issue very quickly became a question of membership of what, and it again became clear that Britain had a distinct outlook on the future shape of the Community.

Britain has generally favoured proposals relating to greater co-operation in EPC (see Chapter 4), but has been opposed to reforms of Community institutions as urged by those who wish to make them more supranational in character. On EPC in the 1980s, the UK has favoured the establishment of a small secretariat in Brussels in order to formalise the existing co-operation on foreign policy issues; a binding commitment by heads of government to consult one another before launching foreign policy initiatives; a commitment to vote the same way within the UN (or to abstain); and the extension of political co-operation to include more security issues. The EPC has been one area where the British have been keen to see both institutional and substantive development and the 1981 British Presidency saw the London Report, which somewhat expanded EPC and improved its mechanisms. Britain has consistently pushed for the member states 'to act with more vigour and greater purpose' in EPC, to demonstrate 'more political will to *act* together'.[74]

Britain has argued for an expansion of the definition of 'security' in EPC but equally has not wished to initiate any fundamental restructuring of the institutions already existing in Europe to deal with defence and military co-operation. Britain has retained the objectives of strengthening 'the European pillar of the Alliance' and improving 'European defence co-operation' but does not see that these objectives have to be confined to a particular institution. Indeed, in June 1984 in a paper to the Fontainebleau European Council, Mrs Thatcher made the general point that there were advantages in 'a flexible Europe' in which not all member states necessarily participated fully in every venture, it being open to member states to join certain ventures 'as and when they are able to do so'.[75]

The Fontainebleau paper also revealed a lack of British enthusiasm for radical reform of the Communities' institutional structure. Mrs Thatcher's proposals for reform in this area were extremely modest and mostly procedural: for example, the European Parliament was to be kept 'better informed' of Council matters; the European Council was not to become a 'Court of Appeal'; there was to be greater co-operation between incumbent, preceding and succeeding Presidencies; and the voting provisions of the treaty were to be 'fully honoured', although 'Member States must be able to continue to insist where a very important national interest is at stake on discussion continuing until agreement is reached'.[76]

The Fontainebleau Council established the Ad Hoc Committee on/ for Institutional Affairs, or Dooge Committee, to examine a range of ideas on the future (see Chapter 1). Britain's representative was Malcolm Rifkind, a junior Foreign and Commonwealth Office minister who was responsible *inter alia* for European Community affairs. Rifkind, like several of his colleagues on the committee, found much from which to dissent in the mainstream report, which was presented to the European Council meeting in Milan in June 1985. Rifkind and the Prime Minister, whom he consulted closely, objected to proposals to allow the Commission president-designate to influence the choice of his future colleagues, to proposals to 'democratise' Community decision making by giving the European Parliament an effective legislative role, and to changes in existing voting practices in the Council. Rifkind also demurred from the call for an intergovernmental conference to negotiate a draft treaty on European union.[77]

These preoccupations were apparent at the Milan European Council meeting in June 1985. The British proposals again focused on EPC and more efficient decision making, it being argued that an intergovernmental conference was superfluous. The unexpected Milan decision to proceed to such a conference was a significant tactical reverse for the British. The Italian Presidency, with the support of Belgium, the

Federal Republic of Germany, France, Ireland, Luxembourg and Holland, attained a majority for the convening of the conference. The recalcitrant states accepted the reverse and participated in the subsequent negotiations, while reserving their position on the outcome. They knew, moreover, that treaty amendments would require unanimity. Britain began to make it clear that it would accept treaty amendments on a pragmatic but limited basis.[78]

The resulting Single European Act was within the parameters of the Conservative Government's policy on Europe. In particular it paved the way for the creation of the post-1992 single market, and the Department of Trade and Industry took up with gusto the task of preparing British businesses for the associated opportunities, challenges and downside risks. To some extent this was a positive British contribution to the development of the Community. In 1984 in her Fontainbleau paper Mrs Thatcher had espoused the merits of creating a 'genuine common market in goods and services', of removing the 'remaining obstacles to intra-Community trade' and the 'internal barriers to business and trade', and of harmonising standards, all of which could lead to the creation of 'what is potentially the largest single market in the industrialized world' and 'the development of a vigorous, efficient and cost effective industrial sector' able to compete with others.[79]

Whilst much of post-1979 British policy towards the Community could have been conducted by a government of either party, certain aspects of the Single European Act, particularly those relating to the removal of the remaining barriers to trade within the Community and the creation of an internal market without internal frontiers, in which the free movement of goods, persons, services and capital is ensured within the provisions of the EEC Treaty, reflect very much the Thatcher Government emphasis upon deregulation and market forces. More generally, they reflect a British preference for measures of negative integration, namely 'the removal of discrimination as between the economic agents of the member countries', as against positive integration, 'the formation and application of coordinated and positive policies on a sufficient scale to ensure that major economic and welfare objectives are fulfilled'.[80]

The distinction between approaches to negative and positive integration underlay important differences of opinion over the interpretation of the Single European Act between Mrs Thatcher on the one hand and Jacques Delors, the Commission President, and several continental European governments on the other. Britain, as has been seen, has been enthusiastic about the internal market and indeed in its promotion and support of that idea has appeared at its most *communautaire* since the premiership of Edward Heath, although there were some British reservations over tax harmonisation. More importantly, certain other components of the Single European Act received neither the same initial attention nor the same enthusiasm in Britain: for example, the so-called 'social dimension' which, as well as new measures to alleviate unemployment, also gave weight to workers' rights to consultation and to participation, and the revived notion of monetary union going beyond the European Monetary System, which the UK has still not joined because 'the time has not been right'.

Both of these positive integration developments were the subject of a great deal of European speech making in 1988, much of which caused deep reservations in the British Government. In particular, statements by Delors on the inevitability of a further shift in decision making to the centre, on the Community soon becoming responsible for initiating three-quarters of European economic and social legislation, and on greater intervention in social policy all caused a flurry with the British Government, although the Labour Party began to see reasons for a certain European enthusiasm. Delors basically argued that an exclusive emphasis upon liberating market forces risked triggering a backlash among voters, and that consequently the Community should build on 1992 to develop common social policies.

In the autumn of 1988, in a tour of three European centres beginning in Bruges, Belgium on 20 September, Mrs Thatcher replied and gave her vision of the future. Whilst certain aspects of her speeches were related to the specifics of 1988, her Bruges speech in particular demonstrated many of the traditional features of British attitudes towards European integration, although expressed in Mrs Thatcher's own style.[81] She was keen to dispose of some 'myths' about Britain and Europe. She spoke of the cultural and historical links and of the common legacies Britain and Europe shared in many areas. Emphasis was laid upon the British contribution to European freedom in two world wars, and upon the fact that 70,000 British servicemen were still stationed on the European mainland. Mrs Thatcher made it clear that Britain sought no alternative to the Community, especially that it did not seek an 'isolated existence' on the fringes of Europe, but she opposed talk of a European super-state and insisted that attention must be given to specific tasks in hand. She showed irritation at 'arcane institutional debates' which were 'no substitute for effective action'. The

Community must, she said, reflect 'the traditions and aspirations of all' of its members. Mrs Thatcher went on to offer some 'guiding principles for the future' development of Europe:

- There must be 'willing and active cooperation between independent sovereign states'. It was not possible to 'suppress nationhood and concentrate power at the centre of a European conglomerate'. Mrs Thatcher said that, whilst she was the first to believe that 'on many great issues the countries of Europe should try to speak with a single voice', this did '*not* require power to be centralised in Brussels or decisions to be taken by an appointed bureaucracy'. Success lay in 'dispersing power and decisions *away* from the centre'. Britain had 'not successfully rolled back the frontiers of the state . . . only to see them reimposed at a European level, with a European super-state exercising a new dominance from Brussels'. She wished to see 'Europe more united' but this had to be done in a way which 'preserves the different traditions, Parliamentary powers and sense of national pride in one's own country'.

- 'Community policies must tackle present problems in a practical way' – for example, although progress had been made in reforming the CAP it remained 'unwieldy, inefficient and grossly expensive'.

- Community policies must 'encourage enterprise' and there must be a greater awareness that the Treaty of Rome 'was intended as a Charter for Economic Liberty'. The aim should be deregulation, free markets, wider choice and reduced government intervention. On monetary matters the key issue 'is not whether there should be a European Central Bank'. Movement of goods and services should be made much easier, but 'it is a matter of plain commonsense that we cannot totally abolish frontier controls' because of drug traffic, terrorism and illegal immigrants.

- 'Europe should not be protectionist.'

- Europe 'must continue to maintain a sure defence through NATO'. Interestingly, Mrs Thatcher again made the general point that defence was 'not an institutional problem. It's not a problem of drafting. It's much more simple and more profound: it is a question of political will and political courage.'

In conclusion, Mrs Thatcher returned to the theme that 'it is not enough just to talk in general terms about a European vision or ideal' and that 'new documents' were not required. They should look to make 'deci-

Table 5.2   UK European election results (June 1989)

	Seats	Votes
Conservative	32	5,244,037
Labour	45	6,153,604
Social and Liberal Democrats	0	986,292
Social Democrats	0	75,886
Scottish National	1	406,686
Plaid Cymru	0	115,062
Green	0	2,292,705

sions . . . rather than let ourselves be distracted by Utopian goals'. In sum, the British approach was 'Let there be a family of nations, understanding each other better, appreciating each other more, doing more together but relishing our national identity no less than our common European endeavour.'[82] The general tenor of this speech was reflected in the Conservative campaign in the elections to the European Parliament in June 1989.

In practice none of the main protagonists on either side of the argument about the future direction of Europe is as extreme in its views as is sometimes made out, but clearly there is a divergence. More broadly, there remains a difference of opinion between Britain and its partners about both the prospects for and the desirability of European union. Whatever the rhetoric, the process of integration has continued to take place progressively over the past decade and since 1973, although clearly there is little prospect for a long time of reaching the stage of a fully integrated political union.

The Bruges speech is particularly interesting in that, for the most part, it could have been delivered, at one time or another, by nearly all British post-war prime ministers. Some of the issues of the last decade, then, have had a perennial British quality. This has been reflected in both the concern that the Europeans would wish to go too far along the integration path and the continuing British problem of how to reconcile its relationship with its Community partners with its desire to have a 'special relationship' with the United States, a problem highlighted by the close relationship between Mrs Thatcher and President Reagan.

What is most intriguing is whether the June 1989 direct election result reflected the beginning of a change in the attitude of the British public to the Community or merely mid-term frustration at the incumbent government. The results were as shown in Table 5.2. In Ulster the Democratic Unionist Party, the Official Unionist Party and the Social Democratic and Labour Party each won one seat.

Notes

1. Sir Anthony Eden, British Foreign Secretary, University of Columbia, 11 January 1952, in Nicholas Mansergh, *Documents and Speeches on British Commonwealth Affairs 1931–52 Vol. 1* (London, Oxford University Press for the Royal Institute of International Affairs, 1953), pp. 1156–7.

2. Uwe Kitzinger, 'Time-lags in political psychology', in James Barber and Bruce Reed (eds), *European Community: Vision and Reality* (London, Croom Helm, 1973), p. 7.

3. Paul Kennedy, *The Realities Behind Diplomacy: Background Influences on British External Policy 1865–1980* (London, Fontana, 1981), p. 20, who quotes R. Hyam, *Britain's Imperial Century* (London, Batsford, 1976), p. 48.

4. Kennedy, op. cit. p. 21.

5. Winston Churchill when Leader of the Opposition, speech quoted in Randolph S. Churchill (ed.), *The Sinews of Peace* (London, Cassell, 1948), p. 202.

6. Winston Churchill when Prime Minister, *House of Commons Debates*, 5th Series, Vol. 515, Cols 889ff, 11 May 1953.

7. Winston Churchill, *The Second World War Vol. 2: Their Finest Hour* (London, Cassell, 1949), pp. 183–4.

8. Clement Attlee, Prime Minister, *House of Commons Debates*, 5th Series, Vol. 450, Cols 1314–19, 5 May 1948.

9. F. S. Northedge, *Descent from Power: British Foreign Policy 1945–1973* (London, Allen and Unwin, 1974), p. 38.

10. Kennedy, op. cit., p. 317.

11. Treaty of Economic, Social and Cultural Collaboration and Collective Self-Defence, signed at Brussels, 17 March 1948.

12. Such assistance being confined to responding to attacks 'in Europe or North America', Article 5 of the North Atlantic Treaty, signed at Washington, 4 April 1949.

13. Miriam Camps, *Britain and the European Community 1955–1963* (London, Oxford University Press, 1964), p. 4.

14. Quoted by Roger Jowell and Gerald Hoinville, 'An unconscionable time deciding' in R. Jowell and G. Hoinville (eds), *Britain into Europe: Public Opinion and the EEC 1961–75* (London, Croom Helm, 1976), p. 7.

15. Clement Attlee, Prime Minister, *House of Commons Debates*, 5th Series, Vol. 477, Col. 472, 5 July 1950.

16. Camps, op. cit., p. 339.

17. *Guardian*, 2 January 1989.

18. Camps, op. cit., p. 274.

19. *Council of Europe: Official Report of Debates, Eleventh Ordinary Session of the Consultative Assembly*, January 1960, pp. 760–4.

20. Camps, op. cit., p. 293.

21. Harold Macmillan, Prime Minister, *House of Commons Debates*, 5th Series, Vol. 645, Cols 928ff, 31 July 1961.

22. Ibid. For the initial debate see Vol. 645, Cols 928ff and 1480ff.

23. 'Labour and the Common Market: statement by the National Executive eCommittee, 29 September 1962', Document 20 in Uwe Kitzinger, *The European Common Market and Community* (London, Routledge and Kegan Paul, 1967), pp. 168–76.

24. Heath's speech was issued as a White Paper: 'The United Kingdom and the European Economic Community', London, HMSO, Cmnd 1565, November 1961.

25. European Economic Community, Commission, *Report to the European Parliament on the State of the Negotiations with the United Kingdom*, Brussels, 26 February 1963.
26. Harold Wilson, Prime Minister, *House of Commons Debates*, 5th Series, Vol. 735, Col. 1540, 10 November 1966.
27. R.H. Crossman, *The Diaries of a Cabinet Minister Vol. II (1966–68)* (London, Hamilton and Cape, 1976), pp. 113, 336–7.
28. Harold Wilson, *The Labour Government 1964–70: A Personal Record* (Harmondsworth, Penguin, 1974), pp. 499–500.
29. William Wallace, *The Foreign Policy Process in Britain* (London, Royal Institute of International Affairs, 1975), p. 86.
30. Crossman, op. cit., *Vol. III (1968–70)*, p. 612.
31. Harold Wilson, Prime Minister, *House of Commons Debates*, 5th Series, Vol. 746, Cols 310ff, 2 May 1967. The debate was on the motion that the House approve the White Paper, 'Membership of the European Communities', London, HMSO, Cmnd 3269, 1967. The Government also published a White Paper on the 'Common Agricultural Policy', Cmnd 3274, and the 'Constitutional and legal implications of UK membership', Cmnd 3301.
32. R. H. Turton, *House of Commons Debates*, 5th Series, Vol. 746, Col. 1108–14, 8 May 1967.
33. President de Gaulle, press conference, 27 November 1967, *Keesing's Contemporary Archives*, Vol. 16 (1967–8) (Keynsham, Keesing's, 1968), pp. 22519–21.
34. 'Britain and the Economic Communities: an economic assessment', London, HMSO, Cmnd 4289, 1970.
35. Harold Wilson, Prime Minister, *House of Commons Debates*, 5th Series, Vol. 795, Cols 1080–97, 10 February 1970.
36. The Labour Party General Election Manifesto 1970.
37. The Conservative and Unionist Party General Election Manifesto 1970.
38. The Liberal Party General Election Manifesto 1970.
39. Keesing's, op. cit., Vol. 18 (1971–2), 24469.
40. 'The United Kingdom and the European Communities', London, HMSO, Cmnd 4715, 1971.
41. Keesing's, op. cit., Vol. 18 (1971–2), p. 24903.
42. Harold Wilson, Leader of the Opposition, *House of Commons Debates*, 5th Series, Vol. 283, Cols 2080–95, 2096–106, 28 October 1971.
43. House of Commons Debates, 5th Series, Vols 831–840 *passim*, February–July 1972.
44. F.S. Northedge, 'Britain and the EEC: past and present', in Roy Jenkins, (ed.), *Britain and the EEC* (London, Macmillan, 1983), p. 26.
45. Labour Party General Election Manifesto February 1974.
46. Conservative and Unionist Party General Election Manifesto February 1974.
47. Liberal Party General Election Manifesto February 1974.
48. Keesing's, op. cit., Vol. 20 (1974), p. 26382.
49. Labour Party General Election Manifesto October 1974.
50. Conservative and Unionist Party General Election Manifesto October 1974.
51. Liberal Party General Election Manifesto October 1974.
52. Harold Wilson, Prime Minister, *House of Commons Debates*, 5th Series, Vol. 888, Cols 1456ff, 18 March 1975.
53. Ibid., Vol. 889, Cols 821–1370, 7 April 1975.
54. Ibid., Vol. 889, Cols 1021–4, 1025–33, 1274–86, 1295–6, 7 April 1975.
55. *Britain's New Deal in Europe* (HMSO, 1975).

56. *Why You Should Vote No* (HMSO for National Referendum Campaign, 1975).
57. *Why You Should Vote Yes* (HMSO for Britain in Europe, 1975).
58. Harold Wilson, Prime Minister, *House of Commons Debates*, 5th Series, Vol. 893, Cols 29–30, 9 June 1975.
59. A delegate to the 1976 Labour Conference, quoted in David Butler and David Marquand, *European Elections and British Politics* (London, Longman, 1981), p. 46.
60. 'Direct elections to the European Assembly', London, HMSO, Cmnd 6394, 1976.
61. European Assembly Elections Act (May 1978).
62. Labour Party General Election Manifesto May 1979.
63. Labour Party Manifesto for Direct Elections to the European Parliament June 1979.
64. Conservative and Unionist Party General Election Manifesto May 1979.
65. Liberal Party General Election Manifesto May 1979.
66. Labour Party General Election Manifesto June 1983.
67. Labour Party Manifesto for Direct Elections to the European Parliament June 1984.
68. Labour Party General Election Manifesto June 1987.
69. L.J. Robbins, *The Reluctant Party: Labour and the EEC 1961–1975* (Ormskirk, G.W. and A. Hesketh, 1979).
70. M. Butler, *Europe: More than a Continent* (London, Heinemann, 1986), p. 95.
71. Helen Wallace, 'The British Presidency of the EC Council of Ministers: the opportunity to persuade', *International Affairs*, Vol. 62, No. 4 (autumn 1986), p. 585.
72. House of Lords, *Fifth Report of Select Committee on the European Communities: 'The European Monetary System'* (London, HMSO, 1983), para. 76.
73. Wallace, op. cit., p. 585.
74. Margaret Thatcher, Prime Minister, 'Europe: the future', paper presented to European Council at Fontainebleau on 25–6 June 1984, reproduced in *Journal of Common Market Studies*, Vol. 23, No. 1 (September 1984), pp. 73–81.
75. Ibid.
76. Ibid.
77. Patrick Keatinge and Anna Murphy, 'The European Council's Ad Hoc Committee on Institutional Affairs (1984–85)', in Roy Pryce, (ed.), *The Dynamics of European Union* (London, Croom Helm, 1987), pp. 217–37.
78. Richard Corbett, 'The 1985 Intergovernmental Conference and the Single European Act', in Pryce (ed.), op. cit., pp. 238–72.
79. Thatcher, 'Europe: the future', op. cit.
80. J. Pinder, 'Positive integration and negative integration: some problems of economic union in the EEC', *World Today*, Vol. 24 (1968), pp. 88–110.
81. *Speech Given by the Rt Hon. Mrs Thatcher at the Opening Ceremony of the 39th Academic Year of The College of Europe, Bruges, 20 September 1988* (British Embassy Press Service).
82. Ibid.

6

The Policies of the Community

In the EEC Treaty, three policies are described as 'common':

- the common commercial policy (Article 113);
- 'a common agricultural policy' (Article 43);
- 'a common transport policy' (Article 74).

Article 130(b) talks about 'the common policies' without specification. Article 130(f) refers to common policies, especially in competition and trade. Part Three of the treaty is entitled 'Policy of the Community' and sets out a number of policy areas, some added by the Single European Act. It would be difficult to establish a hard and fast distinction between something called a 'common policy' and another called a 'Community policy'.

Common Commercial Policy (CCP)

The Common Commercial Policy has one distinctive feature: it assigns exclusive competence to the Community. The member states may not negotiate commercial agreements with third countries even if such agreements do no damage to the common customs tariff or to Community legislation concerning imports and exports. Only the Community can act and Article 113 says how it acts. The Commission makes recommendations to the Council which issues a 'directive' adopted by qualified majority (voting is used). The Commission then negotiates and reports back to the Council. The text which the negotiations have produced is initialled by the negotiators on both sides and is thus fixed. The Council concludes the negotiations, deciding by qualified majority, and signs on behalf of the Community. The member states keep a close watch on the negotiations (they are present, silently observing, during the sessions). Parliament is informed by the Council of the opening of the negotiations, by the Commission of the way the negotiations are moving, and by the Council prior to signature (Westerterp procedure). These commercial agreements may be multinational, the Community being one participant among many, or they may be bilateral. They may be non-preferential, where they essentially provide a rendezvous for the two sides to meet at intervals, or they may be preferential, heading towards or creating a free trade area, consistent with the pertinent rules of the General Agreement on Tariffs and Trade (GATT).

In the 1970s both the member states and the Community began to conclude 'economic co-operation agreements'. They did not fall within the exclusive competence of the Community, so that member states could negotiate in their own name, for example with oil producers and state trading countries. The Community concluded economic co-operation agreements with countries such as India and Canada, where non-preferential agreements would have had only ceremonial value. Economic co-operation opened up possibilities for Community aid for development, or the mutual encouragement of investment, or technology transfer. These agreements are concluded under Article 235, the reserve legislative power, and the results are submitted to the European Parliament for a (non-binding) opinion.

From early days the Community held out the possibility of association under Article 238. Associate status, as it has developed, takes different forms. The earliest, the Greek and Turkish Association Agreements, were explicitly a preparation for possible membership of the Community. The Yaoundé Conventions (1963 and 1969), with the former African colonies of the Six, were not a prelude to membership and they involved some reciprocity. In return for preferential access to the Community market, the African countries made tariff and quota concessions to the Community, although they could also withhold them to further their own economic development. The Lomé Convention (1975), never described as an association agreement although concluded under Article 238, made away with reciprocity. Other association agreements do not envisage Community membership and are preferential. In addition to trade provisions, they usually contain financial protocols under which the Community pledges itself to grant aid for development. Aid under Lomé is drawn from the European Development Fund, which is not budgetised; other development aid is entered in the General Budget of the European Communities. The Parliament is informed of the opening and progress of association negotiations. The results are initialled (Commission) and signed (Council), but before the agreements can be concluded Parliament must, by virtue of the Single European Act, give its assent (*avis conforme*) expressed by the vote of the majority of its members – not of members present and voting. If the majority is not attained, the Council cannot conclude the agreement.

There is continuous Community participation in discussions and negotiations in the General Agreement on Tariffs and Trade (GATT), in the UN Conference on Trade and Development (UNCTAD) and in the Organisation for Economic Co-operation and Development (OECD), as well as in international commodity agreements. The Community has no full-scale trade agreements with the USA and Japan. Trade relations are conducted within GATT and in frequent bilateral consultations. These often concern crises in the Community's relations, especially with the USA: the 'chicken war' over the Community's treatment of chicken pieces imported from the USA; the steel battle over the limitation of exports to the USA; controversy over the supply by member states of equipment for the Soviet gas pipeline; the 'pasta war', in which the USA retaliated against allegedly objectionable practices by cutting its pasta imports; the textile problem, under which the Community intervened to limit certain imports from the USA; the Airbus wrangle, a question of whether member state governments were subsidising the sale of Airbus planes to US users; and the ban on the use of hormones in livestock, which threatens US exports. The general background is of sustained US criticism of the Common Agricultural Policy because of its allegedly damaging effects on US exports and on the stability of world agricultural trade, and of Community attacks on successive Trade Bills which pass through the US Congress and are protectionist.

Trade policy and the member states' external policies interact, especially at times of international crises. In 1980 the bulk of world opinion condemned Iran for taking and holding American hostages. While adopting political sanctions, the Community did not take trade measures. In January 1980, following the Soviet invasion of Afghanistan, the Council adopted two economic measures: cancellation of the food aid programme for Afghanistan, but provision of emergency aid for Afghan refugees; and a decision that exports to the USSR should not replace US exports which had been embargoed. In April 1982, following the Argentine invasion of the Falkland Islands, the Council imposed an embargo on imports from the Argentine. The use of a commercial policy instrument (Article 113) as a political weapon was controversial and insecure, and the foreign policy aspect itself created internal difficulties in some member states. In each of these intersections, policy and procedure were dictated by the circumstances of the moment and give little guide to what might happen in future hypothetical situations.

The Soviet bloc countries for a long time refused to recognise the existence of the European Communities, dismissing them as the side-kick of NATO. It was, however, an open secret that by the early 1970s the vice-minister of foreign trade of every Soviet bloc country except the Soviet Union and East Germany (which is a special case, since the Federal Republic admits imports from the Democratic Republic free of duty) had visited Commission Headquarters privately, usually to make arrangements for the management of imports of agricultural produce into Community countries. In 1974 the Secretary General of the Council of Mutual Economic Assistance (COMECON) Nikolai Fadeyev, made an overture to the Council Presidency suggesting the conclusion of an arrangement between the two bodies. A Commission team visited Moscow in February 1975 and there were further meetings, including two at Commissioner level, up to 1981 when they stalled. The problem was of asymmetry. COMECON is not responsible for conducting the external trade relations of its members. It wanted, however, to enter into treaty relations both with the Community and with its member states. The Community was prepared to deal with COMECON on matters for which the latter had competence, but contractual commercial relations had to be between the EEC and the individual Soviet bloc countries. In the sterility of the Brezhnev years nothing moved. Formally, the Community's commercial relations with Czechoslovakia, Poland, Romania and Hungary were governed by GATT, to which they belonged. As before the Fadeyev opening, so after: various sectoral agreements were concluded with Romania, Poland and Bulgaria (treatment of imports of textiles), and with Romania, Czechoslovakia, Hungary and Bulgaria (imports of steel under the conditions of crisis in the Community). In 1977 a Community delegation headed by David Owen met a delegation from the USSR to discuss fisheries questions. In 1980 Romania broke COMECON ranks and concluded a trade agreement with the EEC (Article 113) notably setting up a joint committee to meet at intervals and examine problems and prospects.

With the advent of the Gorbachev era, the atmosphere changed, and after much negotiation – including the search for a formula to describe the status of Berlin – the Community and COMECON concluded in June 1988 a 'Declaration of Intent' on future relations. This does not say much itself; it does however, mark the end of the Soviet bloc non-recognition of existence of the European Communities, and it opens the way to the Communities' settled policy of transacting commercial questions directly with the Soviet bloc countries. Exploratory discussion opened on the possibilities for an EEC–USSR co-operation agreement. Trade negotiations with Hungary had already begun and were carried to a conclusion. Similarly, negotiations with Czechoslovakia pressed on. Discussions with Bulgaria moved towards a possible trade and co-operation agreement; the same with Poland. In July, East Germany began to explore possible treaty relations. The non-European COMECON countries – Cuba and Vietnam – did not join in the movement. In parallel, the Soviet bloc countries began to establish diplomatic relations with the European Communities and to accredit ambassadors to them. In September 1988 the President of the European Parliament, Lord Plumb, visited Moscow – another first.

The People's Republic of China, making its own distinctive foreign policy, had no inhibitions about the Community from the 1970s and even expressed the hope that the UK would remain a member. Sir Christopher Soames, then Commissioner for External Relations, was quick to take the opportunity to visit Beijing in 1975. It was announced that official relations would be established and an outline agreement was transmitted to the Chinese authorities. Negotiations for a trade agreement opened in 1977 and it came into force on 1 June 1978. Among its provisions is the setting up of a joint committee. Its meetings in Beijing and in Brussels have provided a basis for visits of substantial delegations, including on the Community side exporters and on the Chinese side representatives of the foreign trade organisations and exhibitions of Chinese products. The Community also provides technical assistance in the energy field, and trains Chinese interpreters.

Although the Community is exclusively responsible for the conduct of the Common Commercial Policy, there are one or two vestiges of the national role.[1] Member states feeling themselves under pressure of particular imports have obtained from the suppliers – of textiles, of motor vehicles, etc. – 'voluntary restraint' arrangements. These are not easily compatible with the singleness of the Community market, which is from the mid-1980s a priority objective. Some old pre-CCP bilateral trade agreements, which the member states concerned would otherwise be obliged to denounce, are authorised to continue because they do no harm to the CCP, and their disappearance could have a negative effect politically. Member states can also continue to negotiate economic co-operation agreements with third countries – although the wave of such endeavours of the 1970s is now over – provided they do not contain trade provisions and subject to a mild consultation/information procedure with the Commission and the other member states.

The Community has exclusive responsibility for anti-dumping action. Dumping occurs when the export price of a product is lower than its fair or normal value. This latter serves as a benchmark against which the extent of any dumping is assessed. On a complaint by a Community producer the Commission investigates and if dumping is established it either obtains assurances from the exporters that true prices will be used or proposes that the Council decide to impose anti-dumping duties. The Commission acts within the GATT Anti-Dumping Code. Foreign suppliers often contest the Council's decisions in the European Court of Justice.

Alongside the trade concessions which the Community grants to developing countries in its agreements with them, it also gives autonomous benefits in its Generalised Preference Scheme. This scheme, under which developed countries give tariff preferences to products (and some produce) exported from developing countries, grew out of GATT discussions in the 1960s. The Community reviews its preferential list and list of beneficiaries annually. Early Community relations with the African, Caribbean and Pacific (ACP) countries have been discussed in Chapter 1. The Lomé Convention of 1975 was replaced by Lomé II in 1981 and by Lomé III in May 1986. The negotiation of Lomé IV began late in 1988. Lomé Conventions provide non-reciprocated tariff concessions, development aid (under the European Development Fund), stabilised export earnings ('Stabex'), and mining co-operation ('Sysmin'). Stabex and Sysmin compensate for losses of export earnings by reference to a fixed base. The institutions of the Lomé Convention are the Committee of Ambassadors, the Council of Ministers and the ACP–EEC Joint (Consultative) Assembly.

There are arrangements similar to Lomé for twenty-five overseas countries and territories, dependencies of Britain, France, the Netherlands and (since Greenland left the Communities) Denmark. Under the 'overall Mediterranean approach', the Community has 'co-operation agreements' under Article 238 with Cyprus, Malta, Turkey, Algeria, Egypt, Israel, Jordan, Lebanon, Morocco, Syria, Tunisia and

Yugoslavia. It also has co-operation agreements with the Yemen and with the Gulf Co-operation Council under Articles 235 and 113. It has no agreements with Iraq or Iran. (See also Appendix 6.4.)

Common Agricultural Policy (CAP)

An agricultural policy in which countries with agricultural populations protect their farmers against price competition from outside suppliers has a social dimension. A shift of population from a low-income or otherwise unattractive farming sector towards the urban and industrial sector can be regarded as changing a natural national character which society may wish to preserve. It may also involve unwelcome economic and ecological cost where land ceases to be tended and reverts to wilderness and where pressure develops for the provision of social facilities in towns and for building roads, factories and houses in areas regarded as a national heritage of beauty. Agriculture also has weight in national politics. Partly because of the tradition of government interest in them, farmers are usually well organised in coherent lobbies and pressure groups, have representatives in legislatures and are able to exercise a 'farm vote' often considered crucial to a party's electoral success.

In developed countries such as Europe, total demand for food is largely inelastic and is satisfied. Elsewhere in the world, despite the 'green revolution' of the 1960s, vast populations which are dependent on water that never comes as rain or that inundates and ruins the fields live in famine. Food then enters the arena of international politics, becoming a form of aid to the Third World and giving support to the idea that areas such as Europe with a capacity to expand agricultural output beyond their own needs could become, commercially or charitably, suppliers to the world.

The hallmark of the Community agricultural support system is the guaranteed price. In principle, the price should be at a level which calls for production sufficient to meet at least the major part of demand and to ensure that relative income on the land does not fall behind income in other sectors. Independently of price, farming output is characterised by a secular productivity gain, based on applied research which makes better use of inputs and cuts costs, and is in the grip of weather conditions. These factors make forward output planning inexact –

productivity and weather sometimes combining to produce more than foreseen; weather or natural disasters sometimes reducing supplies below expected yields. If imports are not regarded as a buffer, one way of evening out year-to-year surplus and deficit is storage. Private or state stores take unsaleable produce off the market and release it when the market is running short. Moreover, protection against price competition from outside suppliers should go to the specific products grown in the country, but it can also spill out to substitution products, such as imported animal feedstuffs, or to alternative products, such as fruit and vegetables grown elsewhere but competing for consumer preference or imported out of the main domestic season.

World market prices are pretty well notional. At most times the quantities in international trade are surpluses, sold for what they will fetch (costs having been covered on the domestic market) and often subsidised. Because of geography Community farming is more inten- sive than much farming elsewhere, and because of history the average unit size of holding is smaller than elsewhere, resulting in relative diseconomies of scale. This means that the cost of Community farming feeds into prices which are higher than they would be in a theoretical free market or in one where supplies could be obtained from outside opportunistically.

The financing problem is universal. An OECD report of 1987, *National Policies and Agricultural Trade,* studied agricultural policy in Australia, Austria, Canada, the EC, Japan, New Zealand and the United States. It showed that for 1979–81 their assistance to agriculture accounted for over one-third of the value of their agricultural output. Roughly half of the assistance was state-provided finance; the other half was the economic rent consumers paid in higher prices. The trend was upward.

In the Communities' beginnings a common market without agricul- ture was unthinkable. It would have cut out of the operation of the common market a large slice of output and it would have distorted competition among the food-processing industries and, through diver- gent food prices, in unit wage cost in industry. Agriculture had to be in.[2] The guidelines were mapped out at a conference held in Stresa in July 1958 bringing together the representatives of governments, the Com- mission and national farmers' organisations in the Six. It was accepted that the family character of the farm unit should not be undermined. Agricultural prices were to be brought to a common level and for this purpose agricultural markets would have to be managed. Prices would normally be above the world market price; thus unless there was some support, Community agriculture would not compete. Self-sufficiency was not a declared aim but security of supplies was already a treaty objective. These analyses crystallised in the three principles of the CAP which the Council adopted in June 1960:

- the single market (free movement of agricultural goods);
- Community preference (protectionism);
- joint financial responsibility (Community funding for the disposal of produce which could not be sold on the market).

After the principles came the mechanisms. They differ importantly from one agricultural product to another and in their details are matters for the practitioner and specialist (for whom they are amply documented). But in general terms the operation (which, it is emphasised, varies from one product to another) is as follows. An annual price is fixed around April–May. It may be called a target price. It is the price which the farmer should realise in the market. If the farmer obtains the price, the system is in balance. The market is not a true one because consumers cannot make choices and are probably paying more than a true market would charge them. If, however, the market price is less than the fixed price because consumers have enough, and if the price disparity goes beyond a certain point, the farmer can withdraw his offer from the market and sell it to a CAP agency at an intervention price.

Intervention agencies of different kinds exist in all member states. Contrary to prevailing belief, they are financed not by the Community but by national governments: or, perhaps better put, they were so financed when they began. From the General Budget the Community pays part of the cost of storage (rent, heating or cooling, transport, insurance, wages, maintenance, etc.), some depreciation (taking account of natural deterioration and of the inflated book-value of purchases to intervention), and the difference between what the agency paid (allowance made for depreciation already accounted for) and what it collects when it sells the produce. Sales are for export (in the hands of exporting firms, who are accordingly remunerated partly by their clients and partly by the Community budget) or to the Community itself as food aid for developing countries in food deficit, for sale at reduced prices to needy social groups in member states ('Christmas butter'), or, more rarely, for 'denaturing' – destruction.

Imports are not allowed to perturb Community production which can sell at the fixed price, or to bid the market price down, thereby provoking higher sales to intervention. A threshold price is set consisting of the world market price, the cost of transport to the Community frontier, the cost of distribution to an inland consuming centre and the margin to make up the intervention price. The difference between the threshold price and the (lowest) import offer is charged on the imports concerned as a levy. The agricultural levies accrue to the Community budget. Conversely, where a farmer (or dealer) exports Community produce, he obtains as 'restitution' drawn from the agricultural section of the Community budget the difference between the world price (or the rock-bottom sale price) and the Community price.

There are market organisations (under Community regulation) for the following products:

Cereals	The intervention system just described.
Sugar	A system of production quotas, partly price guaranteed, partly subject to a levy on production and partly for export without support.
Certain fruit and vegetables	Intervention, known as withdrawal, partly operated by the producers' organisations. Imports must respect reference prices.
Olive oil and vegetable fats	Intervention and direct aids to producers (based on a tree count) and to consumers – in this case the processors of the raw material.
Wine	Protection against imports accompanied by a price grid. A minimum price can be brought in below which wine may not be sold. Other prices can trigger intervention. There is financial aid for private storage and for distillation. To reduce production, grubbing-up premiums can be paid.
Dairy products	Intervention. To reduce output, milk production is subject to quota. There are also measures to promote better consumption. A tax on margarine, proposed more than once by the Commission, has not been accepted.
Pig meat	Private storage aided in preference to intervention.

Beef	Guide pricing and intervention.
Sheep meat	A system of premiums to make up the difference between a reference price and the forecast market price. A variable slaughter premium is paid in the UK. It is 'clawed back' if the sheep meat is exported to another member state.
Certain oilseeds, cotton, tobacco	Direct aids paid to producers, partly to compensate for a lower level of import protection, itself derived from wider commercial policy considerations.
Flax and hemp, hops, silkworms, seeds	Production subsidies.

No market organisation exists for potatoes[3] or for agricultural alcohol.

The day-to-day management of the agricultural markets is a Commission responsibility. The Commission works in collaboration with a series of management committees, consisting of representatives of member states' agriculture ministries. The committees give opinions, if necessary by vote, on the execution measures which the Commission proposes. This is one of the smoothest-running parts of Community work: over the years the member state representatives and the Commission have developed a high level of co-operation and mutual understanding. Table 6.1 illustrates this, there being no unfavourable opinions on Commission proposals in 1987.

In the financial negotiations of 1987/8 one of the objectives pursued was to limit the Community's commitment to support farm prices by limiting the guaranteed quantities. There had been similar endeavours in the past, by agreements – difficult to sustain – to reduce guaranteed prices in order to discourage production (for example, of cereals) and by the imposition of quotas or co-responsibility levels which made producers pay towards the cost of surpluses. Alongside the tighter budgetary controls applied in 1988, 'stabilisers' were introduced by wholesale amendment of the regulations for market organisation. In general terms, and varying in their form from one product to another, stabilisers fix upper limits to guaranteed quantities. At the same time, additional income aids were introduced together with a scheme for payments to 'set aside' land and leave it out of production. (For the budgetary side, see Chapter 3.)

Table 6.1   Commission–Management Committee relations 1987

	Meetings	Favour-able opinion	No opinion	Unfavour-able opinion
Management Committee for Cereals	50	829	49	0
Management Committee for Pigmeat	12	43	1	0
Management Committee for Poultrymeat and Eggs	13	67	4	0
Management Committee for Fruit and Vegetables	14	79	1	0
Management Committee for Wine	32	50	12	0
Management Committee for Milk and Milk Products	33	229	39	0
Management Committee for Beef and Veal	25	137	8	0
Management Committee for Sheep and Goats	9	11	0	0
Management Committee for Oils and Fats	25	136	9	0
Management Committee for Sugar	50	125	11	0
Management Committee for Live Plants	5	5	0	0
Management Committee for Products Processed from Fruit and Vegetables	12	27	8	0
Management Committee for Tobacco	7	16	0	0
Management Committee for Hops	2	4	0	0
Management Committee for Flax and Hemp	3	4	0	0
Management Committee for Seeds	6	10	0	0
Management Committee for Dried Fodder	10	12	2	0
EAGGF Committee	17	14	2	0
Standing Committee of Feedingstuffs	3	6	0	0
Standing Veterinary Committee	26	99	1	0
Standing Committee on Seeds and Propagating Material for Agriculture, Horticulture and Forestry	8	21	0	0
Standing Committee on Agricultural Structures	9	103	0	0
Community Committee of the Farm Accountancy Data Network	2	1	0	0
Standing Committee on Agricultural Research	2	2	0	0
Standing Committee on Plant Health	12	9	1	0
Standing Committee on Zootechnics	2	1	0	0
Committee on Forest Protection	2	5	0	0
Ad hoc Committee on STM	2	3	0	0

Source: Commission of the EC, *Twenty-First General Report on the Activities of the European Communities 1987* (OOP, 1988), p. 240.

One of the guiding principles of the CAP is common pricing. Prices are expressed in the Community's monetary unit, the ECU, and are translated into national currencies. If the national currency is revalued, the price of a product at the new ECU exchange rate will fall and farmers will lose income. To avoid the opposition that this could provoke, states can hold their local prices unchanged, using 'green rates'. At these green rates the selling price is now higher in all other currencies than the ruling ECU price yields in these currencies; and if the produce were exported to another member state, it would cost more in the local currency than the local produce. This phenomenon, which would split the common agricultural market, brought about the system of Monetary Compensation Amounts (MCAs) under which levies (taxes) are charged on imports into a member state which is using a green rate for the products concerned, whilst its exports benefit from a premium. Over time the system of MCAs has undergone much tinkering and refinement to become vastly complex, far from neutral in its effects on trade, and intensely controversial in price-fixing negotiations among the member states and between them and the Commission. (In the most cynical manifestation a state could hold out for a politically popular low Community ECU price but hold up its national prices by devaluing its 'green rate'. The more positive rationale of green rate charges is that a devaluation is the only way in which a state with relatively high inflation can maintain the real – and presumably intended – effect of an agreed increase in a common agricultural price.) MCAs are regarded as a temporary, necessary evil in an unstable financial world and all policy decisions are supposed, by agreement, to be aimed at eliminating them.

The results obtained from thirty-odd years of the CAP, possibly the part of the European Communities which has provoked most debate and acrimony, point in several directions. The interpretation of them depends largely upon the observer's particular desiderata. Self-sufficiency – or more – exists for common wheat, barley, wine, meat, vegetables, milk-powder and butter. Since 1973 the UK has passed from being a net importer of cereals to becoming a net exporter. As compared with market fragmentation, the single market has encouraged specialisation: trade in agricultural products between the member states increased fourfold between 1973 and 1985.

Farm incomes, which according to the treaty are to be safeguarded, have fluctuated from year to year and from member state to member state: overall in the mid-eighties they were in real terms at about the level of the early seventies. Of course, nobody can say whether, taking account of the economic recession, they would have been better or worse if there had been a different CAP or none at all. In the latter case it is a safe bet that there would have been national uncommon agricultural policies.

Food prices have increased less rapidly than consumer prices as a whole and this is often held up as an example of the virtues of the CAP. No doubt if food prices had been higher, national price indices would have deteriorated, but this kind of statement gives no guide to whether Community food prices are reasonable. Input costs and productivity improvements or deteriorations are specific to sectors and it may not be a virtue in sector A or a vice in sector B if A prices rise more slowly than B prices.

Farming employment has perhaps been sustained generally. This would have counted as a negative effect in the sixties: one of the aims of the Mansholt plan which the Commission put out in 1968 was to facilitate movement off the land. With the mass unemployment levels of the 1970s and 1980s and allowing always for the subtleties of the labour market, farming employment at least provided a pool of jobs.

The Common Agricultural Policy is often criticised for its unsettling effect on the agricultural trade of the rest of the world. Some effects there must be but:

- the Community's share of world agricultural exports has remained stable;
- Community imports from the rest of the world rose in value by over 140 per cent between 1973 and the mid-1980s.

Inside the Community, the most vocal criticism of the CAP concerns its resource cost. A much-quoted study (*The Political Economy of International Agricultural Policy Reform*, Australian Department of Primary Industry, 1980) suggested that the additional cost of higher food prices together with the higher levels of taxation needed to finance the CAP was up to £550 a year for a non-farming family of four. The cost to the Community budget is disproportionate: 60 per cent of the budget is for agriculture, 27 billion ECUs in 1988. Half the budgetary cost goes in storing and disposing of surplus food. In 1987 those stocks reached a book-value of 11 billion ECUs against a possible realisable value of some 4–5 billion ECUs, representing a resource loss of up to 7 billion ECUs, comparable to the annual spend on regional and social policy.[4] In addition to EAGGF Guarantee there is EAGGF Guidance, spending some 1.5 billion ECUs a year on a number of schemes to improve the structure of agricultural production.

Common Fisheries Policy (CFP)

The CFP is a relatively recent arrival, not reaching its fully articulated form until 1983.[5] During the late 1970s it was bitterly fought over and much delayed between conception and implementation.

The Common Fisheries Policy has an important chapter for the conservation of stocks to prevent overfishing. Member states may not take national conservation measures. Overfishing is prevented by the comprehensive allocation to interested member states of quotas within Total Allowable Catches (TACs) and by regulating fishing areas and fishing equipment such as mesh sizes. Local dependent communities receive special consideration.

The market organisation places emphasis on the management role of fisherman's organisations, and gives them certain powers over non-members. There are guide and withdrawal prices, and quality standards.

Some traditional fishing grounds of Community fishermen are in waters under the jurisdiction of third countries, and vice versa. The Community negotiates fisheries agreements for, in some cases, reciprocal access to defined quantities and species, and in other cases, the payment of a fee for fishing rights.

No other common or Community policies are articulated as fully as the CCP and the CAP.

Common Transport Policy

Transport was one of the headings picked up in the Messina communiqué of 1955 as needing joint effort. Transport and agriculture are the only sectors of the economy to have titles devoted to them in the original EEC Treaty. They make a roughly equal contribution to Community GDP, and transport is both the carrier of goods circulating freely and the basis of the existence of industries such as vehicle and aircraft manufacture and shipbuilding. By the early 1980s, however, progress towards defining something that could be described as a common transport policy had been slow.

The EEC Treaty itself (Article 84(1)) applies its transport title only to rail, road and inland transport, and until 1973 it was argued that air and sea transport were outside the treaty. The Court judgment in Case 167/73 stipulated that the general rules of the EEC Treaty applied also to air and sea, and the Council proceeded – by the unanimity required by Article 84(2) – to take a number of decisions affecting sea and air transport. Because the article does not say how it was to be implemented, this was one of the rare cases where the Council could act without first receiving a Commission proposal. This peculiarity was dropped in the Single European Act (Article 16(6)).

One important reason for slow progress – known as the 'policy of little steps', over 100 Council decisions about transport but not adding up to much – was the trouble with the railways. By the beginning of the 1980s 85 per cent of domestic goods transport was going by road and only 7.5 per cent by rail. But the railways trailed clouds of glory from their past (the Prussian Railway had been a unit in the army and senior railway employees wore sabres), served social as well as purely economic purposes (carrying commuters and people living in outlying communities), and were state subsidised (about 20 billion ECUs a year in the early 1980s, about the same as the budgetary cost of the CAP). Thus the Commission concluded:

In most European countries the railways are indispensable . . . However, with their extensive organisation and extraordinary appetite for subsidies, the railways are also one of the Council's main problem areas. Both these factors suggest that the common transport policy hinges on finding a solution to the problems of the railways.[6]

In September 1982 the European Parliament, after a long series of debates which deplored the negligible progress towards a common transport policy, broke new ground by taking the Council to Court for its failure to lay down the foundations of a common policy. The Court (Case 13/83, judgment given on 22 May 1985) held that the Council was in breach of the treaty. On the other hand, the Court found that the treaty did not define the common policy sufficiently precisely to enable the Court to say, as Parliament wished, exactly what was missing. It recommended the Council to work towards a common transport policy.

The Council responded in the area of road transport. In December 1984 it tackled a dossier which had long lain on its desk: the maximum weights and dimensions of goods vehicles. Different rules in different countries block traffic flows. The Council was able to agree on common standards, except for the maximum weight on the driving axle, completing the task – with temporary derogations for the UK and Ireland, where road architecture would not admit the largest sizes – in July 1986 (*Official Journal*, L217, 5 August 1986; L221, 7 August 1986). The study of balancing fiscal charges on road transport, which had previously been a precondition of harmonisation, was to continue. On 30 July 1986 the Council crossed another bridge. Road transport among the member states was governed by quotas, which protected national carriers and possibly also held down the density of traffic on some of the main axes which are a charge on national and local authority budgets. The Council now decided that quotas should be increased, to reach a free market situation by the end of 1992, the 'single market' achievement year (Council Regulation No. EC 1841/88, *Official Journal*, L163, 30 June 1988). For the railways there is not much that Council decision can do except encourage realistic tariff structures. Inland waterways, an asset from which much was expected after the war, are underused and in decline.

The Commission and the European Parliament are enthusiastic supporters of a Community Transport Infrastructure Fund. The Council has been reserved and the relatively small amounts which have found their way into the Community budget have tended to be underused in the absence of a secure legal base for execution. Such a fund remains a parliamentary priority.

Air transport within the Community has been high cost and high tariff as compared with route costs elsewhere in the world. Most states see a national airline as part of the national identity, carrying the name and the flag abroad. In December 1987, after more than five years of hard Council negotiations, the Council agreed on a package of measures to liberalise air transport and to reduce fares. The measures include:

- fares to be discounted, within limits, without requiring prior approval;
- capacity to be adjusted, also within limits, without prior approval;
- new services and new routes to be available;
- services between main and regional airports to be started without bilateral negotiations;
- the 'fifth freedom' for an airline in member state A to carry passengers between an airport in member state B and one in member state C.

The package, whose strongest supporter alongside the Commission was the UK, was another plank in the common policy platform. It also included agreement, or explicit recognition, that the rules of competition apply to air transport services. This was the Commission's *locus standi* in 1988 when it intervened in the allocation of routes following the merger of British Airways and British Caledonian.

In the sea transport sector, the Community's efforts in recent times were partly directed to upholding the interests of the Community fleet in UN discussion of codes, often providing for flag discrimination. On 22 December 1986 the Council adopted four comprehensive regulations on sea transport. Regulation 4055/86 EEC provides for a free market in the provision of shipping services:

- by ships flying member state flags and plying between member states (by 31 December 1989);
- by ships flying member state flags and plying between member states and third countries (by 31 December 1991).
- by other ships between member states and between them and third countries (by 1992).

Regulation 4056/86 EEC determines the application of the competition rules in Articles 85 and 86 of the EEC Treaty to sea transport; it provides for the possibility of exemption from the general ban on agreements among carriers. Regulation 4057/86 EEC introduces a kind of 'anti-dumping' tax on unfair tariffs by third country ship owners to the detriment of Community ship owners. (The first application of this was in the summer of 1988.) Regulation 4058/86 EEC provides for the member states to take co-ordinated action against a third country or its operators if they limit or threaten to limit free access of Community ships to certain traffics.

Road safety is an important part of the policy. The year 1986 was named European Road Safety Year. On 14 November 1985 the Council overhauled the social legislation which governs drivers' working hours. The earlier versions of this legislation introduced the tachograph, which measures lapsed time, speed and distance and was originally resisted in Britain as being the 'spy in the cab'. In 1989 the Commission proposed a batch of road safety measures, including a standard maximum alcohol level in blood. The European Parliament, in giving its opinion on such measures, asked that courts should have the right to disqualify drivers whose licences were issued by other member states.

Research and technological development

In some fields of research, knowledge doubles every five years. Scientific journals publish three million articles a year and 90 per cent of all scientific workers since the beginning of science in medieval alchemy are alive today.

The Euratom Treaty has eight articles devoted to research. The ECSC Treaty contains one reference to research. The original version of the EEC Treaty is silent on research but the 'catch-all' Article 235 was used to get some programmes going. The Single European Act in 1987 added a Title on research and development (VI, Article 130(f)–(q)) and budgetary effect was given to it. This underpins the drive towards the single market (by harmonising product standards and test methods), encourages information exchange and industrial co-operation, flags priorities and reduces overlap.

Under Euratom the Community set up a Joint Research Centre (JRC) at Ispra on Lake Maggiore. Its original remit was nuclear fission energy. By the early 1970s the member states concluded that this kind of collective research – apart from work on reactor safety – was no longer required and the JRC diversified its activities. Meanwhile, on Commission proposals, the Council began to agree to research programmes, especially in information technology. The European Strategic Programme for Research and Development in Information Technology (ESPRIT) was an early result in 1984. ESPRIT is a series of projects for which the Community gives funding provided there are participants from at least two member states. ESPRIT became a model for the administration of programmes in other fields. Fusion research, on which Britain had been engaged since the 1950s, became a Community concern in 1977 when the Joint European Torus (JET) project was inaugurated at Culham (currently the only Community body physically situated in the UK).

In 1987, in parallel with the drafting and ratification of the Single European Act, the Council adopted a framework programme for 1987–91 bringing together into a single whole the different pieces of Community R & D activity (see Table 6.2). The framework programme is proposed by the Commission, is the subject of a parliamentary opinion and is decided by the Council (unanimity is required). It contains cost estimates but they are not immediately budgetary, although they obviously have a strong influence on the budgetary decisions. From the

Table 6.2   Framework programme of Community activities in the field of research and technological development (1987–91)

		million ECUs
1.	**Quality of life**	375
1.1.	Health	80
1.2.	Radiation protection	34
1.3.	Environment	261
2.	**Towards a large market and an information and communications society**	2,275
2.1.	Information technologies	1,600
2.2.	Telecommunications	550
2.3.	New services of common interest (including transport)	125
3.	**Modernisation of industrial sectors**	845
3.1.	Science and technology for manufacturing industry	400
3.2.	Science and technology of advanced materials	220
3.3.	Raw materials and recycling	45
3.4.	Technical standards, measurement methods and reference materials	180
4.	**Exploitation and optimum use of biological resources**	280
4.1.	Biotechnology	120
4.2.	Agro-industrial technologies	105
4.3.	Competitiveness of agriculture and management of agricultural resources	55
5.	**Energy**	1,173
5.1.	Fission: nuclear safety	440
5.2.	Controlled thermonuclear fusion	611
5.3.	Non-nuclear energies and rational use of energy	122
6.	**Science and technology for development**	80 80
7.	**Exploitation of the sea bed and use of marine resources**	80
7.1.	Marine science and technology	50
7.2.	Fisheries	30
8.	**Improvement of European S/T co-operation**	288
8.1.	Stimulation, enhancement and use of human resources	180
8.2.	Use of major installations	30
8.3.	Forecasting and assessment and other back-up measures (including statistics)	23
8.4.	Dissemination and utilisation of S/T research results	55
	Total	5,396

Source: Research and Technical Development Policy Periodical, 2/1988, OOP, p. 26.

framework programme, specific programmes are derived. They are subject to the co-operation procedure, in which the Parliament is consulted twice, and are adopted by the Council by qualified majority. This procedure, which it was feared might be cumbersome, has in fact worked with conspicuous success.

Scientific information is exchanged via the Euronet–Diane computer networks, giving access to data bases and data banks.

Social policy

In its original text the EEC Treaty is cautious about anything resembling a common or Community social policy. In the negotiation phase there had been alarm and counter-alarm: alarm that prospective members whose labour costs included relatively low social security contributions might have a competitive edge, and counter-alarm that they might have to harmonise their labour costs upwards to the detriment of their competitiveness.

The original Title III 'Social Policy' bears the hallmark of compromises. A social policy is said to exist, but it is squarely in the hands of the member states. The Council is mentioned only once (Article 121) and then only on procedure. Article 117, the scene-setting provision, presupposed that social objectives would ensue directly from the dynamism of the common market, as well as from an in-built market force favouring harmonisation (that is, labour would move to where it would be best off). In so far as causality can be inferred, the dynamism worked: between 1958 and 1972 wages increased by 70 per cent in Luxembourg, 91 per cent in Belgium, 97 per cent in France, 111 per cent in the Netherlands, 115 per cent in Germany and 144 per cent in Italy.

Equal pay, demanded by Article 119, became a Community canon despite hesitation and backsliding. Migrant workers (from other member states) were covered by social security provisions. The Social Fund, named in the treaty, was set up; successive revisions of its objectives took it beyond 'rendering the employment of workers easier and increasing their geographical and occupational mobility' and into measures acting against the rising tide of unemployment and for the benefit of particular groups such as young people, the handicapped, the long-term unemployed and women workers. Safety and health at the workplace – which is both a kind of human right and a factor affecting competition – also commanded attention and gave rise to directives concerning exposure to or working with harmful substances or energy sources.

A more controversial part of a social development programme concerns intervention in support of workers' rights, which became the rebalancing of power between workers and employers and the rethinking of state (or Community) responsibilities. Those who have reservations about the value or justification of this type of intervention dismiss it as 'social engineering'. One of the more notable endeavours of the late 1970s was the Vredeling draft directive, a Commission proposal which aimed at giving workpeople explicit and defined rights to be consulted in the affairs of complex companies,[7] typically multinationals with irons in fires in several member states. These proposals, and others (like the draft fifth company law directive) concerning employee representation on boards, were opposed particularly but not exclusively by Britain, which contended that such matters were not appropriate for top-down legislation but belonged to negotiations within industries or firms.

The Single European Act was greeted as adding a caring, social dimension to the purely entrepreneurial aspects of the single market. The argument was that 'ordinary people' needed to be given a stake in the single market and that the adaptations which it would force on firms could damage employment in some areas whilst favouring growth and welfare generally. While the 'social dimension' became a major concern of some member states, others viewed it as the condemned 'social engineering'. The Commission's first collected body of suggestions (Marin Memorandum, September 1988) were cautious – excessively so for some but nevertheless 'the writing on the wall' for others. The Commission, in *The Social Policy: Looking Ahead to 1992* (OOP, 1988), argued that 'Contractual policy must remain the basis of the European social model.' The idea of a 'European Social Charter' was met with reserve in some member states and elsewhere was hailed as a manifesto. Controversy rages over whether such an instrument should exist at all; and whether, if existent, it should be legislative or purely declaratory.

Social affairs created their own organs. They are discussed in a specialised council, which meets two or three times a year. A Standing Committee on Employment brings together employees' and employers' representatives, representatives of publicly owned enterprises, ministers of employment (not meeting as the Council) and the Commission. They discuss measures to stimulate investment and employment, the impact on the labour force of new technologies, training schemes, etc. The Commission, acting on Article 118(b), has promoted discussions between the two sides of industry (in the language of Brussels 'the social partners') in a series of meetings which it has convened known as the 'Val Duchesse dialogue'.

Competition policy

Competition policy is a field where:

- competence is shared between the Community and member states' authorities, perhaps both become involved in the same case;
- the Commission, not (generally speaking) the Council, takes the Community decisions, subject to reference to the Court of Justice.

Competition policy is principally concerned with three types of phenomenon:

State aids: subsidies, grants and relief to enterprises, whether publicly or privately owned. State aids which distort competition are banned but on application to the Commission can be authorised, possibly subject to conditions, if there is justification for them. Justification can include the demands of regional policy, conformity with a planned programme of structural adjustment (shipbuilding), support for the launch of a venture with promise to improve competitiveness, etc.

Trusts, cartels, abuse of dominant market positions: the classic anti-trust fields, involving on the one hand agreements among enterprises to rig markets to the detriment of consumers, and on the other predatory behaviour based on market or financial strength. They come into play when trade between member states is affected or when there is abuse of a dominant position within the common market or in a substantial part of it. Exemptions can be and have been given to agreements among enterprises which satisfy the tests set out in Article 85(3), such as exclusive dealership arrangements.

Merger control. Whilst in some member states (for example, Britain and Germany) there is explicit control over mergers of enterprises, no such provision exists in the EEC Treaty, although the competition articles (85 and 86) might apply and state financial involvement, if any, might fall foul of Articles 92 and 93. The Commission made in the 1970s and revised in the mid-1980s a proposal for an instrument of merger control, which would give it the say over mergers of a given size. This proposal is still before the Council (1989).

In applying the provisions of competition law the Commission has extensive powers to require the production of information and to carry out on-the-spot investigations with or without prior notice ('dawn raids') to those concerned. 'Until 1978 the Commission conducted surprise investigations in only a few cases. The situation has changed somewhat . . . the Commission now likes to gather the maximum amount of evidence of suspected infringements.'[8]

Community competition law can apply to enterprises outside the Community, having no branches or subsidiaries inside the Community but selling to customers within the Community. This principle of extra-territorial application was confirmed by the European Court of Justice in the Woodpulp cartel case (September 1988).

Economic and monetary policy

The EEC Treaty is about creating a customs union, known familiarly as the Common Market. The Single European Act catches up with ongoing activities to give them a treaty basis and it completes the common market by attacking the non-tariff barriers which outlasted the abolition of customs duties and import quotas within the union.

According to some, enough is enough, or enough for the time being. According to others, the common or single market is not enough for an economic community. The argument is that, while a single market will enable the factors of production to move freely, it does little to affect the extent to which and the ways in which state governments intervene to manage the economy of their countries. Their actions affect growth rates, employment levels and investment decisions in time and space. Moreover, since the opening of markets makes the separate economies more interdependent, the results of the economic management in one may spill over into the others, for good or for ill. Rather than leave these effects simply to the laws of the market to absorb, it is argued that the member states should, as a minimum, pursue compatible 'conjunctural' policies in the short term and, in time, should reach economic union. Economic union means the taking, by the authority responsible there-for, of decisions which directly affect the citizen's welfare, and therefore implies sensitivity and a certain consensus regarding the aims to be pursued. Economic union is correspondingly not easily dissociable from the creation of a central political authority of some kind, where central does not necessarily mean strongly centralised.

The twenty-year debate about economic integration has tended to be marked by two discussions. The first is oversimplified, but conveniently so, by being represented as one between 'economists', who believe that the way forward is to adopt policies which will reduce regional disparities in growth, inflation, employment and investment, and 'monetarists' who believe that the use of instruments which promote stability among the different currencies in use in the constituent parts of the union will, as a first stage, create the conditions for closer integration. When a sufficient stability has been reached, a common currency and a banking apparatus for managing it internally and externally will be possible. Most 'monetarists' would accept that the price of exchange rate stability may be damage to some local economies as part of the process of adjustment.

This is the starting point of a second debate: what concurrent measures need to be taken to enable all to participate in the prototype of economic and monetary union? To some extent this debate mirrors another which is strictly independent of the monetary issue. It is a debate which arises with every enlargement. Geographically the six new members are peripheral, and economically five of them (not Denmark) were below Community average performance. Part of the negotiations before or after enlargement has been about directing help towards them. In the UK and Irish cases the recognisable outcome was the Regional Development Fund. In the Greek case it was the Integrated Mediterranean Programmes. In the Iberian case it is the doctrine of 'cohesion', along with the strengthening of all the (redistributive) structural funds and some measures which recognise the special vulnerability of Portugal.

The guidance given in the EEC Treaty on this complex of questions is thin. At the time economies were in growth, although not without problems, and governments preferred to keep their hands free – after all elections are partly won on parties' economic performances and promises. Member states are enjoined to regard their short-term economic policies as a matter of common concern (Article 103); to run their economies in pursuit of the three virtues of equilibrium in the balance of payments, full employment and low inflation (Article 104); to co-ordinate their economic policies (Article 105); to use their best endeavours to free capital movements (Article 106); and to treat exchange rate policy as another matter of common concern (Article 107). These requirements leave member state governments wide room for national manoeuvre.

In 1969 the Commission brought out the first substantial plan for concerted action, named after the Commissioner responsible, Raymond Barre. The Barre plan called for the joint definition, by consultation, of medium-term strategies and for mutual financial help when a member state gets into trouble which might oblige it to jeopardise the continuing functioning of the common market. The Werner Report (whose author was the Luxembourg Prime Minister) of October 1970 was more monetarist than the Barre plan. It looked forward to fixed and unchangeable parities among national currencies, at which stage a single currency could (not must) be introduced. In this circumstance there would need to be a single decision-making centre for economic management and central banks acting in accordance with Community policy.

By the end of the 1960s there were signs of a phase change in world economic conditions. Cyclical crises were leaving behind them a rising level of built-in unemployment. Inflation was moving beyond the 3 per cent mark which was regarded as a sign and stimulant of growth. Monetary instability hit the EEC countries with the traumatic devaluation of the French franc in August 1969 and the revaluation of the Deutschmark in October.[9] In the days of fixed positions against the US dollar, devaluations and revaluations, and the wave of rumour preceding them, were truly awesome events. At their meeting in the Hague in 1969 the six heads of state or government decided that 'a plan by stages should be drawn up with a view to the creation of an economic and monetary union'.[10]

The case for a stabilisation plan was reinforced in the summer of 1971 when the convertibility of the dollar was formally suspended. With the eclipse of the post-war Bretton Woods agreement, which had fixed official and durable parities, a new arrangement was concluded in Washington at the Smithsonian Institute to fix central rates with allowable margins of fluctuation (the tunnel). The Council of the European Communities asked central banks to remain within narrower bands (the snake). The pound sterling and the Scandinavian crowns also joined but by 1977 only the countries of the so-called DM zone had held on – the mark, the Dutch guilder, the Belgian franc and the Danish krone. The others could not hold the fixed rate under the pressure of inflation at different rates, speculation against them and the presumed benefit of floating freely, which on at least one theory is itself a corrective.

At the beginning of 1977 Roy Jenkins, himself a former finance minister, became president of the Commission. In May of that year the

Committee which the previous Commission had appointed under Sir Donald MacDougall published its report, *The Role of Public Finance in European Integration*. The report was not a formula for monetary union, but it examined the role of public finance in a state, in a community and in a federation. This, therefore, was of the economists' school, and concerned especially the redistributive or equalising function of public finance, which is also a policy instrument to reach and sustain economic union. After careful preparation and on the 300th day of his office, 27 October 1977, Jenkins, speaking at the temple of European integration, the European University Institute of Florence, called for economic and monetary union to be put back at the top of the Community agenda.

The result was not entirely the one for which he had called. The German Chancellor, Helmut Schmidt, and the French President, Valéry Giscard d'Estaing, both former finance ministers and on close terms with each other, set out to devise a system for monetary stability. The technical work was entrusted to a German, a French and a British official (Kenneth Couzens of HM Treasury), but the United Kingdom was unable to make the necessary precommitments and the work became Franco-German. A first public showing occurred at the European Council meeting in Copenhagen in April 1978, more substance was given at the meeting in Bremen on 7 July 1978, and the system was established at Brussels on 5 December 1978 with a starting date of 1 January 1979. This date could not be kept because of tense negotiations into the New Year on agricultural prices – which would be reduced in national currencies if the new accounting basis of the European Monetary System (EMS), the ECU, were to be applied directly to them – but on 13 March 1979 the EMS began. In the preparatory discussions attention had been given to the 'concurrent measures' necessary to cushion the less prosperous countries against possible adverse affects. The three countries which contended that they needed this facility were the UK, Ireland and Italy. But Britain decided that it would not participate and Ireland and Italy received compensatory finance in the form of soft loans and other inducements.

The EMS exchange rate mechanism is a hybrid – not entirely Community, not entirely outside it. It was created by a resolution of the European Council followed by a decision of the Council and an agreement between the participating central banks. It consists only of those member states which elect to join it. Apart from Britain, Greece and Portugal have not done so. But all member states have the option to join; non-member states, including those who were in the snake, do not.

The EMS itself is not based on treaty articles. Although Jenkins broke the ice, the system was not the one formally proposed by the Commission under Article 235 of the EEC Treaty. The exchange rate mechanism of the EMS is not part of the *'acquis'* of the Community.[11]

The EMS exchange rate mechanism is in two parts. One is a parity grid in which each currency has a parity with every other. This parity may fluctuate by 2.25 per cent (Italy 6 per cent). If it goes further, members must intervene. In a bilateral system two countries will exhaust their margins at the same time. The intervention obligation falls on both – the one going strong (which should sell its currency) and the one going weak (which should buy its currency). The second mechanism is a divergence indicator. It uses the ECU, which is composed of a basket of currencies of all member states weighted for their economic importance. When a currency deviates from the ECU by 75 per cent of the spread of divergence (that is, its relationship to the ECU is no longer what its current weighting would make it, and the change in their relationship is greater than 75 per cent of the currency's possible fluctuation under the bilateral parity grid) the country is required to take appropriate steps. These can if necessary include fixing a new parity grid and a new weighting of the ECU.[12] To help countries to intervene in the exchange markets there are a very short-term credit facility, a short-term support facility and medium-term financial assistance.

The participants in the EMS pronounce themselves satisfied with the stability it has given them, in an unstable financial world, in its first years of life. Britain continues to remain outside and to pursue an exchange rate policy which is either subordinate to other domestic monetary policies (the free float, without a predetermined target and without intervention triggers) or is formally independent of the EMS and uses its own targets for sterling parities. Britain has repeatedly said that it will join the ERM 'when the time is right'.

The concurrent measures which emerged from discussion were relatively limited in scale. At one point it had been suggested that they should work through an increased Regional Fund but this suggestion was not pursued. The problem of regional disparity remained and according to some was growing worse. Regional disparity was criticised *per se* (because it meant that some Community citizens had a deplorably low standard of living and uncertain prospects) and because it was an obstacle to economic and monetary union, a road leading, on some maps, to political union. The divisive effect of these disparities came out strongly in the Dooge Report and notably in the Note annexed to it in which the Greek representative, Ioannes Papantoniou, emphasised the importance of *cohesion*. Economic and social cohesion became a clarion call of the Single European Act. The practical application of the received principle was the decision, in the context of *Making the Single European Act Succeed*, to double the budgetary commitment appropriations in the structural funds (Regional Development, Social and Agricultural Guidance) between 1988 and 1993. A doubling of the Regional Fund over five years was also a long-standing demand of the European Parliament.

At its meeting in Hanover in June 1988, the European Council:

- recalled that in the Single European Act the member states had confirmed the objective of the progressive realisation of economic and monetary union;
- entrusted to a committee, chaired by the president of the Commission, the task of studying and proposing concrete stages leading towards this union;
- decided to examine the means of achieving this union at its meeting in Madrid in June 1989.

For an understanding of the debate which these decisions opened it is important to have in mind that the European Council was not asking Jacques Delors and his colleagues on the committee, who included the governors of central banks, what they thought about economic and monetary union and whether it was realisable. They were unambiguously asked to propose 'concrete stages leading towards Union'.

The Committee reported in April 1989. In terms of the artificial distinction drawn above, the report is more 'monetarist' than 'economic'. Under the latter heading it notes that arrangements already exist, in the form of ongoing Council–Commission activity, to secure greater economic co-ordination and convergence. This chapter does not therefore require new institutions, but does need a considerable strengthening of rules – for example, guidance and later legally binding requirements relating to the size of annual national budget deficits and their financing.

It had been stated in the Single European Act (Article 102A) that 'insofar as further development in the field of economic and monetary union necessitates institutional changes' these would need to be carried out by treaty revision. They could not be secured by Commission proposal and Council decision, but only by calling a conference of representatives of the member states under Article 236, negotiating a new treaty and submitting it to national parliaments for ratification.

On the monetary side, therefore, the *Report on Economic and Monetary Union* is concerned both with policy formulation and with institutional reform. It stresses that a greater convergence of economic performance is needed and that there must be parallel advancement in economic and in monetary integration, in order to avoid imbalances which could cause economic strains and loss of political support for developing the Community further into an economic and monetary union. While acknowledging that economic and monetary union implies far more than the single market programme, it also notes that the full liberalisation of capital movements – an essential ingredient of that programme – and the integration of financial markets create a situation in which the co-ordination of monetary policy would have to be strengthened in any case.

Much of the report is devoted to the steps to be taken to create and operate a proposed 'European System of Central Banks' (ESCB). In this new Community institution, centralised and collective decisions would be taken on the supply of money and credit as well as on other instruments of monetary policy, including exchange rates. These decisions would be consistent with and would articulate in the monetary sphere, the economic policy of Community authorities. Obviously, on top of the convertibility of Community currencies which already exists, and the capital liberalisation which is to come in the single market, there would be in the monetary union the elimination of margins of fluctuation among member states' currencies and the irrevocable locking of exchange rate parities. As soon as possible after this is achieved national currencies should be replaced by a single currency. The ESCB should, according to the report, be independent of instructions from national governments and Community authorities (including the European Council). It would submit an annual report to the European Council and European Parliament. Although the report does not say so, it is to be assumed that the controlling authorities of the ESCB would seek to have and hold the support and confidence of these two bodies and would listen to what they might have to say to them.

The debate about economic and monetary union quickened in the summer of 1989 in the context of the third direct elections to the European Parliament (15 and 18 June 1989) and the meeting of the European Council in Madrid on 26–7 June. The British Government continued to express its reservations. While upholding co-operation in economic and monetary policy (part of the title of Article 102(a) of the EEC Treaty, as amended by the Single European Act – the rest of the title, placed in brackets, is 'Economic and Monetary Union') it regarded the Delors Report as unrealistic. The Conservative Party manifesto for the 1989 European elections said:

We support practical steps of this kind to promote closer economic and monetary co-operation. On the other hand, as the recent report of the Delors Committee makes clear, full economic and monetary union would involve a fundamental transfer of sovereignty. It would require new European institutions to administer a common currency and decide interest rates, and a considerable degree of central control over budgetary policy. The report, if taken as a whole, implies nothing less than the creation of a federal Europe. Such ideas go way beyond what is realistic or desirable in the foreseeable future. Indeed to think in these terms is not only unrealistic but damaging, for it distracts political attention and energy from the Community's central current task – completing the single market by 1992.[13]

Although the results of the election were a rebuff to the Conservatives, those who gained in the election in Britain were probably not far from the Conservative position.

In the run-up to the Madrid meeting of the European Council it appeared that a large majority of the member states were in favour of following the Delors Report and that some insisted on what was known as 'automaticity': all stages in the Delors Report hang together and the decision to begin implementation implied and required a continuous process and progress to the end result. The discussion of EMU effectively monopolised the Madrid meeting. The outcome was a compromise, such that all could consider that they had secured their aims. It was agreed that the 'first stage' should begin on 1 July 1990, and that preparatory work should be carried out for an intergovernmental conference to lay down the subsequent stages. This is the Intergovernmental Conference envisaged by Article 236 of the EEC Treaty to amend the treaty. A decision to convene an intergovernmental conference can be taken by simple majority (seven member states voting for), but the agreement of all member states is necessary for the conference to have a successful outcome. Preparatory work began under the French Presidency – strong advocates of economic and monetary union – in July 1989.

Environment policy

It has been said that the environment was discovered and the environmentalist born about 1965.[14] The EEC Treaty does not say a word about the environment or about a policy for it. When, however, concern about the damage being done to the environment became a political preoccupation in Europe as elsewhere, and since environmental problems straddle frontiers, it was proper that the Economic Community should become involved. In 1973 it adopted the first Action Programme on the Environment, followed by programmes in 1977, 1983 and 1987, running up to 1992.[15] These programmes took the form of Council resolutions, which are not legally binding and are regarded as indicative rather than as implying that everything mentioned in them will actually happen.

The constitutional difficulty about environment policy is that the member states and the Community continue to exercise competence concurrently. One side-effect of this – the main effect was protracted argument about who can do what – was that ultimate agreements on environmental measures were minimal standards which individual member states could surpass, thereby damaging the intended unity of the policy and of the market. A practical difficulty is the different perception of the weight to be given to environmental protection and improvement as opposed to other factors such as cost, industrial investment, job creation, economic growth, and central and local government spending.

The first series of Community environmental measures concerned the purity of water intended for different uses – drinking, bathing, supporting fish-life, etc. On this there was a divergence of view over the objective. Most member states thought that the effective way to control water was to establish emission standards – that is, to work on what goes into water. The UK dissented: it stood for a quality objective – that is, what is the water actually like? The compromise was to admit both concepts and to work out equivalences between them, along with test methods for each.

Atmospheric pollution was not taken up until much later, from 1980. There was growing public concern in northern Europe over the destruction of forests and the damage inflicted on the environment and on wildlife by acid rain. There were also public heath anxieties – for example, from lead in petrol – although mention of public health tended to excite additional controversy over the division of competence between the Community and its member states, some of which insisted that there was no Community competence. Measures discussed or adopted included the limitation of (especially sulphurous) emissions from large power stations and heat-raising plants; car exhausts; and the inert gases (CFCs) used in aerosols and other applications and found to be attacking the ozone layer. Concern began to be felt about the 'global climate' change and the interconnections between phenomena like rising temperature and increased concentrations of carbon dioxide in the atmosphere ('greenhouse effect').

Other environmental measures concerned noise levels – of aircraft and motor vehicles. (Separately, and not strictly part of the environment programme, there were proposals and decisions concerning noise at the workplace and the protection of workers against hearing loss.) Another noise source with which the Community concerned itself was the noise of lawnmowers. This – like the mythical Euro-sausage of *Yes, Minister* fame – is often held up as showing the ridiculous side of European integration. Why bother with such trivia? In fact, the work was initiated by British industrial interests which feared that they would be shut out of markets if national governments adopted excessively tight standards.[16]

The environmental action programmes also took up the dumping of waste and especially of dangerous waste. The discovery in 1983 that forty-one barrels of highly contaminated soil from the Seveso explosion in Italy were somewhere adrift without anyone seeming to know where or what was to happen to them came as a shock and give impetus to Community action.

The programmes also concerned themselves with wildlife. In 1976 the Commission broke completely new ground by proposing a directive on the protection of wild birds. The Council adopted it on 2 April 1979 (*Official Journal*, 103, 2 April 1979). The massacre of baby seals for their pelts provoked public outcry in 1982. In a rare reversal of roles, however, it was not the Commission but the European Parliament which took the initiative and virtually induced the Commission to propose a draft regulation banning imports of the skins of baby seals and objects made therefrom. The Council adopted a directive in March 1983.

In the field of the prevention of pollution, rather than in repairing damage already done, the Community opened up relatively small budgetary provisions, largely for research, but it also held fast to its central principle: the polluter pays. It discussed for five years, and finally adopted in 1985 a directive instituting a Community system of

Environment Impact Assessments (Official Journal L175, 5 July 1985). In general terms this measure requires public authorities responsible for licensing certain kinds of development project to consider, in relation to a set of criteria, the impact which the project, if realised, would make on the environment. The directive also provides for information to be made available to the public. This directive was regarded as a landmark in the Community approach to the conservation of the environment.

The absence from the EEC Treaty of mention of the environment meant that the measures adopted had as their legal basis the 'catch-all' Article 235. The Single European Act provides in the three articles (130(r)–(t)) of Title VII a new treaty basis for decisions about the environment. The principles are set out in Article 130(r), para. 2:

- preventive action should be taken and environmental damage should as a priority be rectified at source;
- the polluter should pay.

Article 130(s) is the operational legal basis. It provides for the Council to take decisions unanimously after consulting the Parliament and the Economic and Social Committee. This is the classic consultation procedure, not involving the two phases of the new co-operation procedure. Article 130(s) also provides, however, that the Council can decide unanimously that there are some matters in which it can decide by qualified majority. There is no parallel for this facility elsewhere in the treaty, as amended by the Single European Act. Finally, Article 130(t) harks back to the principle of environment measures being minima: it allows for member states to go beyond them and it refrains from laying down any procedure which they must follow if they decide to do so.

In addition to the new Title VII which is dedicated to the environ- ment, the Single European Act offers, in Article 100(a), another instrument for the protection of the environment. This new article is the key to progress towards the single market by 1992. As compared with the old Article 100, it introduces:

- the co-operation procedure, giving Parliament two readings;
- qualified majority voting.

But there is a reminder of the 'minimum standards' doctrine in Article 100(a), para. 4. A member state, which presumably was outvoted when it argued that the proposed Community measure was not rigorous enough, can apply additional national provisions 'on grounds . . .

relating to the protection of the environment' if:

- it notifies the Commission;
- the Commission confirms that the provisions are not a means of arbitrary discrimination or a disguised restriction on trade (for example, they do not protect a national producer against import competition).

In the first year of application of the Single Act, involving thirty measures which ran the full course of the co-operation procedure, no use was made of Article 100(a), para. 4.

Energy

Although the ECSC Treaty and the Euratom Treaty have a direct concern with two major energy sources, energy policy as a subject is not mentioned in the EEC Treaty or in the Single Act. The Council's annual reviews of its activities refer modestly to the 'Development of a Community Energy Policy'. The quadrupling of oil prices in 1973 and the subsequent tripling in 1979 certainly concentrated the Community's mind, and mention is made of energy problems regularly in the published conclusions of European Councils. But these preoccupations do not seem to have inspired the Community to equip itself with a full-dress energy policy.

Generally speaking, meetings of the Council (Energy) have received communications, rather than legislative proposals, from the Commission. Members have exchanged views and agreed on objectives, the latest of which run to 1995. They are (Council resolution of 16 September 1986; *Official Journal*, C24, 25 September 1986):

- the development of Community energy resources in satisfactory economic conditions;
- the diversification of the Community's outside sources of energy supply;
- flexibility for energy systems;
- effective crisis management measures, especially for crude oil;
- a vigorous policy of energy conservation and rational use;
- diversification among the different forms of energy.

Among the reasons for the adoption of relatively open positions and of

Table 6.3 Energy consumption and dependence in the member states: 1963, 1973, 1983

	Energy consumption in 1983		Percentage dependence on energy imports		
	Per capita (toe)	Total (m toe)	1963	1973	1983
Federal Republic of Germany	4.0	276	23.7	56.5	51.2
Belgium	4.1	41	52.0	88.0	73.3
Denmark	3.2	17	96.8	99.6	86.6
France	3.2	174	53.6	79.6	61.8
Greece	1.6	16	–	–	64.9
Ireland	2.2	8	74.8	84.4	62.6
Italy	2.2	125	72.3	84.3	81.2
Luxembourg	7.7	3	99.7	99.6	98.7
Netherlands	3.3	57	67.7	22.0	7.2
United Kingdom	3.4	191	29.7	53.1	–17.4
Eur. 10	3.2	876	41.6	64.3	41.9

Source: The Economy of the European Community (OOP, 1984), p. 37.

aims rather than measures is the different degree of dependence on energy imports in the member states (see Table 6.3). Another reason may be the need for flexibility in the face of the fluctuation of the energy market, where shortages are succeeded by surpluses and where prices gyrate. A third reason may be the wish of member states to keep the management of their own energy policies, including the external relations aspects, in their own hands. (One example of this in 1975 was the insistence of the UK in participating in its own name at the International Energy Conference, although the Community was also to be represented as such.)

In 1985 the Council adopted a regulation (EEC No. 3640/85; *Official Journal*, L350, 27 December 1985) on the provision of financial support for demonstration projects – 'a mainstay of the Community's energy strategy'.[17] These covered the development of alternative energy sources, energy saving and the liquefaction and gasification of solid fuels. The scheme runs to 31 December 1989. The experiences gained from these projects are analysed and disseminated through the Community's 'information market' (an institution which used to be the title of one of the Commission's Directorates General and has a budget of 36 million ECUs over two years).

Industry

The Community does not proclaim an industrial policy. If any part of it did so, a number of member states might declare that they do not believe in such things. However, the Common Commercial Policy, the rules of competition, the research and technological development, the free circulation of goods in the upcoming single market, the energy objectives, the co-ordination of economic policy, the social policy, the operation of the European Investment Bank – all have a bearing on conditions in Community industry.

Until the Research and Development Programme took off, Community concern with industry tended to be with those where the workforce and/or production were in decline, such as shipbuilding, steel and textiles. In such industries there was a form of planning for contraction, on the basis of equality or equity of misery, and arrangements for state aid to be authorised, if member states wanted to give it, under defined conditions and as part of the phasing-out operation. In the case of steel, the Community operated a crisis plan with price fixing (to prevent undercutting), production quotas and agreements with third countries under which they restricted their exports to the Community. The quotas were phased out by 1988.

Outside the 'sunset' industries, Community enterprises are helped by the widening of their home market, by harmonised technical standards which avoid low production runs, by the encouragement and part-financing of research including pre-competitive co-operative research, and by the opening up of public purchasing – where typically 90 per cent of purchases are from national suppliers. Industrial enterprise is encouraged by deregulation. Special attention is given to small and medium-sized firms. Every Commission proposal is accompanied by a fiche which assesses the impact that the proposal may have on small and medium-sized firms. Some Community industries have benefited from anti-dumping duties imposed on damaging imports, especially of electronic consumer goods from Japan and Korea. Textile and clothing firms in the Community, as elsewhere, are protected from disruptive competition from low-cost producers by quota restrictions maintained under the Multi-Fibre Agreement, which is a world-wide managed market.

Regional policy

The Communities' regional policy shows concern for those of its regions which are economically backward, especially the peripheral areas, and for those which are in industrial decline. With the aim of avoiding competitive subsidisation it defines the intensity of regional aid which national governments can offer, and it provides grant aid under the Regional Development Fund to help to correct regional disparities. Regional Fund aid may be for financing productive enterprises (including tourist assets) or it may be for infrastructure such as road building. Projects are put forward by their sponsors with support from the competent national authority and are selected by the Commission according to need.

The single market

The completion by the end of 1992 of the single market is a top priority for the Community. The comprehensive programme for the removal of non-tariff barriers to the movement of goods and for the free circulation of capital, services and people was set out in the Commission's White Paper of June 1985 associated with the name of Vice-President Lord Cockfield.[18] The procedural changes in the Single European Act were designed in part to accelerate progress, especially by majority voting. There are different ways of adding up how many proposals are either in the White Paper or are so close to it as to count in the programme, but they total about 300 and concern:

- removal of physical and technical barriers (for example, veterinary regulations and those concerning pressure vessels, tower cranes, use of asbestos, etc. which being divergent impede cross-frontier trade);
- conditions for providing services (banking, insurance, insider trading, etc.);
- free movement of capital;
- unification of company law and other regulations (trademarks, the European company, structure of public limited companies, etc.);
- fiscal approximation (VAT coverage and rates);
- suppression of internal frontier controls (common visa policy, no passport control).

The European Council meeting in Rhodes in December 1988 observed that about half of the proposals for the creation of the single market had been adopted. Apart from the normal difficulties inherent in reconciling arrangements which have grown up separately, there were particular problems over:

- VAT, where some member states, facing a movement down to a common level, fear loss of revenue; some are concerned about losing their freedom to vary rates; and the UK is opposed to the disappearance of zero-rating on, for example, children's clothing and food;
- the free movement of people, and the suppression of border checks – seen by some as weakening the effort to reinforce security in the fight against terrorism, drug trafficking, illegal immigration and internationally organised crime.

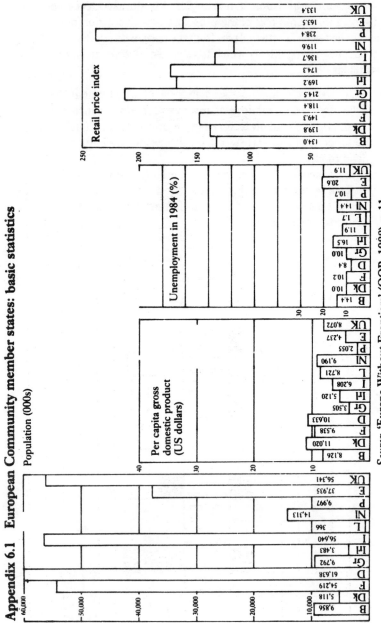

Appendix 6.1   European Community member states: basic statistics

Population (000s)

Per capita gross domestic product (US dollars)

Unemployment in 1984 (%)

Retail price index

Source: 'Europe Without Frontiers' (OOP, 1988), p.11.

Appendix 6.2   Foreign trade of the Community of Twelve (billion ECU)

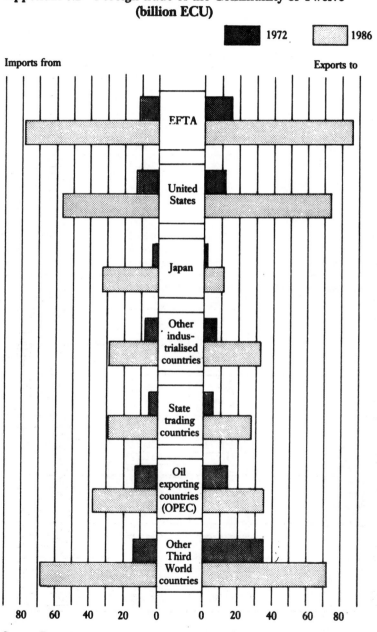

Source: Commission of the EC, *The European Community in the World* (OOP, 1988), p.4.

Appendix 6.3   EC external trade (billion ECU)

	1986	1987
Intra-EC	459.7	485.7
Imports (extra-EC)	334.6	339.2
USA	56.6	56.3
Japan	33.2	34.5
EFTA	78.7	82.4
LDCs	107.7	108.2
OPEC	38.5	34.7
Med. basin	28.3	29.1
ACP	19.6	16.4
State trading	29.5	30.1
Exports (extra-EC)	341.9	338.9
USA	75.2	71.8
Japan	11.4	13.6
EFTA	87.2	90.2
LDCs	107.6	104.6
OPEC	35.3	29.6
Med. basin	36.3	34.1
ACP	16.0	13.8
State trading	27.6	25.4

Source: Eurostat external trade monthly statistics (OOP).

Appendix 6.4   EEC agreements with third countries[1]

	Date of signature	Offical Journal Reference	Treaty article
Northern Europe			
Austria	22/1/72	L300/72 p. 93	113
Finland	5/10/73	L328/73 p. 1	113
Iceland	22/7/72	L301/72 p. 1	113
Norway	14/5/73	L171/73 p. 2	113
Sweden	22/7/72	L300/72 p. 96	113
Switzerland	22/7/72	L300/72 p. 189	113
Southern Europe			
Cyprus	19/12/72	L133/73 p. 1	238
Malta	5/12/70	L61/71 p. 1	238
	27/10/77	L304/77 p. 2	238
Turkey	12/9/63	L217/64 pp. 3685, 3705	238
Yugoslavia	2/4/80	L41/83 p. 1	–
			Also signed by member states
	31/3/81	L147/81 p. 5	113
	10/12/87	–	238

State trading countries

China	21/5/85	L250/85 p. 1	113
Czechoslovakia	Negotiated October 1988		113
Hungary	Negotiated October 1988		113
Romania	28/7/80	L352/80 pp. 5, 21	113
CMEA (COMECON)		L157/88 p. 35	235

Middle East

Algeria	26/4/75	L263/78 p. 1	238
Egypt	18/1/77	L266/78 p. 1	238
Israel	11/5/75	L136/75 p. 1	113
	8/2/77	L270/78 p. 1	238
Jordan	18/1/77	L268/78 p. 1	238
Lebanon	3/5/77	L267/78 p. 1	238
Morocco	27/4/76	L264/78 p. 1	238
Syria	18/1/77	L269/78 p. 1	238
Tunisia	25/4/76	L265/78 p. 1	238
Yemen	9/10/84	L26/85 p. 1	113/235
Gulf Co-operation Council	15/6/88	L54/3 p. 1	113/235

The Americas

Canada	6/7/76	L260/76 p. 1	113/235
Brazil	18/9/80	L281/82 p. 1	113/235
Mexico	15/7/75	L247/75 p. 10	113/114
Uruguay	2/4/73	L333/73 p. 1	113/114
Andean Group (Venezuela, Colombia, Peru, Bolivia, Ecuador)	17/12/83	L153/84 p. 1	113/235
Centramerica (Costa Rica, El Salvador, Guatemala, Honduras, Nicaragua, Panama)	12/11/85	L172/86 p. 1	113/235

Asia and ACP

Bangladesh	19/10/76	L319/76 p. 1	113/114
India	23/6/81	L328/81 p. 5	113/235
Pakistan	23/7/85	C81/85 p. 3	113/235
Sri Lanka	22/7/75	L247/75 p. 1	113/114
ASEAN (Indonesia, Malaysia, Philippines, Singapore, Thailand, Brunei)	7/3/80	L144/80 p. 1	113/235
ACP (Lomé III)	8/12/84	L86/86 p. 1	238

---

[1] Excluding: ECSC agreements; fisheries, technological, environmental and services agreements; textiles and agricultural product agreements; enlargement protocols.

[2] The ACP states which signed the Third Lomé Convention are: Antigua and Barbuda, Bahamas, Barbados, Belize, Benin, Botswana, Burkina Faso, Burundi, Cameroon, Cape Verde, Central African Republic, Chad, Comoros, Congo, Djibouti, Dominica, Equatorial Guinea, Ethiopia, Fiji, Gabon, Gambia, Ghana, Grenada, Guinea, Guinea-Bissau, Guyana, Ivory Coast, Jamaica, Kenya, Kiribati, Lesotho, Liberia, Madagascar, Malawi, Mali, Mauritania, Mauritius, Mozambique, Niger, Nigeria, Papua New Guinea, Rwanda, Saint Christopher and Nevis, Saint Lucia, Saint Vincent and the Grenadines, Samoa, Sao Tome and Principe, Senegal, Seychelles, Sierra Leone, Solomon Islands, Somalia, Sudan, Suriname, Swaziland, Tanzania, Togo, Tonga, Trinidad and Tobago, Tuvalu, Uganda, Vanuatu, Zaire, Zambia and Zimbabwe.

Source: Bureau des Traités (Commission, 1988).

Appendix 6.5   Some agricultural data

I   Main characteristics

	Eur. 12		Highest		Lowest	
	1980	1986	1980	1986	1980	1986
Share of agriculture in employed civilian working population (%)	8.8	8.3	Greece 27.0	28.5	UK 2.3	2.6
Utilised agricultural area per holding (ha)[1]	12.5	8.9	UK 64.5	65.1	Gr 3.6	Gr/Port 4.3
Share of agriculture in GDP (%)	3.7	3.5	Greece 16.5	16.6	UK 2.1	1.8
External trade balance in food and agricultural products 1986 (million ECUs)	−23,997		Denmark +1,078		UK −5,560	

[1] Cf. Canada 1981: 145 ha.

II   Some trade statistics

(a) Community trade in agricultural products (000 million ECUs)

Year	Imports from non-member countries	Exports to non-member countries	Intra-Community trade
1973	24.0	7.4	15.5
1975	25.4	9.5	20.8
1980	42.2	19.6	35.8
1981	45.2	26.4	41.4
1982	48.3	25.9	47.6
1983	50.7	26.8	50.7
1984	58.6	31.7	57.1

(b) Percentage increase of Community imports from main non-member countries (1973–84)

Industrialised countries:	+116%
Developing countries:	+194%
State trading countries:	+185%

(c) Pattern of imports of food and other agricultural products (Eur. 10)

	1973	1975	1980	1984
Value (000 million ECUs)	24.0	25.4	42.2	58.6
Breakdown (%):				
Industrialised countries	49.0	48.3	48.2	43.7
Developing countries	40.7	42.6	44.1	49.0
State trading countries	10.3	9.1	7.7	7.3

Source: The Common Agricultural Policy and its Reform (OOP, 1987), p. 38.

(d) Market shares and trade balances

	1973	1980	1985	1986
Eur. 12 share of world agriculture exports (%)	9.5	11.5	12.1	12.3
Eur. 12 excess of agricultural imports over exports (%)	11.6	34.0	20.6	22.6

Source: 'The agricultural situation in the Community', 1987 Report (OOP).

III Productivity

(a) Yields of some of the main products in the Community of Ten 1970–84

	1970	1975	1980	1984
Cereals (excl. rice) (100 kg/ha)	34.4	38.8	47.6	58.1
Sugarbeet (100 kg/ha)	410.1	411.3	471.4	515.8
Wine and must (Hl/ha)	60.04	51.51	59.54	59.41
Milk (kg/cow/year)	3,648	3,708	4,186	4,242

Source: The Common Agricultural Policy and its Reform (OOP, 1987), p. 64

(b) Degree of self-sufficiency (percentage share of internal production in total consumption; figures in excess of 100% indicate a surplus). *Source*: Commission of the EC, *A Community of Twelve: Key figures*(OOP, 1989), p. 25.

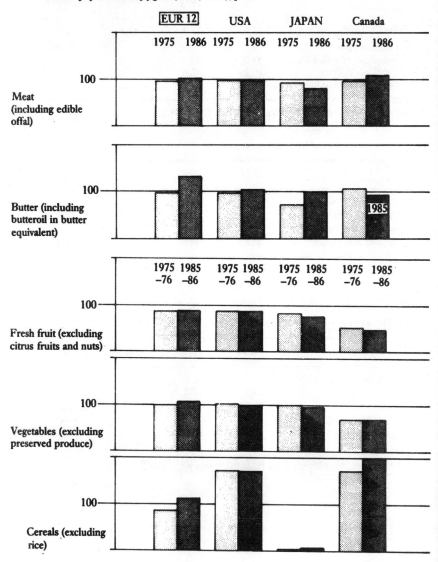

IV   Prices

(a) International food consumer prices 1985 (Eur. 12 = 100)

USA	124.0
Japan	155.6
Canada	115.5
Australia	85.3
Austria	118.8

Source: 'The agricultural situation in the Community', 1987 Report (OOP), p. 34

(b) Trend of food and all-item consumer prices index

	1973–79 (ave.)	1979–81 (ave.)	1982
Consumer Prices	+11.3	+12.5	+11
Agricultural Prices	+ 8.4	+ 8.8	+11.2

Source: *National Policies and Agricultural Trade* (OECD, 1987).

V   Budgetary costs of the CAP

(a) Expenditure under the Common Agricultural Policy (million ECUs)

	1983[1]	1984[1]	1985[1]	1986[2]	1987[2]
EAGGF Guarantee section	15,811.6	18,346.5	19,744.2	22,137.4	22,988.5
EAGGF Guidance section (payments)	728.0	676.2	719.6	773.5	847.1
Total gross expenditure	16,539.6	19,022.7	20,463.8	22,910.9	23,835.6
Ordinary levies	1,347.1	1,259.9	1,121.7	1,175.5	1,763.9
Sugar levies	948.0	1,176.4	1,057.4	1,111.5	1,438.6
Total net expenditure	14,244.5	16,586.4	18,284.7	20,623.9	20,633.1

Source: 'The agricultural situation in the Community', 1987 Report (OOP), p. 95.
Notes:
[1] Eur. 10
[2] Eur. 12.

VI   Farm income

(a) Development of farm incomes per person (Eur. 10) (100 = average 1979/1980/1981)

Year	Net value added per person	Year	Net value added per person
1975	103	1981	99
1976	105	1982	109
1977	104	1983	104
1978	107	1984	109
1979	107	1985	103
1980	97	1986	104

Source: 'The agricultural situation in the Community', 1987 Report (OOP), p. 49.

(b) EAGGF Guarantee expenditure by member state (million ECUs)

	Total	B	Dk	D	Gr	Sp	F	Irl	I	L	Nl	P	UK
Eur. 10													
1982	12,405.6	355	559	2,030	685	–	2,869	500	2,507	3	1,425	–	1,286
Eur. 12													
1986	22,137.4	979	1,066	4,401	1,387	241	5,447	1,214	3,069	2	2,277	31	1,987
Share (%)	–	4.4	4.8	19.9	6.3	1.2	24.6	5.5	13.9	–	10.3	–	9.0

Source: Court of Auditors.

Appendix 6.6   Data banks

The Commission has set up a number of data banks which give statistical information as well as information about Community legislation in several policy fields. The list of data banks to which access is possible is extended from time to time. Information about the data banks is available from the Commission's local offices.

Agrep: Inventory of agricultural research projects in the European Community.

Celex: Inter-institutional data base for Community law.

Comext: Data base of external trade statistics for the Community and its member states.

Cronos: Data base of macroeconomic time series for the member states and major partners.

EABS:* Documents published in connection with scientific and technical research.

Ecdin: Environmental chemicals data and information networks – chemicals reacting with the environment.

Endoc:* List of environmental information and documentation centres in the member states of the Community.

Euristote:* List of university theses and projects on the various aspects of European integration.

Enrep:* Environmental research projects in the European Communities.

Eurodicautom:* Terminology data bank.

Dianeguide:* Summary of data bases offered by Euronet-Diane.

FSSRS: Statistical data base giving the results of a regular survey of the structure of agricultural holdings.

Pabli: Progress of Community development operations.

Regio: Statistical data base showing the social and economic situation of the various regions of the European Community.

SCAD: Central computerized documentation service – List of official Community publications, acts adopted by the institutions other than those which are valid for a limited period only, and articles selected from over 1,200 periodicals in co-operation with Parliament's documentation service.

TED: Tenders electronic daily. This contains the invitations to tender published in the 'S' supplement to the *Official Journal*.

* Access free of charge.

Appendix 6.7 Economic and monetary union: key texts

I Communiqué issued by the Heads of State or of Government of the Countries of the enlarged Community at their meeting in Paris on the 19th and 20th October 1972. Cmnd 5109

The Heads of State or of Government reaffirm the determination of the Member States of the enlarged European Communities irreversibly to achieve the economic and monetary Union, confirming all the elements of the instruments adopted by the Council and by the representatives of Member States on 22nd March 1971, and 21st March 1972.

The necessary decisions should be taken in the course of 1973 so as to allow the transition to the second stage of the economic and monetary Union on 1st January 1974 and with a view to its completion not later than 31st December 1980.

The Heads of State and Government reffirmed the principle of parallel progress in the different fields of the economic and monetary Union.

II Preamble to the Single European Act 1986

Whereas at their Conference in Paris from 19 to 21 October 1972 the Heads of State or of Government approved the objective of the progressive realization of Economic and Monetary Union . . .

III European Council, Hanover, 27–8 June 1988: Presidency Conclusions (extract)

The European Council recalls that, in adopting the Single Act, the Member States confirmed the objective of progressive realization of Economic and Monetary Union.

They therefore decided to examine at the European Council meeting in Madrid in June 1989 the means of achieving this Union.

To that end they decided to entrust to a Committee the task of studying and proposing concrete stages leading towards this Union.

The Committee will be chaired by Mr Jacques Delors, President of the European Commission.

Notes

1. The exclusive competence of the Commission to speak for the Community is not contested, but de Clercq, External Relations Commissioner and a former minister of the Belgian Government, remarked in 1988 that when there is a GATT ministerial meeting it would be too much to expect the trade ministers of EC member states (which formally remain GATT contracting parties) to be silent.
2. For the other side of the coin – the prospective effect on UK wage costs of CAP price levels – see D. Jay, *After the Common Market* (London, Penguin, 1968).
3. A national market organisation for potatoes exists in Britain (in 1988).
4. By the autumn of 1988, following the rise in world prices and shortages after the protracted North American drought, Community stocks had been heavily drawn down, at relatively low cost.
5. The CFP negotiations of 1977 gave rise to the only occasion on which the UK practised the 'empty chair' by declining to attend a Council meeting held in Berlin, on the grounds that the UK was being unfairly treated in contemporaneous agricultural negotiations.
6. The European Community's *Transport Policy Periodical*, 3/84, OOP, p. 21.
7. The Vredeling proposal is memorable for the vast amount of counter-lobbying which it provoked when the European Parliament came to deliver an opinion on it.
8. 'Powers of investigation in the enforcement of competition law', *OOP Periodical* 1985, p. 33.
9. Giving rise to the first Monetary Compensation Amounts.
10. Communiqué of the Conference of the Heads of State and Government of the European Community's Member States, 2 December 1969, The Hague, *Bulletin of the European Communities*, 1–1970, pp. 11–18.
11. This has led to the proposition that there are now three European systems: the Communities, Political Co-operation and the Monetary System.
12. The worked out example given on p. 50 of *The Economy of the European Community* (OOP, 1984) is:

The divergence threshold for a currency with a weighting in the ECU of 20% is reached when it deviates from the ECU central rate by

$$\frac{2.25 \times (100 - 20) \times 0.75}{100} = 1.35\%$$

13. See *Leading Europe into the 90s*, Conservative Central Office, May 1989, pp. 34–5.
14. Especially by the shock-wave sent out by the publication in the USA in 1962 of Rachel Carson's book, *The Silent Spring*.
15. *Official Journal* references: C112, 20 December 1973; C139, 13 June 1977; C46, 17 February 1983; C328, 7 December 1987.

16. Lawnmower noise is a sensitive subject. In many Belgian communes it is an offence to use garden power-tools on a Sunday or public holiday.
17. *Thirty-Third Review of the Council's Work* (OOP, 1985), p. 71.
18. Various organisations are keeping a tally of Single Act progress. A handy guide is prepared by the British Chamber of Commerce for Belgium and Luxembourg, Brussels. The Department of Trade and Industry in conjunction with Profile Information has a data base called Spearhead. Access is via, for example, Celex and Telecom Gold. The European Parliament publishes checklists in its Action Taken series (Directorate General for Research).

7

Conclusion

On European union

The European Community can, if its decision takers so wish, continue as the Treaty of Rome stipulates towards 'an ever closer union among the peoples of Europe' (Preamble, first line). This could be considered to give effect to 'making concrete progress towards European Unity' (Single European Act, Article 1, first paragraph). Its members can, as the Single European Act says in the first paragraph of its preamble, 'continue the work . . . to transform relations as a whole among their States into a European Union'. This is not a new commitment and it was not new when it was undertaken in Stuttgart in 1983. The inclusion of it in the Single Act in February 1986 was a recommitment.[1]

European union is an expression without precise significance unless the user defines it with some care, as Leo Tindemans did in his 1975 report, or as the European Parliament did in its Draft Treaty of European Union.[2] Otherwise, as the European Court of Justice observed in 1975, 'it is not yet clear what the expression imports'.[3] In October 1988 the European Parliament could still complain that the Council's Annual Report on Economic Union was singularly uninformative.[4]

The exact constitutional and institutional structures of a European union are a matter of choice and of negotiation if Europe is going down that road. There is also a choice not to go such a road, but rather to give priority, over a lengthy period, to completing and cementing the Communities, Political Co-operation, other intergovernmental co-operation of the Twelve and 'another Europe' in which some or all of the Twelve, with or without the Community, develop co-operation of different kinds with third countries. All this could arguably be called further European integration.

A reading of the series of papers and reports which appeared in the first half of the 1970s concerning European union[5] might almost suggest that what was then being far-sightedly suggested as the stuff of 'European union' is not too far from what is today programmed to be the European Community of the 1990s: a directly elected Parliament participating in legislation; a European Council making light of distinctions between Community action and member states' co-operation; a form of European political co-operation with a treaty base; a European Monetary System which makes for exchange rate stability and uses a monetary instrument (also used privately to measure value, less as a means of exchange); a Council where a good number of decisions are taken by qualified majority vote; a Commission whose president is appointed after consultation with the European Parliament; and a market which is so truly common as to be single.

Meanwhile, however, time has moved on and the terms of the discussion have changed. In late 1988 the discussion re-opened on what the destination is to be. Debate is handicapped by the emotion excited by words like 'supranational' (usually with sympathetic vibrations), 'super-state' (usually pejorative),[6] 'sovereignty' (positive) and 'nationalism' (negative). If the debate were without emotion it would be so much the poorer. It is, after all, about how and by whom people want to be governed. Wars have been fought for less.

A European Union which was a new state would, it is to be supposed, do what a twentieth-century state does, which means that whatever its structure – and 'federal' and 'confederal' are words which unfortunately are not rigorously defined either – there would be a unitary principle somewhere in it. To clarify the starting point of a debate which this chapter will certainly not conclude, it is useful to reflect on the boundary conditions which might distinguish a future European Union from the 1993 model European Community.

The first consideration has to be constitutional, although constitutions are not ends in themselves: under what structure of government does the citizen participate in the decisions which are taken in his or her name? Most of the discussion turns on the future relationship between different political forces, those mediated by:

- the unanimous or majority tendencies and actions of the governments of the member states of the Union, represented by and accountable to their national electorates;

- the majority view of the European Parliament whose members are also accountable to their voters at five-year intervals;
- the collegial advocacy and the authority of the Commission, however appointed, and to whomever it is answerable.

The member states are not at all responsible to the directly elected European Parliament; and the Council has not gone very far down the road of submitting itself to European parliamentary control. Another way of saying the same thing is that the Council, holding the Community's legislative power, has not wanted to share much of that power with the Parliament. There is only the tiny germ of a true bicameral system in Parliament's final decision – within constraints – on the level of non-compulsory expenditure in the budget, and in the assent procedure for Article 238 agreements and for new members under Article 237. The European Parliament has also acquired some influence, but no veto, over legislation.

In a more fully developed structure it is empirically unusual and perhaps organically unnatural for the lower house (for example, a future European Parliament) to be the revising chamber which pronounces on bills normally originating in a higher chamber (for example, a Council of the European Union). The House of the People (that is, the European Parliament) would want a larger share of the power than this kind of projection would allow. In order to exercise it, it would need a continuity of purpose which cannot easily be secured by the fluctuating alliances within the present European parliamentary parties as at present constituted. Since a plurality seems unlikely, and proportional representation is not conducive to it, a reasonably stable coalition with an ideological base would be needed. The House of the People, and the whole system, may also need an executive to propose the programme and see it through. This gives colour to the idea that at least the chief executive's should be an elective post.[7]

The second minimal distinguishing attribute of European union is that it should practise economic management in regard to the level of employment, prices and growth. Although central, the management need not be centralised – there could be a lot of devolution. But a central, unitary management of the economy, and one in which the factors of production can circulate freely, gives rise or emphasis to the problem of regional disparity. Conditions are not everywhere equal: there are areas of prosperity and areas of deprivation. Unless some steps are taken to provide for redistribution of wealth, the use of resources will be allocative – drawn towards the geographical areas which offer the best prospects. This allocative principle, unless tempered, will incite opposition to integration from those who are not favoured by it. Thus the MacDougall Report:

The [pre-federal] Community's economic policies are assumed to include intervention in some industries as well as structural and redistribution policies designed to bring about a greater convergence of economic performance and fortunes between Member States and regions – in the absence of which further integration of any fundamental kind would be unattainable.[8]

This is not a one-off operation – the balance between allocative and redistributive decision making has to be maintained. For as MacDougall also pointed out, unless the Community budget becomes much larger there is no automatic off-set for a fall in a region's external sales via lower tax and insurance payments to the centre and via the regional receipt of higher social security benefits (p. 12). In the same order of ideas the authors of *Efficiency, Stability and Equity*, the Padoa-Schioppa Report commissioned by President Delors in 1987 (OUP), considered that 'in a larger and more differentiated Community redistributive functions performed through the budget and the lending instruments of the Community should be considerably developed in size and made more effective in their purpose and design' (p. x). On this Delors commented, 'Is it sufficient to increase the redistributive capacity of the Community budget or must we look at the quality of the transfers themselves, at their real economic effectiveness?' (Preface, p. vi). In other words, allocative decisions seem also to be needed within the redistributive functions.

The MacDougall Report attempted an estimate of the resources necessary to have a significant redistributive effect: the *Ausgleich*, to use the Federal German concept. The benchmark is that up to 1992 1.2 per cent of GNP will be available to the Community budget for all purposes. (It was 0.7 per cent when the MacDougall Report was written.) The MacDougall Report thought that in a small public sector federation central expenditure would need to be about 5–7 per cent of GNP, plus 2.5–3 per cent of GNP if defence expenditure became a federal responsibility (p. 20).

A third distinguishing feature or boundary condition of European union is an economic and monetary policy, even an economic and monetary union. This too is not new: neither is it so old as to be obsolete. At the meeting of the European Council in Hanover in June 1988, the participants recalled that 'in adopting the Single Act the Member States confirmed the objective of progressive realisation of Economic and Monetary Union' (Conclusions, Section 5, 'Monetary Union'). On this, however, the Padoa-Schioppa Report, like the MacDougall Report a decade before, is cautious. MacDougall:

If only because the Community budget is so relatively very small there is no such [automatic redistributing] mechanism in operation on any significant scale as between Member countries, and this is an important reason why in present circumstances, monetary union is impracticable. (p. 12)

Padoa-Schioppa:

While recognising that a monetary union has several first-best properties from an economic point of view the Group does not advocate a precipitous move in this direction. There would have to be further adaptation of attitudes among private agents (employers and trade unions) as well as of political attitudes for monetary union to be a sufficiently low-risk proposition. (p. 10)

The Hanover meeting of the European Council was also cautious. It appointed a committee under the chairmanship of Delors to study and propose the concrete stages leading towards this (monetary) union, and asked for the report to be available at the European Council's meeting in Madrid in June 1989.[9]

The functions of an economic and monetary union would include:

- Decisions on public spending priorities, of the kind finally settled in the UK by the 'Star Chamber' procedure. This implies a large consensus on objectives, or the acceptance of leadership in their selection. The union need not be responsible for anything like all public expenditure but it needs to be able to influence a large part of it in order to avoid those regional disparities which would contradict the *Ausgleich* and distort other decisions.

- The creation or reduction of credit; the management of inflation, including its regional variation; the maintenance, or otherwise, of planned exchange rates between the currency unit which the union uses in its national accounting and (if they continue to exist) national currencies.[10] Even in a deregulated economy all these decisions will influence the volume and location of investment, including inward investment, the condition of the labour market, economic growth and the end-division of added value.

The division of added value again implies a consensus or an acceptance of leadership in social policy, in fields usually thought to be of the closest interest to voters. This puts the union, as the EEC's first president said of it, squarely in the business of politics.

The exchange rate/single currency proposition bristles with problems. If a variable interregional exchange rate disappears, apart from the cushion of transport costs, regional prices cannot rise and high-cost regional production cannot compete. Some US sages accept that it is then the factors of production which must move and they compare the rigidity of the labour market in Europe with internal US emigration. The contemporary equivalents of the Okies of the thirties are the blue-collar workers in their campers moving to where the work is. But it is a different proposition for Europeans – even those who, in Norman Tebbit's memorable phrase, 'get on their bikes' – to move to an area where the language, education, social values and cultural and recreational possibilities are completely different, and where they may become an ethnic minority of the kind with which they may already have had friction at home. If there is no exchange rate variation to cushion, however expensively and temporarily, corporate and personal earnings, the redistributive function will have to take more of the strain to prevent disinvestment, job loss and enforced emigration towards reception areas which are likely to be congested and socially difficult. Perceived adverse effects could lead to political disenchantment with the Union.

In fact, while much effort has been expended on measuring the cost of the benefits of the single market, with an overall positive judgement, the economic and welfare case for European union has not been presented with the same thoroughness; and there is the chicken-and-egg problem of knowing what kind of European union to measure.

A fourth minimum attribute of a European Union would be the common foreign policy of which Leo Tindemans spoke. The Union would need it practically and psychologically, to feel itself as a single whole in its dealings with the world outside. In its fully developed form, the foreign policy of the Union would be unitary and, as in existing models, centralised: there cannot be separate foreign policies for different parts of the territory of the Union, and in order to be valid international interlocutors the Union's representatives and negotiators must be able to commit the Union, subject always to whatever are the Union's internal rules of ratification of international agreements – which could involve a parliamentary stage. This is, however, a long way from Single European Act political co-operation. The jump is even further if defence and military security are regarded as essential components of a foreign policy. In his 1975 report, Tindemans declared that as long as the European Union has no common defence policy it remains incomplete.[11] For the immediate future, however, he was careful to go not much further than 'exchange of views' and co-operative arms procurement. The member states have so far eschewed the latter and gone some way, with careful footwork, on the former. But national thinking remains strong: in Denmark where a formula concerning the non-admission of nuclear weapons into Danish waters provoked (at least partly) the 1988 summer elections, or in France where the President of the Republic reaffirmed on 11 October 1988 that 'we are part of an alliance . . . but the decision to be taken is ours alone . . . ours is a strategy of independent nuclear deterrence',[12] or in Ireland which upholds its non-membership of military alliances. For the time being it does not look as if the possible candidates for membership of the Union will go beyond being 'Ready to coordinate their positions more closely on the political and economic aspects of security' (Single European Act, Article 30(6)(a)).

In an anecdote, Tindemans showed the *realpolitik* of January 1987. He recalled (*Europa zonder Kampas*, p. 80) that Jacques Delors had suggested that the heads of government should hold a special meeting to compose a reply to President Gorbachev's proposals on disarmament. Several member states told him that they would refuse an invitation to attend any such meeting. Further, at the Conference of Member States in December 1985, the military aspects of security policy had been specifically excluded from Political Co-operation. Again, only eleven of the member states belong to NATO and only five of them had accepted the positioning of Euro-missiles: UK, Italy, the Federal Republic of Germany, Belgium and the Netherlands. Others had refused. France was a special case. One member state had participated in discussions with other countries about nuclear-free zones in Europe. How then could there be a common view on the opening stages of the negotiations between Washington and Moscow?

The underlying notion of this section – that there can be a passage from Community to Union 'when the time is right' – may even be fatally flawed, especially in the British setting:

When broad questions are asked some 70 per cent of the UK respondents are in favour of the general idea of European unity, but they do not link that concept specifically to the European Community and its particular institutions. Once specific questions are asked about the European Community and its institutions that goodwill vanishes. There is a distinction between the European Community and the general idea of European cooperation.[13]

The European destination is still unknown.

A question of perspective

The issue of European union illustrates the importance of perspective in any attempt to assess the significance of the European Communities in their current form and stage of development, and in assessing whether that form and stage are merely a phase in *Europe: Journey to an Unknown Destination*,[14] or whether that journey has already come to an end. Perspective is also crucial in any assessment of what has already been achieved on that journey.

There have always been sceptics as to the practicality of attempting or making the journey, and those sceptics have not been confined to the United Kingdom. In the late 1940s, for example, Sean Lemass, who was later responsible for the Irish application in 1961, still had 'doubts as to the practability of maintaining a permanent organization for European cooperation'.[15] Even in the late 1950s British sceptics still believed that the new European Economic Community, which came to life in 1958, was a mere flash in the pan, it being perceived that it would not last long especially, but not only, because of the lack of British participation. If it were to survive it was felt that it would probably be in a watered-down form, reverting to a general free trade agreement arrangement, as had been and was being discussed in the OEEC, and with central institutions being bereft of real power and authority, rather like the Council of Europe by that time. In 1958 no one knew quite what to expect and, as seen earlier, some expected Euratom to be significant. The negotiations leading to the two Treaties of Rome had been difficult, with success being by no means guaranteed. At several points during the negotiations, and indeed during the preceding decade since the halcyon days at The Hague in 1948, the entire journey could have been derailed, the entire enterprise scuttled. There was no inevitability about the destination or the smoothness of the journey, then, later or now.

It is thus important to record the fact that some thirty years later the Communities still exist and from some perspectives flourish. The company making the journey has expanded, from the original six to nine in 1973, to ten in 1981, and to twelve in 1986. The company now encompasses some 322 million people, a greater population than that of either the United States (237 million) or the Soviet Union (275 million). It comprises the world's largest trading unit, having some 18 per cent of world trade compared to the 17 per cent of the United States and the 9 per cent of Japan. Indeed, if intra-Community trade is included, the share of world trade involving the Twelve approaches some 40 per cent. More than 130 states have diplomatic relations with the Community as such, while some 120 or so agreements relating to trade, aid and economic co-operation have been signed between the Community and other states. In addition, the Community participates in some thirty multilateral agreements.[16]

The Community has clearly become a pole of attraction to others, a phenomenon that has become more pronounced with the onset of the single internal market in 1992. As shown in Chapter 1, that prospect has stirred several European non-members into re-evaluating their position. Sweden and Austria, for example, have begun to wonder whether neutrality is the insurmountable obstacle they previously affirmed, whilst the Norwegians have begun to re-examine the arguments of 1972 Community as a fact of life and to come to terms with that reality. However, events in 1989 have completely opened up the question of the nature of their relations with the Community, and, indeed, the future institutional relationships which might exist in Europe as a whole.

A hundred, even fifty years ago, it would have been inconceivable that twelve European and sixty-six African, Caribbean and Pacific (ACP) states would freely and voluntarily sign trade and aid agreements such as Lomé. It would have been impossible to conceive of twelve fractious, blooded European states, including France, Germany and Britain, taking a common position in harmony at a multilateral conference on Co-operation and Security in Europe (CSCE); these same states now, on a range of issues, voting in common at international forums like the United Nations, with one of their number regularly speaking on behalf of all and negotiating for all; moreover, these same states allowing a Commission to take their place and speak on their behalf in the General Agreement on Tariffs and Trade (GATT) and elsewhere, the group speaking with one voice in many trade and commodity negotiations. Although many have been disappointed that there has not been greater cohesiveness among the company on the journey, more evidence of common, united action and purpose, that Europe's potential to play a world role has been hindered by its fissile tendencies and lack of agreement on the formation of a common foreign and security policy, such considerations ought not to obscure what progress has been made in travelling forward, not only in terms of a voice in the world but in a range of other matters as well.

It may be that it is difficult to find examples of federations of states which had existed for any length of time or in any real sense as independent, sovereign states, but the Community exists and is, perhaps, a greater advance towards international co-operation and integration on a voluntary basis by states than has ever been seen before. The Community is different from the purely intergovernmental institutions of the late nineteenth and early twentieth centuries in which member states refused 'to accept any formal limitation on their sovereignty, insisting on the maintenance of a national veto.'[17] In those first practical steps towards the creation of permanently existing international organisations, co-operation was limited to collaboration among independent, sovereign states and the powers of institutions were heavily circumscribed. The states remained as distinct entities, and indeed were intended to remain as such, the objective of organisations being to help those states perform their roles better, not to portend or imply the withering away of the state. The states were subject to no superior authority or law, and domestic law was solely the preserve of the organs of the state, especially the government. Whilst the new organisations had 'secretariats', they were literally that: a group for taking notes, preparing meetings in a formal sense and recording the decisions of others. Those secretariats did not take decisions.

In late twentieth-century Europe the situation is very different. The philosophical ideas of Sully, Penn, Simon and Cattaneo discussed in Chapter 1 have been transformed into living institutions and systems. The role of at least one secretariat has been transformed. Now the European Commission's permission is required before a state can derogate from its obligations under Community law. States are no longer free to decide for themselves whether special problems or circumstances entitle them to suspend or deviate from their obligations to others. On 18 May 1982 further evidence was provided of how different is the Community: while states have allowed themselves to be outvoted on occasion, much to their chagrin the British were outvoted by seven of their partners on a matter upon which the British claimed the veto applied.[18] While the shock of May 1982 has not produced the traumas it might have, being something of an aberration, the key point is that a member state, in this case Britain, was put in the position of having to accept that to which it was resolutely opposed. In the Community system, all the member states have found themselves, at one time or another, circumscribed in their behaviour. This is a revolutionary change in the conduct of international politics in international institutions.

States have always had their freedom of decision and action constrained by the limitations on their own power set by the power of others, but the institutionalised and legitimised way in which this occurs in the Community system is rather different and new. It suggests that it is perhaps possible to talk of the evolution of a supranational authority, albeit that the full force of supranationalism has not been achieved. The Community is beginning to shape up to the requirements of supranationalism, namely that 'a supranational organization is one which (a) bypasses the nation-state's authority and deals directly with the citizen; which (b) takes over some functions traditionally exercised by the nation-state; and (c) is in the position to originate decisions not only on behalf of the State but despite it'.[19] As compared to the mid-1960s when this definition was proposed, progress has been made on all three dimensions. It must be noted that the Community can only operate within its spheres of competence and that (a) and (b) do not mean it has replaced the state. In fact it is (c), however, which has remained the most problematical, and of course it remains the case that, despite the 1982 aberration, states retain the *de facto*, if not the *de jure*, power to exercise a veto over a wide range of issues, and that little can be done over their strong objection. Notwithstanding this, whatever their intentions and behaviour, in the Single European Act the member states have again committed themselves to an expansion of qualified majority voting, and the areas where a *de jure* veto power remains have been narrowed, now involving fundamental, constitutional-type questions within the Community, such as enlargement, any redistribution of power among the institutions and any move into new, unchartered areas of policy.

Furthermore, although states can still in practice stop decisions, policies and agreements being reached, they have found it all but impossible to go back on decisions and policies previously introduced. In other words, governments are now constrained in their decision making and, apart from retaining the unilateral right to abrogate their commitments and membership, states are no longer sovereign in the traditional sense. J.D.B. Mitchell observed that 'already by 1973, the Treaty of Rome had become a constitution having its effects within the internal law of the whole Community and having consequentially effects . . . on the constitutional situation and internal law of each' of the member states.[20] As noted in Chapter 2, certain decisions are 'directly applicable', as is made clear in Article 189 of the EEC Treaty. Moreover, in addition to the ENEL case referred to earlier, other cases such as the seminal *Van Gend en Loos* and *Simmenthal* have clearly established that Community law does enjoy primacy over national law.[21] Community law now pervades much of the legal systems of the twelve member states and is, therefore, part of the environment of every court. Furthermore, given the treaty – the legal position regarding qualified majority voting – some Community institutions can enjoy primacy, in some cases, over national governments. This position was hardly imaginable to many a generation ago. Although there remains the practical legacy of the 1965–6 crisis, any comparison with the extent of collaboration and co-operation in the period before the formation of the Communities is striking and significant. To some extent, albeit on a minor scale, the Community can now make the 'authoritative allocation of values', in Easton's memorable phrase, within the various national societies which go to make up the Community.[22]

Also striking is the creation, existence and evolution of the European Parliament. Whatever the debate about its precise powers and functions (Chapters 2 and 3), it is a novel feature of the international environment that millions of citizens from twelve states should vote for their directly elected representatives to a European Parliament, some 110 million voting in 1979 and 115 million in 1984. Whilst the turnouts of 61–2 per cent may have disappointed those with lingering 1940s aspirations, that should not divert attention from the significance of such elections being held for such a body in the first place. That turnout, incidentally, was higher than the turnout in recent US presidential elections. Without becoming whimsical, the symbolic coming together of 518 MEPs from twelve states ought not to be underestimated, especially given their ability to question the actions (and inaction) of governments, to thwart the will of governments over some aspects of the budget, and, under the Single European Act, to be awkward about the passage of Community legislation. Too often the focus is upon the constraints the Parliament faces, its limitations, at the expense of any appreciation of what an innovative, far-reaching experiment it has proved to be, and how unique it remains.

As well as these institutional changes, the Community has transformed relationships between its member states, and it has transmogrified the environment in which those relationships occur. Leading up to the Franco-Prussian War of 1870 there was no international organisation in existence for promoting a peaceful settlement of international disputes or for providing a mechanism for such settlement between these or any states. Similarly, there was no organisation or mechanism capable of stopping the second and third conflicts in 1914 and 1939. Between 1870 and 1945 millions had died because of conflict between the French and their neighbours to the east, yet on 9 May 1950

Robert Schuman, the French Foreign Minister, could talk of the contribution that an organised and living Europe could bring to civilisation by maintaining peace. He and Monnet, who submitted the plan to him, tackled that central problem of Franco-German relations, specifically advocating the *rassemblement* of the nations of Europe and, crucially, 'the elimination of the age-old opposition of France and Germany. Any action taken must in the first place concern these two countries.' Of course, Schuman also went on to say that by establishing solidarity of production of coal and steel it is plain that 'any war between France and Germany becomes not merely unthinkable, but materially impossible'.[23] That central aim has now been achieved, at least with respect to the greater part of Germany.

Whilst critics might argue that the Community has done little to contribute to the avoidance of a truly 'European' war, its contribution in the Franco-German area should not be gainsaid. Similarly, although it has not solved all the problems existing between Dublin, Belfast and London, common membership of the Community does provide potentially a mechanism whereby old sores can be circumvented, with old bilateral battles being subsumed by the Community process. The impact of the Community may make the border less of an issue in the future. In other words, several parts of the Community which have been violently opposed to each other for decades have been brought into a new pattern and environment of relationships.

In considering the question of perspective, it is perhaps worth recalling the motivations underlying the moves for European unity after the war, in addition to the central Franco-German issue. Those promoting a vision of a united Europe were concerned firstly about the repair of material destruction, economic recovery and growth. The advocates of a fundamental change were preoccupied with both immediate and long-term concerns. The latter focused on war prevention, on how to bring traditionally warring powers actively together in a new relationship. The former focused on the immediate necessity for action given that continental Europe was a 'charnel-house' – that is, a vault of dead bones.[24] Half a century on it is easy to gloss over the situation in Europe in May 1945, but Richard Mayne has provided a salutary and grim picture of the reality:

In the cities, the skyline was jagged with destruction: amid the ruins and craters, rubble and wreckage blocked the streets . . . machinery rusted in the bombed-out factories . . . Roads were pitted with shell-holes . . . Much of the countryside was charred and blackened . . . in some areas, unchecked by peasant bows and arrows, herds of wild pigs roamed the land for forage.

Yet amid the destruction there were people . . . Sheds on weekend vegetable plots became houses; cellars and caves were turned into houses . . . The survivors . . . for them, this wasteland of rubble, rags and hunger was a prison without privacy or dignity; and like all prisons it smelled . . . of sweat and vomit, dirty socks and excrement; of decay and burning and the unburied dead.[25]

Beyond doubt the Communities have contributed significantly to the socioeconomic transformation of Europe, so that today the 322 million citizens of the Twelve enjoy a very high standard of living relative to the rest of the world, with a gross domestic product per capita which is some 270 per cent of the world average, and with high levels of personal utility consumption and acquisition, levels which trail only North America, Japan and Scandinavia. As already noted, the Community is an economic giant, and its citizens (in general) are the inheritors of and the participants in 'the affluent society'. This has brought other benefits too, such as a transformation in life expectancy levels.

The second concern of those promoting a united Europe was for military defence against the Soviet Union and protection from American economic strength. Here the record is rather more mixed. More than a generation after the Western Europeans turned quaking to the United States for support in the late 1940s, over 300,000 American military personnel are still in Europe. There remains little doubt that, despite the British and French strategic nuclear systems, most people in Western Europe feel that the Community states, individually or even collectively, could do little to resist a Soviet attack, and that the British and French strategic systems are not sufficient to deter a conventional attack in Europe. In this sense Europe remains fundamentally reliant upon the American nuclear commitment at strategic, theatre and tactical levels as part of NATO's doctrine of flexible response and as an element of the coupling of Europe and America. This coupling is still widely perceived as necessary, especially given the apparent continuing preponderance of Soviet conventional forces.

In this sense the European states are really in no better position than they were a generation ago, being unable to provide for a basic prerequisite of their citizens' needs – security. On the other hand, as against the expectations of many a generation ago, Western Europe has been neither swamped nor intimidated by the Soviet Union. Moreover, not only has there been the development of the British and French nuclear systems, but with economic recovery Europeans generally have also begun to make a greater contribution to their own defence. In the late 1980s, 90 per cent of the manpower, 95 per cent of the divisions, 85 per cent of the tanks, 95 per cent of the artillery and 80 per cent of the combat aircraft stationed in Europe are provided by the Europeans, as are 70 per cent of the ships in European waters and the Atlantic.[26]

None the less, security has remained a difficult issue for the Twelve, as we have seen in Chapter 4. That chapter also indicated signs of an evolving European identity on security and defence issues, partly because of disenchantment with the quality of American leadership and partly because of an awareness of particular European interests and perspectives on major issues. The danger is real, however, that this identity may find its expression in non-Community forums, like a reinvigorated Western European Union (WEU), or the Independent European Programme Group (IEPG), or the informal Eurogroup within NATO, thus exacerbating the problems identified by Robert Goebbels of Luxembourg (Chapter 2). There are clear signs of this with regard to the attempt to breathe new life into the WEU. It has, for example, enlarged to include Spain and Portugal and in October 1987 it issued 'The common platform on European security interests' which *inter alia* declared: 'We remain determined to pursue European integration including security and defence and to make a more effective contribution to the common defence of the West.'[27]

If not swamped by the Soviets, then neither have the Europeans been suffocated by the economic embrace of the Americans, despite occasional alarms that they might. As late as 1967 J.J. Servan-Schreiber in *Le Défi Americain*[28] expressed concern at the danger of American technological and economic penetration, concerns that returned in the 1980s, for example, in connection with the British debate over American or European solutions to the Westland helicopter problem.

There have, of course, been problems in the relationship with the United States, such problems surfacing periodically in 'chicken wars', disputes over the European contribution to a gas pipeline for the Soviets, and hormone-injected meat. The main problem has been American concern at the perceived protectionist nature of much Community activity, especially with regard to the Common Agricultural Policy, coupled with divergences over security questions. More than a decade ago, President Nixon drew attention to the potential for serious dispute: 'can the principle of Atlantic unity in defence and security be reconciled with the European Community's increasingly regional economic policies?'[29] The question remains of whether the crises in the transatlantic relationship are transient, as they have been in the past, or whether a structural change is beginning to take place as the USA becomes more concerned about its other, Pacific, shore.

The problem for the Europeans is how far they can assert their cohesion, their identity, without damaging their relations with third parties, and without, in particular, weakening the American commitment to protect them. It may, however, be counted as a success that West Europeans still face that dilemma some forty years after the signing of the North Atlantic Treaty. Europeans have not succumbed to the alternatives of either total estrangement from the United States or subservience to it.

The vision of a united Europe was thirdly inspired by concern for a role in the world. The problem of relations with the United States will remain of vital importance to Europeans and the objective clearly is not to become divorced from the Atlantic partnership since that would be counterproductive in terms of security and anathema to the majority of European opinion. The objective is rather to evolve a European identity, through European Political Co-operation (as discussed in Chapter 4) so as to become more equal partners with the United States – as both Kennedy and Monnet envisaged in 1962, Monnet calling for a 'relationship of two separate but equally powerful entities, each bearing its share of common responsibilities in the world'.[30] Again, perspective is important since, whilst that symmetry in position has not been achieved, it is clear that the asymmetry has been reduced.

As was seen in Chapter 4, Europe was once the cauldron of international relations but it has had to adjust to the loss of empires and the movement of truly global power to two extra-European superpowers. Stutteringly, Europeans have tried to adapt to the new realities and to begin to establish a new role for themselves, albeit on a smaller scale than before. EPC has been a significant element in this development and even more important has been the Community's impact through its external relations activities, as shown in Chapters 4 and 6. Again, despite all the tensions, it is increasingly possible to identify the emergence of a particular European view and contribution. Whilst the citizens of Europe focus on centrifugal predispositions of the Twelve, states outside the Community are struck by its strength, its relative cohesion, and its centripetal tendencies. Whilst it still has far to go to become a 'superpower in the making',[31] it is becoming increasingly less accurate to regard the Community as an economic giant but a political dwarf.

A fourth ingredient was a belief in Europe and the European ideal. This clearly relates to much of the foregoing, but in general terms it might be regarded as the one area where the ratchet effect has failed to work – instead of there being evidence of general advance, despite occasional slippage, with respect to the European ideal, the process seems to have been one of gradual, if not steady, decline. In terms of the hearts and minds of many of its citizens, the imperatives, the faith, the *cri de coeur* underlying the European ideal have been somewhat dimmed. The belief in the construction of a new Europe involving a new pattern of political relationships, as an experiment, has been distorted as the economic instruments identified to achieve political change and objectives have gradually become regarded as more important than the objectives themselves. The means are in danger of consuming the ends. The fact that the true nature of the European Community cannot be understood simply by focusing on the provisions of the founding treaties has been obscured. As the cohort who lived through the ravages of war, despair and destruction died, it was replaced by a new generation of citizens and adults which was brought up to focus on the economic dimension of the Community. In the 1970s, however, the sheen went off the economic miracle as progress ran into the wall of OPEC price increases and world recession. Given this, the shortcomings of the Community appear only too apparent to the new generations of Europeans.

Indeed, when considering perspective, the shortcomings are also apparent if the current situation is compared to the aspirations of the founding fathers. Their motivation was not the price of eggs, bacon or steel but rather a revolution in international behaviour. When some resistance groups met in Geneva in 1944 they talked of the need 'to go beyond the dogma of absolute sovereignty of the state and unite in a single federal organization',[32] while at the Congress of Europe at The Hague in 1948 resolutions referred to 'the urgent duty of the nations of Europe to create an economic and political union in order to assure security and social progress'.[33] Schuman in May 1950 saw his proposals on coal and steel as 'a first step in the federation of Europe'.[34] As against such passionate appeals, it can be argued that states have been reluctant to 'transfer and merge some portion of their sovereign rights' as demanded at The Hague,[35] and sceptics can also argue that despite elections there has been little real movement towards European union or federation. It can further be argued that the member states appear to have reverted back to intergovernmentalism to some extent and have at regular intervals shied away from any transfer of power with regard to crucial decisions. But again perspective is important, for as has been shown 'some portion' of sovereignty and 'some portion' of the freedom to take decisions have been transferred, and whatever the limitations unique direct elections have been held.

It may be that to some extent the Community has become a victim of its own success, that as it has partially, or in some cases fully, achieved some of its basic objectives, particularly in the economic sphere, many have begun to feel that the need for radical solutions has passed, that a somewhat patched-up system of states could suffice, that the Community has achieved enough to satisfy its members – that is, they know that the current stage of development is not the optimal solution to Europe's problems and needs, but to many it is reasonably satisfactory and 'good enough'. The economic rejuvenation of post-war Europe has lessened the perceived need to continue with political rejuvenation, with some such as the British perceiving no linkage between the two at all. With economic recovery since 1945 and a return to political stability and peace have come the renewed arrogance of national political systems and some desire to restore as much autarky as is possible in an interdependent world.

One is reminded of the distinction between a pessimist and an optimist: the pessimist sees a glass as half empty, but the optimist sees it as half full. That may be a somewhat trite analogy but it is important not to become too preoccupied with the declining glamour, euphoria and bezazz of the Community idea. It can be demonstrated that compared to the 1880s and 1890s, to the 1920s and 1930s, or even to the 1940s much progress has been achieved, that the glass is becoming full. The Community states have achieved a degree of interdependence that would be difficult and economically costly to unravel. The notion of a 'European reflex' does not apply only to EPC as whole sectors of national governmental activity have acquired a European dimension and different domestic departments are forced to ensure that their initiatives and decisions are compatible with Community policy. Individual societies and states have discovered that there is no going back, that whilst not necessarily enamoured with the Community the alternatives are much less attractive, a fact accepted reluctantly by the British Labour Party in the 1980s (as shown in Chapter 5) and more positively by the Danes and the Irish in their referendums on the Single European Act.

Schuman and Monnet who launched the Communities were aware, as Schuman put it in his seminal speech of May 1950, that 'Europe will not be made all at once, or according to a single plan. It will be built through concrete achievements which first create a *de facto* solidarity', that his own proposal was 'the first concrete foundation of a European federation indispensable to the preservation of peace'.[36] It is possible to be too impatient with respect to the progress of the foundations of the new Europe, but it has clearly been demonstrated in the preceding chapters that a number of foundation stones have been laid, that a *de facto* solidarity is being created. Further such steps are being laid daily as the Community conducts its business in a routine fashion. Other steps are more than routine, of course, such as the progress towards the objective of creating a single 'common' market, an objective dating back to the 1950s, reaffirmed in 1985, and proposed for fruition by December 1992, or at least in the 1990s. At this time according to the Single European Act will be created 'an area without internal frontiers in which the free movement of goods, persons, services and capital is ensured in accordance with the provisions of this Treaty'. Since that time, progress has been made.

One final point on perspective, a point highlighted by the Single European Act and the focus on a single common market, is that it must always be borne in mind that the Community experiment does involve that element of 'journey to an unknown destination', and does encompass more than a common market, a mere economic arrangement. As Walter Hallstein, the first president of the EEC Commission, once said, 'We are not in business at all; we are in politics',[37] a point reiterated by one of Britain's first Commissioners during the 1975 referendum campaign when George Thomson emphasised that the Community 'wasn't to make capitalism more efficient. It was to make war unthinkable.'[38] The very word 'community' is symbolic of the nature of the endeavour. European construction is not solely about economic transactions or a single integrated market but about the future nature of the political relations between states and peoples.

Where the Community stands today, then, depends very much upon the perspective used. If one compares the situation as the Community enters the 1990s with the aspirations of the founding fathers much remains to be done, but let it not be forgotten that there is another perspective, namely that of 1870, 1914 and 1939. The fundamental rationale remains:

They shall beat their swords into plowshares, and their spears into pruning hooks: nation shall not lift up sword against nation, neither shall they learn war any more.

Notes

1. The pamphlet put out by the anti-market National Referendum Campaign (1975) opened with the affirmation:

   > For the British people, membership of the Common Market has been a bad bargain. What is worse, it sets out by stages to merge Britain with France, Germany, Italy and other countries into a single nation. This will take away from us the right to rule ourselves which we have enjoyed for centuries.

   An early and lapidary account of the Conservative Government's views on European union was given by Douglas Hurd in 1981 when in the British Presidency and as a Foreign and Commonwealth Office minister he was responsible, among other things, for relations with the European Parliament (1981):

   > Union is not a commitment to a federal system or to the progressive erosion of national sovereignty.
   >   In our view, 'union' amounts to the development of an ever-closer framework of cooperation between the sovereign states of the Community in all areas where this cooperation can be shown to be useful. It does not entail . . . the creation of any new institutions or increase in the formal powers of existing ones. (Quoted in G. Clark, *Your Parliament in Europe*, UK Information Office of European Parliament, 1984, p. 33).

2. Report on European Union by Leo Tindemans, December 1975, *Bulletin Supplement*, 1/76; *A New Phase in European Union* (European Parliament, May 1985).
3. Suggestions of the Court of Justice on European Union, *Bulletin Supplement*, 9/75, p. 17.
4. Planas Resolution, 27 October 1988, Point 1.
5. Apart from Tindeman's report see Attainment of the Economic and Monetary Union, *Bulletin Supplement*, 5/73; Commission, Report on European Union, *Bulletin Supplement*, 5/75.
6. 'No more than the existing Communities have done so, European Union is not to give birth to a centralising super-state', Commission, Report on European Union, op. cit., p. 10, para. 12.
7. For a discussion of possible institutional structures see Commission, Report on European Union, op. cit., p. 30, paras 95–111. More recently there have been proposals that a 'President of Europe' should be elected.
8. On 4 October 1988 Lord Cockfield, Vice-President of the Commission said, 'The developments I have described . . . stake out the path that leads to the single European currency . . . the provocative terms European Central Bank and single currency have been avoided in view of the sensitivities of certain Member States. But no one need have any doubt about what is intended or where we are going (*The Times*).
9. *Report of the Study Group on the Role of Public Finance in European Integration* (OOP, 1977), p. 20.
10. In its 1974 paper, already quoted, the Commission said, 'the ultimate objective should be for monetary resources to be an exclusive field of competence of the Union, just as the common customs tariff is already' (p. 17, para. 36). According to Padoa-Schioppa: 'In the monetary area it is necessary to move towards a European central banking system with considerably enhanced policy coordination and executive responsibilities' (p. 13).

11. In his tantalisingly discreet account of his activities in the Belgian Presidency of 1987, *Europa zonder Kampas*, at present available only in Dutch (Antwerp, Standard Uitgeverij, 1987), Tindemans reaffirms this view.

12. *Le Monde*, 13 October 1988.

13. Secretary-General of Gallup International, which carries out 'Eurobarometer' surveys for the Commission, quoted in the *Independent*, 10 October 1988.

14. Andrew Shonfield, *Europe: Journey to an Unknown Destination* (Harmondsworth, Penguin, 1973).

15. Sean Lemass, *Dáil Éireann Debates*, Vol. CXI, Cols 2003 ff (1948).

16. See *The European Community and the Third World*, European File 15/87 (October 1987); *The European Community in the World*, European File 16/88 (October 1988).

17. Carole Webb, 'Theoretical perspectives and problems', in H. Wallace, W. Wallace and C. Webb (eds), *Policy-Making in the European Community* (Chichester, John Wiley, 1983) 2nd edn, p. 22.

18. See Chapters 1 and 5.

19. Nina Heathcote, 'The crisis of European supranationality', *Journal of Common Market Studies*, Vol. 5, No. 2 (1966–7), p. 141.

20. J.D.B. Mitchell, 'The sovereignty of Parliament and Community law: the stumbling-block that isn't there', *International Affairs*, Vol. 55, No. 1 (January 1979), pp. 34–5.

21. Ibid., pp. 33–46.

22. David Easton, *A Framework of Political Analysis* (Chicago, University of Chicago Press, 1965), Ch. 4.

23. Robert Schuman, 9 May 1950, *Keesing's Contemporary Archives*, Vol. 7 (1948–50) (Keynsham, Keesing's, 1950), pp. 10701–2.

24. Roger Morgan, *West European Politics since 1945* (London, Batsford, 1972), p. 1.

25. Richard Mayne, *The Recovery of Europe* (London, Weidenfeld and Nicolson, 1970) pp. 29–30.

26. Eurogroup, *Western Defense: The Eurogroup Role in NATO*.

27. Communiqué issued after ministerial meeting, Western European Union, 27 October 1987.

28. J.-J. Servan-Schreiber, *Le Défi Americain*, published as *The American Challenge* (Harmondsworth, Penguin, 1969).

29. Speech in Chicago, 15 March 1973.

30. Action Committee for the United States of Europe, 26 June 1962, Michael Palmer, John Lambert *et al.*, *European Unity* (London, Allen and Unwin for PEP, 1968), p. 142.

31. Johan Galtung, *The European Community: A Superpower in the Making* (London, Allen and Unwin, 1973).

32. Uwe Kitzinger, *The European Common Market and Community* (London, Routledge and Kegan Paul, 1967), pp. 29–33.

33. Richard Vaughan, *Post-War Integration in Europe* (London, Edward Arnold, 1976), pp. 35–7.

34. Schuman, op. cit.

35. Vaughan, op. cit., pp. 35–7.

36. Schuman, op. cit.

37. Walter Hallstein, President of the Commission.

38. George Thomson, *Guardian*, 30 May 1975.

Select Bibliography

The following is a selection of published books and articles useful for further reading.

Chapter 1   The construction of Europe

Adenauer, Konrad, *Memoirs 1945–53*, London, Weidenfeld and Nicolson, 1966.
Bond, Brian, *War and Society in Europe 1870–1970*, London, Fontana, 1984.
Brown, George, *In My Way*, Harmondsworth, Penguin, 1972.
Brugmans, H. (ed.), *Europe: Dream, Adventure, Reality*, Brussels, Elsevier, 1987.
Butler, David and Kitzinger, Uwe, *The 1975 Referendum*, London, Macmillan, 1976.
Butler, Michael, *Europe: More than a Continent*, London, Heinemann, 1986.
Callaghan, J., *Time and Chance*, London, Collins, 1987.
Camps, Miriam, *Britain and the European Community 1955–1963*, Oxford, Oxford University Press, 1964.
Camps, Miriam, *European Unification in the Sixties*, Oxford, Oxford University Press, 1967.
de Gaulle, Charles, *Memoirs of Hope*, London, Weidenfeld and Nicolson, 1971.
de Ruyt, J. *L'acte unique européen*, Brussels, Éditions de l'Université Bruxelles, 1987.
Eden, Anthony, *Full Circle*, London, Cassell, 1960.
Fisher, H.A.L., *A History of Europe*, London, Edward Arnold, 1938.
Fondation Paul-Henri Spaak, *Pour une communauté politique européenne*, Brussels, Bruylat, 1984.
Gerbet, Pierre, *La construction de l'Europe*, Paris, Imprimerie nationale, 1983.
Hallstein, Walter, *Die europäische Gemeinschaft*, Dusseldorf, ESCM, 1974.
Hodges, Michael (ed.), *European Integration*, Harmondsworth, Penguin, 1972.
Hoggart, Richard and Johnson, Douglas, *An Idea of Europe*, London, Chatto and Windus, 1987.
Huizinga, J.H. *Mr Europe: A Political Biography of Paul-Henri Spaak*, London, Weidenfeld and Nicolson, 1961.

Jay, Douglas, *Change and Fortune*, London, Hutchinson, 1980.
Joll, James (ed.), *Britain and Europe: Pitt to Churchill 1793–1940*, London, Adam and Charles Black, 1961.
Jouve, Eduard, *Le Général de Gaulle et la construction de l'Europe 1940–1966*, vol. I, Paris, Librairie Générale de Droit et de Jurisprudence, 1967.
Kennedy, Paul, *The Rise and Fall of the Great Powers*, London, Unwin Hyman, 1988.
Kitzinger, Uwe, *Diplomacy and Persuasion*, London, Thames and Hudson, 1973.
Kroebel, Gerhard *et al.*, *European Integration: From the European Idea to the European Economic Community*, 3rd edn, Dusseldorf, German Trade Union Federation, 1963.
Mackay, R.W., *Towards a United States of Europe: An Analysis of Britain's Role in European Union*, London, Hutchinson, 1961.
Macmillan, Harold, *Tides of Fortune 1945–55*, London, Macmillan, 1969.
Mayne, Richard, *The Community of Euorope*, London, Victor Gollancz, 1963.
Medlicott, W.N., *British Foreign Policy since Versailles*, London, Methuen, 1968.
Miljan, Toivo, *The Reluctant Europeans: The Attitudes of the Nordic Countries towards European Integration*, London, Hurst, 1977.
Milward, A.S., *The Reconstruction of Western Europe 1945–51*, London, Methuen, 1987.
Monnet, Jean, *Memoires*, 2 vols, Paris, Fayard, 1969.
Nicolson, Frances and East, Roger, *From the Six to the Twelve*, Harlow, Longman, 1987.
Nicolson, Nigel (ed.), *Harold Nicolson: The War Years 1939–45: Diaries and Letters Vol. II*, London, William Collins, 1967.
Pinder, John and Pryce, Roy, *Europe after de Gaulle*, Harmondsworth, Penguin, 1969.
Pollard, Sidney, *European Economic Integration 1815–1970*, London, Thames and Hudson, 1974.
Saunders, Christopher, *From Free Trade to Integration in Western Europe?* London, Chatham House/PEP, 1975.
Schoutheete, Philippe de, *La coopération politique Européene*, Brussels, Editions Labor, 1986.
Shonfield, Andrew, *Europe: Journey to an Unknown Destination*, Harmondsworth, Penguin, 1973.
Slany, William (ed.), *Foreign Relations of the United States 1955–57: Vol. IV Western European Security and Integration*, Washington DC, US Government Printing Office, 1986.
Spaak, Paul-Henri, *Combats Inachevés*, Paris, Fayward, 1969.
Spanier, David, *Europe our Europe*, London, Secker and Warburg, 1972.
Tugendhat, Christopher, *Making Sense of Europe*, Harmondsworth, Viking, 1986.
Uri, Pierre (ed.), *From Commonwealth to Common Market*, Harmondsworth, Penguin, 1968.
Vaughan, Richard, *Postwar Integration in Europe*, London, Edward Arnold, 1976.

Von der Groeben, Hans, *The European Community: The Formative Years*, Luxembourg, Office for Official Publications of the European Communities, 1987.

Wilson, Harold, *The Labour Government 1964–1970*, London, Weidenfeld and Nicolson, and Michael Joseph, 1971.

Wilson, Harold, *The Final Term: The Labour Government 1974–76*, London, Weidenfeld and Nicolson, and Michael Joseph, 1979.

Commission of the European Communities, *Steps to European Unity 1980*; *European Unification 1987*; Luxembourg, Office for Official Publications of the European Communities.

European Parliament, *Selection of Texts concerning Institutional Matters of the Community from 1950 to 1982*, Luxembourg, European Parliament, 1982.

In the series 'Que sais-je', Paris, Presses Universitaires de France: Deniau, Jean Francois, *Le marche commun*; Masclet, Jean-Claude, *L'union politique de l'Europe*; Barbam, Jean-Louis, *Le conseil de l'Europe*; Bathalay, Bernard, *Le fédéralisme*.

Chapter 2   The institutions at work

Bieber, Roland *et al.* (eds), *An Ever-Closer Union: A Critical Analysis of the Draft Treaty Establishing the European Union*, Brussels, European Perspective Series, 1985.

Budd, Stanley A., *The EEC: A Guide to the Maze*, 2nd edn, Edinburgh, Kogan Page, 1987.

Bulmer, Simon and Wessels, Wolfgang, *The European Council*, London, Macmillan, 1987.

Capotorti, Francesco *et al.*, *The European Union Treaty: Commentary on the Draft Adopted by the European Parliament*, Oxford, Clarendon Press, 1986.

Cocks, Barnett, *The European Parliament*, London, HMSO, 1973.

Council of Europe, *The Protection of Human Rights in Europe*, Strasbourg, The Council of Europe, 1987.

de Ruyt, J. *L'acte unique européen*, Brussels, Editions de l'Université Bruxelles, 1987.

Drew, John, *Doing Business in the European Community*, Sevenoaks, Butterworth, 1983.

Edwards, G. and Wallace, H., *The Council of Ministers of the European Community and the President-in-Office*, London, Federal Trust, 1977.

European Commission, *The Court of Justice of the European Community*, Luxembourg, Office for Official Publications of the European Communities, 1986.

European Commission, *The ABC of Community Law*, Luxembourg, Office for Official Publications of the European Communities, 1986.

Henig, S., *Power and Decision in Europe*, London, Europotentials Press, 1980.

Jackson, R. and Fitzmaurice, J., *The European Parliament*, Harmondsworth, Penguin, 1979.

Jackson, Robert, *The Powers of the European Parliament*, Conservative Group for Europe, 1979.

Lasok, D. and Bridge, J.W., *Law and Institutions of the European Communities*, 4th edn, Sevenoaks, Butterworth, 1987.

Lodge, Juliet (ed.), *Institutions and Policies of the European Community*, London, Frances Pinter, 1983.

Mathijsen, P.S.R.F., *A Guide to Community Law*, London, Sweet and Maxwell, 1972.

Metcalf, L. and Zapiconi, Goni, *Action or Reaction? The Role of National Administrations in European Policy Making*, London, Sage Publications, 1988.

Noel, E., *Working Together*, Luxembourg, Office for Official Publications of the European Communities, 1977.

Nugent, Neill, *Government and Politics of the European Community*, London, Macmillan, 1989.

O'Nuallian, Colm (ed.), *Presidency of the European Council of Ministers*, London, Croom Helm, 1985.

Palmer, M., *The European Parliament*, Oxford, Pergamon, 1981.

Rogers, W. (ed.), *Government and Industry*, revised edn, Chapter 6, London, Kluwer, 1986.

Seiler, Daniel, *Les parties politiques en Europe*, Paris, Presse Universitaire de France, Que sais-je?, 1978.

Wallace, Helen, *The Presidency of the Council of Ministers of the European Community: Tasks and Evolution.* Maastricht, European Institute of Public Administration, 1983.

Wallace, H., Wallace, Wm. and Webb, C. *Policy-Making in the European Communities*, Chichester, John Wiley, 1977 (1st edn), 1983 (2nd edn).

Walsh, A.E. and Paxton, J., *Into Europe*, London, Hutchinson, 1972.

Usher, John, *European Community Law and National Law: The Irreversible Transfer?* London, UACES, 1981.

Chapter 3   The Communities' budget

European Commission, *The Community Budget in Facts and Figures*, 1988 edn, Luxembourg, Office for Official Publications of the European Communities.

Foreign and Commonwealth Office, *The Budget Problem*, London, HMSO, 1982.

House of Commons Session 1987–88, Fifth Report, European Community Finance, 358.

House of Lords, Select Committee on the European Communities:
Community Budget 1986–87, HMSO, HL239;
Court of Auditors, HMSO, HL102.

Le Pertz, Yves, *Investing in Europe's Future*, Oxford, Blackwell, 1988.

Nicoll, W., 'The battles of the European budget', *Journal of the Policy Studies Institute*, Vol. 5, Part 1 (July 1984).

Nicoll, W., 'The budget of the European Community in 1984', *Journal of European Integration*, Vol. 8, Nos. 2–3. (Canada) (1985).

Nicoll, W., 'From rejection to repudiation: EC budgetary affairs in 1985', *Journal of Common Market Studies*, Vol. 25, No. 1 (September 1986).

Nicoll, W., 'EEC budgetary strains and constraints', *International Affairs*, Vol. 64, No. 1 (Winter 1987/88).

Nicoll, W., 'L'accord interinstitutionnel sur la discipline budgétaire et l'amélioration de la procédure budgetaire', *Révue du Marché Commun*, No. 319, (July/August 1988), pp. 373–80.

Nicoll, W., 'The long march of the 1988 budget', *Journal of Common Market Studies*, Vol. 27, No. 2 (December 1988).

Notenboom, Harry, *Het Europees parlement en de financien*, The Hague, SDU Uitgeverij, 1988.

Padoa Schioppa *et al.*, *Efficiency, Stability and Equity*, Chapter 9, Oxford, Oxford University Press, 1987.

Shaw, M., *The European Parliament and the Community Budget*, European Conservative Group, 1978.

Spaventa, L. *et al.*, *The Future of Community Finance*, Centre for European Policy Studies, 1986.

Strasser, D., *Finances of Europe*, 2nd edn, Luxembourg, Office for Official Publications of the European Communities, 1981 (the 5th edn, in French only, was published by Nathan/Labor in 1984).

Chapter 4   European political co-operation

Allen, D., and Pijpers, A. (eds), *European Foreign Policy Making and the Arab–Israeli Conflict*, The Hague, Nijhoff, 1985.

Allen, D., Rummel, R. and Wessels, W. (eds), *European Political Cooperation*, London, Butterworth, 1982.

De Vree, J.K., *et al.* (eds), *Towards a European Foreign Policy: Legal, Economic and Political Dimensions*, The Hague, Nijhoff, 1987.

European University Institute: European Policy Unit, *European Political Cooperation Documentation Bulletin 1985*, Florence, European University.

European Parliament: Political Affairs Committee:
Report on European Political Cooperation, Rapporteur: Mr Erik Blummenfeld PE Doc. 427/77;
Report on European Political Cooperation and the Role of the European Parliament, Rapporteur: Lady Elles PE Doc. 1–335/81;
Report on European Political Cooperation and European Security, Rapporteur: Mr N. Haagerup PE Doc. 1–946/82.

Feld, W. *The European Community in World Affairs*, Boulder, Colo., Westview Press, 1983.

Galtung, J. *The European Community: A Superpower in the Making*, 2nd edn, London, Allen and Unwin, 1981.

Hill, C. (ed.), *National Foreign Policies and European Political Cooperation*, London, Allen and Unwin, 1983.

Hill, C., 'Changing gear in political cooperation', *Political Quarterly*, Vol. 53 (1982).

Hill, C. and Wallace, W., 'Diplomatic trends in the European Community', *International Affairs*, Vol. 55, No. 1 (January 1979).

Holland, Martin, *The European Community and South Africa: European Political Cooperation under Strain*, London, Frances Pinter, 1988.

Hurd, D., 'Political cooperation', *International Affairs*, Vol. 57, No. 1 (January 1981).

Ifestos, P., *European Political Cooperation: Towards a Framework of Supranational Diplomacy*, Aldershot, Gower, 1987.

James, A., *Sovereign Statehood: The Basis of an International Society*, London, Allen and Unwin, 1986.

Jordan, R. and Feld, W., *European Political Cooperation in Europe in the Balance: The Changing Context of European International Politics*, London, Faber, 1986.

Luard, Evan, 'A European foreign policy', *International Affairs*, Vol. 62, No. 4 (Autumn 1986).

Morgan, Roger, *High Politics, Low Politics: Towards a Foreign Policy for Western Europe*, Washington Papers No. 11, London, Sage Publications, 1973.

Morgenthau, H., *Politics Among Nations*, New York, Knopf, 1973.

Schoutheete, Philippe de, *La cooperation politique Européene*, Brussels, Editions Labor, 1986.

Taylor, P., 'The European Communities as an actor in international society', *Journal of European Integration*, Vol. 6, No. 1 (1982).

Taylor, T. *European Defence Co-operation*, London, RIIA, 1984.

Wallace, H., Wallace, Wm. and Webb, C. *Policy-Making in the European Communities*, Chichester, John Wiley, 1977 (1st edn), 1983 (2nd edn).

Wallace, Wm. and Paterson, W. (eds), *Foreign Policy Making in Western Europe*, Farnborough, Saxon House, 1978.

Wallace, W. and Hill, C. (eds), *National Foreign Policies and European Cooperation*, London, Allen and Unwin, 1983.

Chapter 5   The Political Background in the United Kingdom

Bullock, Alan, *Ernest Bevin: Foreign Secretary 1945–51*, Oxford, Oxford University Press, 1985.

Burgess, Simon and Edwards, Geoffrey, 'The Six Plus One – British policy-making and the question of European economic integration, 1955', *International Affairs*, Vol. 64, No. 3 (Summer 1988).

Butler, David and Kitzinger, Uwe, *The 1975 Referendum*, London, Macmillan, 1976.

Camps, Miriam, *Britain and the European Community 1955–63*, Oxford, Oxford University Press, 1964.

Camps, Miriam, *European Unification in the Sixties*, Oxford, Oxford University Press, 1967.

Evans, Douglas (ed.), *Britain in the EEC*, London, Gollancz, 1973.

Evans, Douglas, *While Britain Slept: The Selling of the Common Market*, London, Gollancz, 1975.

Frankel, Joseph, *British Foreign Policy 1945–73*, London, Oxford University Press, 1975.

George, Stephen, *The British Government and the European Community since 1984*, London, UACES Occasional Papers No. 4, 1987.

Goodhart, Philip, *Full-Hearted Consent: The Story of the Referendum Campaign and the Campaign for the Referendum*, London, Davis-Poynter, 1976.

Gregory, F., *Dilemmas of Government: Britain and the European Community*, Oxford, Martin Robertson, 1983.

Howe, G., 'The future of the European Community: Britain's approach to negotiations', *International Affairs*, Vol. 60, No. 2 (Spring 1984).

Jenkins, R., *Britain and the EEC*, London, Macmillan, 1983.

Jenkins, R. 'Britain and Europe: Ten years of Community membership', *International Affairs*, Vol. 59, No. 2 (Spring 1983).

Jowell, Roger and Hoinville, Gerald, *Britain into Europe: Public Opinion and the EEC 1961–75*, London, Croom Helm, 1976.

Judge, David, 'The British Government, European union and institutional reform', *Political Quarterly*, Vol. 57 (July/September 1986).

Judge, David, 'The House of Commons and the completion of the internal market', *Parliamentary Affairs*, Vol. 41, No. 4 (October 1988).

Kennedy, Paul, *The Realities Behind Diplomacy: Background Influences on British External Policy 1965–1980*, London, Fontana, 1981.

King, A., *Britain Says 'Yes': The 1975 Referendum on the Common Market*, Washington DC, American Enterprise Institute for Public Policy, c. 1977.

Kitzinger, Uwe, *Diplomacy and Persuasion: How Britain Joined the Common Market*, London, Thames and Hudson, 1973.

Leifer, M. (ed.), *Constraints and Adjustments in British Foreign Policy*, London, Allen and Unwin, 1972.

Mackay, R.W.G., *Towards a United States of Europe: An Analysis of Britain's Role in European Union*, London, Hutchinson, 1961.

Macmillan, H., *Pointing the Way 1959–61*, London, Macmillan, 1972.

Macmillan, H., *At the End of the Day 1961–63*, London, Macmillan, 1973.

Melissen, J. and Zeeman, B., 'Britain and Western Europe, 1945–51: opportunities lost?', *International Affairs*, Vol. 63, No. 1 (Winter 1986/87).

Moon, J., *European Integration in British Politics 1950–1963*, Aldershot, Gower, 1985.

Northedge, F.S., *Descent from Power: British Foreign Policy 1945–73*, London, Allen and Unwin, 1974.

de la Serre, Francoise, *La Grande-Bretagne et la communauté Européenne*, Paris, Presse Universitaire de France, 1987.

Shlaim, A., *Britian and the Origins of European Unity 1945–51*, Reading, Reading University Press, 1978.

Swift, W., *Great Britain and the Common Market 1957–1969*, New York, Facts on File, 1970.

Tugendhat, C., *Making Sense of Europe*, Harmondsworth, Viking, 1986.

Wallace, H. 'The British presidency of the EC Council of Ministers: the opportunity to persuade', *International Affairs*, Vol. 62, No. 4 (Autumn 1986).

Wallace, Wm, *The Foreign Policy Process in Britain*, London, Allen and Unwin for the RIIA, 1976.

Wallace, Wm, *Britain in Europe*, London, Heinemann, 1980.

Wallace, Wm, 'What price independence? Sovereignty and interdependence in British politics', *International Affairs*, Vol. 62, No. 3 (Summer 1986).

Wilson, Harold, *The Labour Government 1964–70*, London, Weidenfeld and Nicolson, and Michael Joseph, 1971.

Wilson, Harold, *The Final Term: The Labour Government 1974–76*, London, Weidenfeld and Nicolson, and Michael Joseph, 1979.

Young, Simon, *Terms of Entry: Britain's Negotiations with the European Community 1970–1972*, London, Heinemann, 1973.

Chapter 6   The policies of the Community

Common Agricultural Policy

'The agricultural situation in the Community', *Annual Reports*, Luxembourg, Office for Official Publications of the European Communities.

Commission of the EC, *The Common Agricultural Policy and its Reform*, Luxembourg, Office for Official Publications of the European Communities, 1987.

Commission of the EC, 'Reflections on the CAP', *Bulletin of the EC*, Supplement 6/80, Luxembourg, Office for Official Publications of the European Communities.

Duchêne, F., Szczepanik, E. and Legg, Wm., *New Limits on European Agriculture: Politics and the Common Agricultural Policy*, Totowa, Rowman and Allan held, 1985.

Hill, Brian, *The Common Agricultural Policy: Past, Present and Future*, London, Methuen, 1984.

Tracy, Michael, *Agriculture in Western Europe*, London, Granada, 1982.

Common Commercial Policy

Hine, R.C., *The Political Economy of European Trade: An Introduction to the Trade Policies of the EEC*, Hemel Hempstead, Harvester/Wheatsheaf, 1989.

Vignes, D. and Dewost, J.L., *Organisations européennes et Vie Internationale*, Societé Francaise pour le Droit International, Éditions Pedane, 1982.

Wellenstein, E., *25 Years of European External Relations*, Luxembourg, Office for Official Publications of the European Communities, 1979.

Common Fisheries Policy

Leigh, Michael, *European Integration and the Common Fisheries Policy*, London, Croom Helm, 1983.

Wise, Mark, *The Common Fisheries Policy of the European Community*, London, Methuen, 1984.

Common Transport Policy

Commission of the European Communities, *The European Community's Transport Policy*, 2nd edn, Luxembourg, Office for Official Publications of the European Communities, 1984.

Erdmenger, Jürgen, *Vers une politique des transport pour l'Europe*, Brussels, Editions Labor, 1984.

Economic policy

Commission of the European Communities, *The Economy of the European Community*, Luxembourg, Office for Official Publications of the European Communities, 1984.

Commission of the European Communities, *The European Monetary System*, Luxembourg, Office for Official Publications of the European Communities, 1986.

Commission of the European Communities, *A European Financial Area: The Liberalisation of Capital Movements*, Luxembourg, Office for Official Publications of the European Communities, 1988.

Commission of the European Communities, *Completing the Internal Market*, Luxembourg, Office for Official Publications of the European Communities, 1988.

El-Agraa, A.M., *The Economics of the European Community*, 2nd edn, Deddington, Philip Allan, 1985.

Cairncross, A. *et al.*, *Economic Policy of the European Community*, London, Macmillan, 1974.

de Grauwe, P. and Peeters, T., *The ECU and European Monetary Integration*, London, Macmillan, for Catholic University of Leuven, 1989.

Dosser, D., Gowland, D. and Hartley, K., (eds), *The Collaboration of Nations: A Study of European Economic Policy*, Oxford, Martin Robertson, 1982.

Giavazzi, F., Micossi, S. and Miller, M. (eds), *The European Monetary System*, Cambridge, Cambridge University Press, 1988.

Guerrieri, P. and Padvan, P.C., *The Political Economy of European Integration*, Hemel Hempstead, Wheatsheaf, 1989.

Harrop, J., *The Political Economy of Integration in the European Community*, Aldershot, Edward Elgar, 1989.

Hitiris, T., *European Community Economics*, Hemel Hempstead, Harvester Wheatsheaf, 1989.

Journal of Common Market Studies, *The European Monetary System: Special Issue*, Vol. 27, No. 3 (March 1989).

Ludlow, P., *The Making of the European Monetary System*, Sevenoaks, Butterworth, 1982.

Masera, R. and Triffin, R. (eds), *Europe's Money: Problems of European Monetary Coordination and Integration*, Oxford, Clarendon Press, 1984.

Owen, R. and Dynes, M., *The Times Guide to 1992*, London, Times Books, 1989.

Pelkmans, J. and Winters, A., with Wallace, H., *Europe's Domestic Market*, London, Routledge and Kegan Paul for RIIA, 1988.

Puchala, D., *Fiscal Harmonization in the European Communities*, London, Frances Pinter, 1984.

Readman, P. *et al.*, *The European Monetary Puzzle*, London, Michael Joseph, 1973.

Robson, P., *The Economics of International Integration*, 3rd edn, London, Allen and Unwin, 1987.

Swann, D., *The Economics of the Common Market*, 5th edn, Harmondsworth, Pelican, 1984.

Energy

Gasteyger, C. (ed.), *The Future for European Energy Security*, London, Frances Pinter, 1985.

Lucas, N.J.D., *Energy and the European Communities*, London, Europa, 1977.

Environment

Johnson, S. and Courcelle, G., *L'autre Europe 'verte': La politique communautaire de l'environment*, Brussels, Editions Labor, 1987.

Regional Policy

Armstrong, H.W., 'The reform of the European Community regional policy', *Journal of Common Market Studies*, Vol. 23, No. 4 (June 1985).

Croxford, C.J., Wise, M. and Chalkley, B.S., 'The reform of the European Regional Development Fund: a preliminary assessment', *Journal of Common Market Studies*, Vol. 26, No. 1 (September 1987).

Yuill, D., Allen, K. and Hull, C., (eds), *Regional Policy in the European Community*, London, Croom Helm, 1980.

Social Policy

Collins, Doreen, *The European Communities: The Social Policy of the First Phase, Vol. II The European Economic Community 1958–1972*, London, Martin Robertson, 1975.

Collins, Doreen, *The Operation of the European Social Fund*, London, Croom Helm, 1983.

Halloway, J., *Social Policy Harmonization in the European Community*, Aldershot, Gower, 1981.

Chapter 7   Conclusions

Bieber, Roland *et al.* (eds), *An Ever-Closer Union: A Critical Analysis of the Draft Treaty Establishing the European Union*, Brussels, European Perspective Series, 1985.

Bogdanor, V., 'The future of the EC', *Government and Opposition*, Vol. 21, No. 2 (1986).

Brewin, C., 'The EC: a union of states without unity of government', *Journal of Common Market Studies*, Vol. 26, No. 1 (September 1987).

Butler, M., *Europe: More than a Continent*, London, Heinemann, 1986.

Capotorti, Francesco, *et al.*, *The European Union Treaty: Commentary on the Draft Adopted by the European Parliament*, Oxford, Clarendon Press, 1986.

Defarges, P.M., *Quel avenir pour quelle communuaté?*, Paris, 1986.

de Ruyt, J., *L'Acte Unique Européen*, Bruxelles, Editions de l'Universite Bruxelles, 1987.

Everling, U., 'Possibilities and limits of European integration', *Journal of Common Market Studies*, Vol. 17, No. 3 (March 1980).

Hoffman, S., 'Reflections on the nation state in Western Europe today', *Journal of Common Market Studies*, Vol. 21, Nos 1 and 2 (Sept/Dec 1982).

Kaiser, K., Merlini, C., de Montbrial, T., Wellenstein, E. and Wallace, Wm, *The European Community: Progress or Decline?* London, RIIA, 1983.

Lodge, J. (ed.), *The European Union: The European Community in Search of a Future*, Basingstoke, Macmillan, 1986.

Lodge, J. (ed.), *The European Community and the Challenge of the Future*, London, Frances Pinter, 1989.

Nicoll, W, 'Paths to European unity', *Journal of Common Market Studies*, Vol.23, No. 3 (March 1985).

Noel, E., 'The EC: what kind of future?', *Government and Opposition*, Vol. 20, No. 2 (1985).

Pinder, J., 'The European Community and nation-state: a case for neo-federalism', *International Affairs*, Vol. 62, No. 1 (Winter 1985/6).

Pinder, J., *The Single European Act as a Federal Increment: A Critique from a Neo-federalist Perspective*, London, Federal Trust, 1986.

Pryce, R. (ed.), *The Dynamics of European Union*, London, Croom Helm, 1987.

Shonfield, A., *Europe: Journey to an Unknown Destination*, Harmondsworth, Penguin, 1973.

Wallace, H., 'Less than a federation, more than a regime: the Community as a political system', in Wallace, H., Wallace, Wm and Webb, C., (eds), *Policy-Making in the European Communities*, 2nd edn, Chichester, John Wiley, 1983.

Wallace, H. with Ridley, A., *Europe: The Challenge of Diversity*, London, Chatham House Paper No. 29, Routledge and Kegan Paul for RIIA, 1985.

Wallace, Wm, 'Europe as a confederation: the Community and the nation-state', *Journal of Common Market Studies*, Vol. 21, Nos 1 and 2 (Sept/Dec 1982).

Index

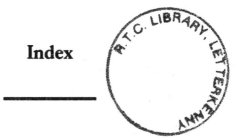